The changing role of the teacher

International perspectives

Norman M. Goble and James F. Porter

A study prepared for the
International Bureau of
Education

unesco NFER Publishing Co. Ltd

Published in 1977 by the
United Nations Educational
Scientific and Cultural Organization,
7 Place de Fontenoy, 75700 Paris, France

Published in 1977 in the United Kingdom
by the NFER Publishing Company Ltd,
The Mere, Upton Park, Slough, Berks SL1 2DQ,
United Kingdom

Printed by Imprimeries Réunies S.A.
Lausanne, Switzerland

ISBN 0 85633 131 7

The designations employed and the presentation of the material in this publication
do not imply the expression of any opinion whatsoever on the part of the
Unesco Secretariat concerning the legal status of any country or territory, or of its
authorities, or concerning the delimitations of the frontiers of any country or territory.

Preface

In late August and early September 1975, the Palais des Nations in Geneva was the setting for the thirty-fifth International Conference on Education (ICE). This conference is sponsored by Unesco and organized by one of its specialized institutions, the International Bureau of Education (IBE). There were over 400 persons at the conference, counting delegates, representatives and observers from Member States of Unesco, and from international, intergovernmental and non-governmental organizations—including representatives of the teaching profession.

Each conference divides its attention between a debate in Plenary on 'Major trends in education' and a discussion in Commission on a special theme which, for the 1975 ICE, was 'The changing role of the teacher and its influence on preparation for the profession and on in-service training'.

It is the special theme which provides the over-all structure of this book, the compilation of which was entrusted by the Secretariat of the IBE to two delegates, both of whom played an invaluable part in the work of the Conference: Mr. Norman Goble (Secretary-General of the Canadian Teachers' Federation) was Rapporteur to the Commission; and Mr. James Porter (Principal of the Bulmershe College of Education, United Kingdom) was one of its Vice-Chairmen. Their terms of reference were broad for, while drawing extensively from the documents provided to the conference and from the discussions and viewpoints of the delegations, they have also given of their long experience in education and their first-hand knowledge of the problems of the teacher in a rapidly changing society.

The book falls into two distinct parts which may be generalized as the 'theory' and the 'practice'. Firstly, Norman Goble has taken the dimensions of the present role of teachers in schools and extrapolated them into a future which is not too distant for the developed countries of the world, and which he believes will be the direction taken by the developing countries as well. It is a world which runs the danger of conflict, ignorance, prejudice, alienation of the young and stubborn resistance to change, but where the teacher's role as change-agent and community worker is considered to be vital as the key to a more equable, secure and prosperous society, and where the responsibility to broaden his own capabilities does not cease to grow. The teacher should equally shun the temptation to turn educational institutions into irrelevant shrines of conservatism and élitist behaviour, which leads to his isolation from society.

The reader will note a change of measure for the second part of the book. James Porter, too, believes in the catalyst role. Teachers are a critical factor in development: they are in a privileged position to break the circle of poverty, ignorance and prejudice in a manner likely to be accepted by the populations concerned; while the multiplier effect of their occupation singles them out as a valuable investment at a time of crushing demand and limited resources. But this demands that certain priorities be established for training and guiding the teacher. Mr. Porter reviews many innovations, techniques and policies in the field of teacher training and makes clear proposals for a three-phase model of education for teachers: personal education; initial teacher training; and, perhaps most important, continuing professional education. Three appendixes report recent strategies for teacher education in the developing world, and a fourth appendix gives the text of the Recommendation adopted at the 1975 ICE.

Although the authors have included many significant sources as references to their chapters, a comprehensive bibliography of the 1975 ICE concludes the book.

The Secretariat records its thanks to the authors for their excellent work which, though not necessarily expressing the views of Unesco, will remain a concrete follow-up to the thirty-fifth session of the International Conference on Education and an invaluable source of guidance and inspiration to those seeking to provide a changing education to a changing world.

Contents

The teacher
in a changing world

by Norman M. Goble

Secretary-General of the Canadian Teachers' Federation

other people in the community and for more involvement in community life;

7. Towards acceptance of participation in school services and extra-curricular activities;

8. Towards accepting a diminution of traditional authority in relation to children—particularly to older children and their parents.

The report adopted at the close of the conference[1] showed, for the most part, strong agreement on these points. It also stressed the need for teacher education to change its orientation to match these priorities, and for a strengthening of the links between theory and the realities of the classroom and the community in which the teacher works.

Especial emphasis was placed by the conference on the need for an ordered programme of in-service education for teachers. It was pointed out that the job of teaching (even without the complications introduced by changes in expectations and functions) is one in which competence and confidence have to be developed through actual experience, and that there are limits to the effectiveness of any pre-service course of preparation, however well conceived. Besides, many countries, especially in the developing regions, are still compelled by circumstances to put teachers into service with inadequate preparation, while most countries have substantial numbers of teachers whose initial training ended at a level well below that which is now normal.

Even if we set aside the need for reform, then, we must recognize that teachers in service are in need of in-service training, either to remedy deficiencies that they have discovered in their professional skills, to develop their potential competence in some specialized field, or simply to raise their level of all-round capability to keep pace with their increasing maturity and judgement. When we add the factor of change in the function of the school, and consequently in the role of the teacher, we see that these same remedial and developmental purposes arise in relation to the entire school system and the entire professional corps, as well as bringing new dimensions to the needs of the individual teacher.

Moreover, the development of a strong in-service education programme creates the opportunity for a much-needed rapprochement

1. See bibliography, item 38.

Introduction

A changing world requires a changing style of education. Young people who are being prepared for entry into adult responsibilities need to be equipped with skills quite different from those which sufficed for their parents. For that matter, adults find it increasingly necessary to extend and renew their own skill and knowledge, so that they can manage their lives successfully in a changing environment. Democratization and developmental needs combine to make demands that exceed, quantitatively or qualitatively, the capacity of traditional systems. The nature of social change, and its causes, vary in their specifics from country to country. What is true in all countries, however, is that there is a pressing need for re-assessment of the function of the school. Three aspects of change are of particular importance in this regard.

One is the fact that in a time of rapid change the store of past knowledge and experience which, in a more stable period, parents drew upon for the guidance of their children, is quite inadequate for that purpose. Parents, indeed, are often more uncertain than their sons and daughters. The same is true of the adult community in general. Traditional values and inherited customs have lost much of their authority over young people and are insufficient as a guide to right action in a rapidly changing milieu. As the confidence and competence of parents, and of the various adult agencies that have traditionally shared in the informal education of the child, grow weaker, there is increasing dependence upon the institutions of formal education.

Secondly, the school itself must adapt to the fact that the new knowledge which is proliferating outside its walls is not only enormously greater in quantity than that which the school has at its own command, but may also be much more vital to the real-life interests of its clients. Not only must the school renew its own stock of knowledge, selecting it according to revised priorities; it must also adapt to the new function of teaching young people to cope with, and make good use of, the mass of knowledge which they will encounter in their daily lives outside the school.

The third essential element in the operation of the school, and in the accomplishment of necessary reform, is the competence of the teacher, and it is therefore of the highest importance that this be appropriately defined and effectively maintained.

What, then, are the essential functions of the teacher in a changing world? What kind of preparation can be devised to ensure that teachers acquire and maintain the competencies necessary for the discharge of those functions?

These were the questions to which the thirty-fifth session of the International Conference on Education (ICE) addressed itself. Held in Geneva from 27 August to 4 September 1975, under the auspices of Unesco, the conference took as its theme *The changing role of the teacher and its influence on preparation for the profession and on in-service training*. In preparation, the International Bureau of Education (IBE) invited reports from the Member States of Unesco, and drew material from them for a series of working papers. Particularly notable was the collaboration of the four major international associations of teacher organizations—the World Confederation of Organizations of the Teaching Profession (WCOTP); the International Federation of Free Teachers' Unions (IFFTU); the World Confederation of Teachers (WCT); and the World Federation of Teachers' Unions (WFTU)—in producing, at the invitation of the IBE, a conference document entitled *The teacher's role and training*.[1]

Delegates to the conference were asked to consider the implications of the search for education of a better quality and greater equality of opportunity, and of the effort to adapt systems of education to changing economic and social needs, in terms of the roles and functions expected of teachers and of coherent policies for teacher education. They were asked to do so in the light of statistical reports which showed the virtual certainty of a massive shortage

1. See bibliography, item 39.

of primary and secondary teachers continuing in the developing regions well into the mid-1980s. They were reminded that most of the developing nations, even to establish universal primary schooling of the most traditional kind, would have to double or treble their output of teachers, thus placing enormous demands upon their frail economies.

The problem, then, is to devise policies and strategies which reach towards a goal appropriate to a changing world, and then to construct a realistic plan of action which achieves as much as can practicably be hoped for, in the most efficient manner possible. The ideals of education, like all other ideals, are no doubt incapable of final realization. To try to formulate them is to do no more than establish a direction of desired change, to provide a basis for judgement about what change is for the better and what is for the worse, and to set a course along which one may strive to advance, stage by feasible stage, in some confidence that each step is an improvement over what came before. Yet the desired goal must be formulated, however unattainable it may seem, for even a small advance towards a good end is manifestly better than a small change in a bad direction or in no direction at all.

On the basis of the reports submitted to the IBE from Unesco's Member States, a 'Working paper' identified the following general trends of change in the role of the teacher:[1]

1. Towards more diversified functions in the instructional process and acceptance of more responsibility for the organization of the content of learning and teaching;
2. Towards a shift in emphasis from transmission of knowledge organization of the pupil's learning, with maximum use of sources of learning in the community;
3. Towards individualization of learning and a changed structure teacher-student relationships;
4. Towards wider use of modern educational technology acquisition of necessary knowledge and skills;
5. Towards larger acceptance of broader co-operation teachers in schools and a changed structure of rel tween teachers;
6. Towards the necessity to work more closely w

1. See bibliography, item 102.

between the teacher education institution and the school. It imposes the need for dialogue between partners who have too often been wary and mutually distrustful, and offers the hope that theory will be put to the test of practice, and practice illuminated and refined by theory, more often and more effectively than has commonly been the case in the past. It is undeniable that much of what the student-teacher can learn in his own studies is meaningless until he tries to apply it in practice—not under direction as a student, but at his own discretion—and valueless unless he is *able* to do so. It is equally undeniable that the prolonged practice of a profession does not, of itself, guarantee any improvement in competence. Teachers, like all other professionals, need to be challenged in their habitual behaviour by encounter with new insights, informed analysis and evolving theory.

Teacher education has the twofold responsibility for responding to change in the role of the teacher and prompting further change. It can only do so if it operates in real and continuous contact with the schools, and if it is conceived as a recurrent process throughout the teacher's working years. The Recommendation adopted by the 1975 conference, and addressed to the Ministries of Education of the Member States of Unesco, observes that 'a comprehensive policy is needed to ensure that teacher education is reorganized as a continuous co-ordinated process which begins with pre-service education and continues throughout the teacher's professional career'.

The conference stressed the importance of a fact that is perhaps more widely acknowledged than utilized: 'the importance of the active participation of the teacher' (these are the words of the *Final report*) 'in the process of innovation'. 'The teacher-learner relationship', says the Recommendation, 'will remain at the centre of the educational process.' No reform, then, can be expected to succeed unless it is fully understood, fully embraced, and effectively implemented by teachers. The full involvement of teachers and their professional organizations in the conception, the planning and the administration of innovation, therefore, is not merely philosophically desirable—it is a practical necessity—and the development in teachers of competence in this role is, in turn, a necessary goal of improvement in teacher education.

These are the ideas which are amplified and explored in detail in this book. The following chapters draw heavily upon, and often

attempt to synthesize, the information supplied to the IBE by the
Member States of Unesco—too frequently, indeed, to permit acknowledgement of sources in any manageable fashion—and owe
much to the excellent work of the IBE staff in compiling conference
documents. They also draw upon the authors' own observations in
their encounters with schools, teachers and administrators in
various countries at various stages of development.

Perhaps it is this element of personal experience which inspires
in the present authors the conviction that the task of reshaping
school systems to emerging needs is too great to be borne by nations
in isolation, that as the peoples of the world grow towards more
intimate contact and closer interdependence it is more and more
necessary that they share their ideas about the development of basic
social institutions, and that the threads of common experience are
more important than the distances they span. In the experience
of every country there is some lesson for all others. And in that fact
lies the need and the justification for the continuance of such activities as the International Conference on Education.

It is unhappily true, and fully recognized by the authors of this
book, that vast numbers of the world's people live in conditions in
which grandiose statements of educational purpose may seem to be
extravagantly unreal. Nations which are faced with crucial problems of hunger, drought, poverty and disease, with extreme difficulties of communication, energy supply and finance, and with a crippling shortage of skilled manpower, may seem to be unready for a
leap into new and demanding styles of schooling.

But it cannot be stressed too often that it is precisely those countries that were the most eloquent advocates, at the 1975 ICE, of the
philosophies expressed here. It is the former colonies that have
been most keenly aware of the irrelevance of the traditional school
to their developmental and cultural needs. It is they who sense most
clearly the urgency of the need to do whatever can be done to make
the teacher effective in the exercise of a new, more relevant role,
rather than to waste scarce resources in trying to refine an institution that is wrong in its basic orientation. It is they who stress most
strongly the need to define new ideals—not in the vain hope of
grasping the ultimate fruits immediately, but as an indication of the
direction in which they must proceed.

School
and society

To speak of change in the role of the teacher is to imply a change in the definition of the functions of the school. It implies, too, that there already exists some generally accepted concept of present role and functions. There are indeed a number of generally-held concepts about what a 'teacher' is and does. Though subject to modification by variations in local circumstances, the role of the teacher, and more particularly of the teacher within the public institution of the school, was established in most parts of the world in very similar terms by the second decade of the present century—so similar, in fact, that it is possible to use phrases like 'the traditional school' and 'the traditional teacher' with every expectation of being understood.

The continuing evolution of societies, however, has led, in the last quarter of a century in particular, to a search for new definitions more appropriate to current conditions and to the aspirations of peoples, and to a widely-expressed conviction that the concepts which satisfied earlier generations are not adequate for the needs of man and society on the threshold of the twenty-first century. More particularly, the concepts which matched the interests of mature industrial powers are clearly inappropriate to the needs and enormous problems of new societies in the post-colonial era.

Obviously the search is not just for a means of predicting what the teacher's role is going to be, as if we were observing some spontaneous and unpredictable natural process, but for a means of causing the kind of change that we want. Changes will occur whether we wish them to or not, and if we await their arrival with passive fatalism we may well have reason to regret having done so. If there is one thing that we should have learned from the advance of scientific knowledge, it is the need to chart probabilities on the basis of a careful analysis of present circumstances, to calculate the probabilities that would be created by various possible alternatives, and then to choose a desired outcome and try to cause it to happen. The report entitled *Learning to be* [1][1], which attracted so much well-deserved attention on its appearance in 1972, repeatedly stresses these points. 'We can and we must,' say its authors, 'given the present state of affairs, inquire into the profound meaning of education ... its powers and its myths, its prospects and its aims' (p. 23). 'Education, being a subsystem of society, necessarily reflects the main features of that society... It by no means follows that for lack of being able to modify and correct social conditions by itself education must remain their passive offshoot' (p. 60). '... it may be the product of history and society, but it is not their passive plaything' (p. 104). 'Failure to adhere to the logical process, moving from policy to strategy and from strategy to planning ... is responsible for education having been too often oriented by chance, guided blindly and developed in anarchic fashion' (p. 172). 'The very substance of education, its essential relationship to man and his development, its interaction with the environment as both product and factor of society must all be deeply scrutinized and extensively reconsidered' (p. 69).

In relation to the role of the teacher, therefore, the task is to identify those factors which determine and define that role and which constrain or inhibit its development, to consider how those factors may be modified in order to shape the teacher's role in desirable ways and to avert undesirable changes, and above all (since a role is an empty and ineffectual concept until it is successfully filled and exercised by a competent actor) to discover how to prepare people to assume this exacting role and play it in such a way that its intended purposes are achieved.

RELATING ROLE CHANGE TO THE ·SOCIAL CONTEXT

There is a kind of basic integrity in the function of teaching which cannot and must not be violated in any definition of the teacher's

1. Numbers in square brackets refer to the references at the end of each chapter.

role. Just as we may say unconditionally that it is the function of a doctor to do such things and dispense such advice as will improve the health of his patient, and that each new discovery about how this can be done is a new and categorical imperative which must not be contradicted by any description of the doctor's 'role', so we must say unconditionally that it is the teacher's duty to promote learning, and that descriptions of 'role' must not pervert that purpose nor inhibit him in discharging that basic function in whatever ways are found to be most effective.

But the teacher's task, to a much greater extent even than that of the doctor, is complicated by the inter-relationship of social factors. The teacher's specific functions are very deeply influenced by the general goals of education in his particular society, and by the way in which time and circumstances modify those goals, changing the answers to such questions as '*What* should people learn? For what purpose?'. Moreover, there is no society in which the school is the only agency concerned with education, or exerting influence upon it. School is a device for formalizing certain aspects of education, so as to achieve specific purposes. Those purposes change from place to place and from time to time. The teacher's role is to a great extent determined by the way in which, in his particular society, the line is drawn between 'upbringing' (the general educational process in which so many formal and informal agencies participate) and 'schooling', and by the nature of the objectives which society assigns to the latter.

There is a third factor of some importance. School is a public institution. All institutions are prone to develop artificialities, and the school is no exception. Because of the internal characteristics of particular institutions, they may not be able to do what is expected of them. On the other hand, they may function very efficiently in ways that were not intended, and produce results that are not in the best interests of their clients. The role of people who work in an institutional setting is influenced, sometimes more deeply than we realize, by the nature of the institution, and it is undeniable that the role of the teacher is shaped to a considerable extent by the characteristics, and the limitations, of the institution of the school.

These inter-relationships operate in two directions. On the one hand, any change in the general goals of education, the assignment of particular functions to the school, or the organization of the institution of public education, will to some extent modify the role of the teacher. (It is of course evident that any economic, social or political change, whether originating within the society or impinging upon it from outside, which changes any of the balances within the social structure will have some effect upon these three elements—general goals, specific assignments to the school, and institutional characteristics.)

On the other hand, if an analytical exercise of the kind referred to earlier leads to the conclusion that a deliberate attempt should be made to change the teacher's role, we must bear in mind that this cannot be effectively done without accompanying changes in the institution of the school, the specific assignments given to the school, and the respective roles of the various informal and formal agencies involved with the school in the process of education. All are interlinked. To speak of a change in the role of the teacher is also to speak of change in the roles of parents, communities, the public communications media, churches, and a host of other agencies and professions. 'The sharing of the responsibilities for providing learning,' says one Asian commentator, 'by the several agencies—the family, the work-place, the temple, the mosque, the shrine, the community and mass media—presents a complex pattern of sharing with overlapping areas of responsibility.' [2] To change one area of responsibility is to affect all. Change is, in fact, occurring all the time, but it is not always taking place rationally or smoothly. Difficulties have been evident, the same writer remarks 'when ... the community and the family transferred certain of their earlier socializing and custodial activities to the school. When this happened, in most contexts, instead of a systematic adaptation to the situation both by the teaching cadres and teacher-educators, the widening of the teacher's role was often reflected in an increase in confusion as to what expertise the teacher needed and how and when it needed to be applied. In short, there was increasing confusion as to the teacher's extended role.'

When there is widespread belief, as seems to be the case at the present time, in the need for substantial and controlled change, and when the conviction is generally established that teachers should be in the forefront of the effort of redefining their own role, it becomes exceedingly important to do everything possible to reduce the confusion referred to.

Introduction

A changing world requires a changing style of education. Young people who are being prepared for entry into adult responsibilities need to be equipped with skills quite different from those which sufficed for their parents. For that matter, adults find it increasingly necessary to extend and renew their own skill and knowledge, so that they can manage their lives successfully in a changing environment. Democratization and developmental needs combine to make demands that exceed, quantitatively or qualitatively, the capacity of traditional systems. The nature of social change, and its causes, vary in their specifics from country to country. What is true in all countries, however, is that there is a pressing need for re-assessment of the function of the school. Three aspects of change are of particular importance in this regard.

One is the fact that in a time of rapid change the store of past knowledge and experience which, in a more stable period, parents drew upon for the guidance of their children, is quite inadequate for that purpose. Parents, indeed, are often more uncertain than their sons and daughters. The same is true of the adult community in general. Traditional values and inherited customs have lost much of their authority over young people and are insufficient as a guide to right action in a rapidly changing milieu. As the confidence and competence of parents, and of the various adult agencies that have traditionally shared in the informal education of the child, grow weaker, there is increasing dependence upon the institutions of formal education.

Secondly, the school itself must adapt to the fact that the new knowledge which is proliferating outside its walls is not only enormously greater in quantity than that which the school has at its own command, but may also be much more vital to the real-life interests of its clients. Not only must the school renew its own stock of knowledge, selecting it according to revised priorities; it must also adapt to the new function of teaching young people to cope with, and make good use of, the mass of knowledge which they will encounter in their daily lives outside the school.

The third essential element in the operation of the school, and in the accomplishment of necessary reform, is the competence of the teacher, and it is therefore of the highest importance that this be appropriately defined and effectively maintained.

What, then, are the essential functions of the teacher in a changing world? What kind of preparation can be devised to ensure that teachers acquire and maintain the competencies necessary for the discharge of those functions?

These were the questions to which the thirty-fifth session of the International Conference on Education (ICE) addressed itself. Held in Geneva from 27 August to 4 September 1975, under the auspices of Unesco, the conference took as its theme *The changing role of the teacher and its influence on preparation for the profession and on in-service training*. In preparation, the International Bureau of Education (IBE) invited reports from the Member States of Unesco, and drew material from them for a series of working papers. Particularly notable was the collaboration of the four major international associations of teacher organizations—the World Confederation of Organizations of the Teaching Profession (WCOTP); the International Federation of Free Teachers' Unions (IFFTU); the World Confederation of Teachers (WCT); and the World Federation of Teachers' Unions (WFTU)—in producing, at the invitation of the IBE, a conference document entitled *The teacher's role and training*.[1]

Delegates to the conference were asked to consider the implications of the search for education of a better quality and greater equality of opportunity, and of the effort to adapt systems of education to changing economic and social needs, in terms of the roles and functions expected of teachers and of coherent policies for teacher education. They were asked to do so in the light of statistical reports which showed the virtual certainty of a massive shortage

1. See bibliography, item 39.

of primary and secondary teachers continuing in the developing regions well into the mid-1980s. They were reminded that most of the developing nations, even to establish universal primary schooling of the most traditional kind, would have to double or treble their output of teachers, thus placing enormous demands upon their frail economies.

The problem, then, is to devise policies and strategies which reach towards a goal appropriate to a changing world, and then to construct a realistic plan of action which achieves as much as can practicably be hoped for, in the most efficient manner possible. The ideals of education, like all other ideals, are no doubt incapable of final realization. To try to formulate them is to do no more than establish a direction of desired change, to provide a basis for judgement about what change is for the better and what is for the worse, and to set a course along which one may strive to advance, stage by feasible stage, in some confidence that each step is an improvement over what came before. Yet the desired goal must be formulated, however unattainable it may seem, for even a small advance towards a good end is manifestly better than a small change in a bad direction or in no direction at all.

On the basis of the reports submitted to the IBE from Unesco's Member States, a 'Working paper' identified the following general trends of change in the role of the teacher:[1]

1. Towards more diversified functions in the instructional process and acceptance of more responsibility for the organization of the content of learning and teaching;
2. Towards a shift in emphasis from transmission of knowledge to organization of the pupil's learning, with maximum use of new sources of learning in the community;
3. Towards individualization of learning and a changed structure in teacher-student relationships;
4. Towards wider use of modern educational technology and the acquisition of necessary knowledge and skills;
5. Towards larger acceptance of broader co-operation with other teachers in schools and a changed structure of relationship between teachers;
6. Towards the necessity to work more closely with parents and

1. See bibliography, item 102.

other people in the community and for more involvement in
community life;

7. Towards acceptance of participation in school services and extra-curricular activities;

8. Towards accepting a diminution of traditional authority in relation to children—particularly to older children and their parents.

The report adopted at the close of the conference[1] showed, for
the most part, strong agreement on these points. It also stressed the
need for teacher education to change its orientation to match these
priorities, and for a strengthening of the links between theory and
the realities of the classroom and the community in which the teacher works.

Especial emphasis was placed by the conference on the need for
an ordered programme of in-service education for teachers. It was
pointed out that the job of teaching (even without the complications
introduced by changes in expectations and functions) is one in
which competence and confidence have to be developed through
actual experience, and that there are limits to the effectiveness of
any pre-service course of preparation, however well conceived.
Besides, many countries, especially in the developing regions, are
still compelled by circumstances to put teachers into service with
inadequate preparation, while most countries have substantial numbers of teachers whose initial training ended at a level well below
that which is now normal.

Even if we set aside the need for reform, then, we must recognize
that teachers in service are in need of in-service training, either to
remedy deficiencies that they have discovered in their professional
skills, to develop their potential competence in some specialized
field, or simply to raise their level of all-round capability to keep
pace with their increasing maturity and judgement. When we add
the factor of change in the function of the school, and consequently
in the role of the teacher, we see that these same remedial and developmental purposes arise in relation to the entire school system and
the entire professional corps, as well as bringing new dimensions to
the needs of the individual teacher.

Moreover, the development of a strong in-service education programme creates the opportunity for a much-needed rapprochement

1. See bibliography, item 38.

between the teacher education institution and the school. It imposes the need for dialogue between partners who have too often been wary and mutually distrustful, and offers the hope that theory will be put to the test of practice, and practice illuminated and refined by theory, more often and more effectively than has commonly been the case in the past. It is undeniable that much of what the student-teacher can learn in his own studies is meaningless until he tries to apply it in practice—not under direction as a student, but at his own discretion—and valueless unless he is *able* to do so. It is equally undeniable that the prolonged practice of a profession does not, of itself, guarantee any improvement in competence. Teachers, like all other professionals, need to be challenged in their habitual behaviour by encounter with new insights, informed analysis and evolving theory.

Teacher education has the twofold responsibility for responding to change in the role of the teacher and prompting further change. It can only do so if it operates in real and continuous contact with the schools, and if it is conceived as a recurrent process throughout the teacher's working years. The Recommendation adopted by the 1975 conference, and addressed to the Ministries of Education of the Member States of Unesco, observes that 'a comprehensive policy is needed to ensure that teacher education is reorganized as a continuous co-ordinated process which begins with pre-service education and continues throughout the teacher's professional career'.

The conference stressed the importance of a fact that is perhaps more widely acknowledged than utilized: 'the importance of the active participation of the teacher' (these are the words of the *Final report*) 'in the process of innovation'. 'The teacher-learner relationship', says the Recommendation, 'will remain at the centre of the educational process.' No reform, then, can be expected to succeed unless it is fully understood, fully embraced, and effectively implemented by teachers. The full involvement of teachers and their professional organizations in the conception, the planning and the administration of innovation, therefore, is not merely philosophically desirable—it is a practical necessity—and the development in teachers of competence in this role is, in turn, a necessary goal of improvement in teacher education.

These are the ideas which are amplified and explored in detail in this book. The following chapters draw heavily upon, and often attempt to synthesize, the information supplied to the IBE by the Member States of Unesco—too frequently, indeed, to permit acknowledgement of sources in any manageable fashion—and owe much to the excellent work of the IBE staff in compiling conference documents. They also draw upon the authors' own observations in their encounters with schools, teachers and administrators in various countries at various stages of development.

Perhaps it is this element of personal experience which inspires in the present authors the conviction that the task of reshaping school systems to emerging needs is too great to be borne by nations in isolation, that as the peoples of the world grow towards more intimate contact and closer interdependence it is more and more necessary that they share their ideas about the development of basic social institutions, and that the threads of common experience are more important than the distances they span. In the experience of every country there is some lesson for all others. And in that fact lies the need and the justification for the continuance of such activities as the International Conference on Education.

It is unhappily true, and fully recognized by the authors of this book, that vast numbers of the world's people live in conditions in which grandiose statements of educational purpose may seem to be extravagantly unreal. Nations which are faced with crucial problems of hunger, drought, poverty and disease, with extreme difficulties of communication, energy supply and finance, and with a crippling shortage of skilled manpower, may seem to be unready for a leap into new and demanding styles of schooling.

But it cannot be stressed too often that it is precisely those countries that were the most eloquent advocates, at the 1975 ICE, of the philosophies expressed here. It is the former colonies that have been most keenly aware of the irrelevance of the traditional school to their developmental and cultural needs. It is they who sense most clearly the urgency of the need to do whatever can be done to make the teacher effective in the exercise of a new, more relevant role, rather than to waste scarce resources in trying to refine an institution that is wrong in its basic orientation. It is they who stress most strongly the need to define new ideals—not in the vain hope of grasping the ultimate fruits immediately, but as an indication of the direction in which they must proceed.

School and society

To speak of change in the role of the teacher is to imply a change in the definition of the functions of the school. It implies, too, that there already exists some generally accepted concept of present role and functions. There are indeed a number of generally-held concepts about what a 'teacher' is and does. Though subject to modification by variations in local circumstances, the role of the teacher, and more particularly of the teacher within the public institution of the school, was established in most parts of the world in very similar terms by the second decade of the present century—so similar, in fact, that it is possible to use phrases like 'the traditional school' and 'the traditional teacher' with every expectation of being understood.

The continuing evolution of societies, however, has led, in the last quarter of a century in particular, to a search for new definitions more appropriate to current conditions and to the aspirations of peoples, and to a widely-expressed conviction that the concepts which satisfied earlier generations are not adequate for the needs of man and society on the threshold of the twenty-first century. More particularly, the concepts which matched the interests of mature industrial powers are clearly inappropriate to the needs and enormous problems of new societies in the post-colonial era.

Obviously the search is not just for a means of predicting what the teacher's role is going to be, as if we were observing some spontaneous and unpredictable natural process, but for a means of causing the kind of change that we want. Changes will occur whether we wish them to or not, and if we await their arrival with passive fatalism we may well have reason to regret having done so. If there is one thing that we should have learned from the advance of scientific knowledge, it is the need to chart probabilities on the basis of a careful analysis of present circumstances, to calculate the probabilities that would be created by various possible alternatives, and then to choose a desired outcome and try to cause it to happen. The report entitled *Learning to be* [1][1], which attracted so much well-deserved attention on its appearance in 1972, repeatedly stresses these points. 'We can and we must,' say its authors, 'given the present state of affairs, inquire into the profound meaning of education ... its powers and its myths, its prospects and its aims' (p. 23). 'Education, being a subsystem of society, necessarily reflects the main features of that society... It by no means follows that for lack of being able to modify and correct social conditions by itself education must remain their passive offshoot' (p. 60). '... it may be the product of history and society, but it is not their passive plaything' (p. 104). 'Failure to adhere to the logical process, moving from policy to strategy and from strategy to planning ... is responsible for education having been too often oriented by chance, guided blindly and developed in anarchic fashion' (p. 172). 'The very substance of education, its essential relationship to man and his development, its interaction with the environment as both product and factor of society must all be deeply scrutinized and extensively reconsidered' (p. 69).

In relation to the role of the teacher, therefore, the task is to identify those factors which determine and define that role and which constrain or inhibit its development, to consider how those factors may be modified in order to shape the teacher's role in desirable ways and to avert undesirable changes, and above all (since a role is an empty and ineffectual concept until it is successfully filled and exercised by a competent actor) to discover how to prepare people to assume this exacting role and play it in such a way that its intended purposes are achieved.

RELATING ROLE CHANGE TO THE SOCIAL CONTEXT

There is a kind of basic integrity in the function of teaching which cannot and must not be violated in any definition of the teacher's

---

1. Numbers in square brackets refer to the references at the end of each chapter.

role. Just as we may say unconditionally that it is the function of a doctor to do such things and dispense such advice as will improve the health of his patient, and that each new discovery about how this can be done is a new and categorical imperative which must not be contradicted by any description of the doctor's 'role', so we must say unconditionally that it is the teacher's duty to promote learning, and that descriptions of 'role' must not pervert that purpose nor inhibit him in discharging that basic function in whatever ways are found to be most effective.

But the teacher's task, to a much greater extent even than that of the doctor, is complicated by the inter-relationship of social factors. The teacher's specific functions are very deeply influenced by the general goals of education in his particular society, and by the way in which time and circumstances modify those goals, changing the answers to such questions as '*What* should people learn? For what purpose?'. Moreover, there is no society in which the school is the only agency concerned with education, or exerting influence upon it. School is a device for formalizing certain aspects of education, so as to achieve specific purposes. Those purposes change from place to place and from time to time. The teacher's role is to a great extent determined by the way in which, in his particular society, the line is drawn between 'upbringing' (the general educational process in which so many formal and informal agencies participate) and 'schooling', and by the nature of the objectives which society assigns to the latter.

There is a third factor of some importance. School is a public institution. All institutions are prone to develop artificialities, and the school is no exception. Because of the internal characteristics of particular institutions, they may not be able to do what is expected of them. On the other hand, they may function very efficiently in ways that were not intended, and produce results that are not in the best interests of their clients. The role of people who work in an institutional setting is influenced, sometimes more deeply than we realize, by the nature of the institution, and it is undeniable that the role of the teacher is shaped to a considerable extent by the characteristics, and the limitations, of the institution of the school.

These inter-relationships operate in two directions. On the one hand, any change in the general goals of education, the assignment of particular functions to the school, or the organization of the institution of public education, will to some extent modify the role of the teacher. (It is of course evident that any economic, social or political change, whether originating within the society or impinging upon it from outside, which changes any of the balances within the social structure will have some effect upon these three elements— general goals, specific assignments to the school, and institutional characteristics.)

On the other hand, if an analytical exercise of the kind referred to earlier leads to the conclusion that a deliberate attempt should be made to change the teacher's role, we must bear in mind that this cannot be effectively done without accompanying changes in the institution of the school, the specific assignments given to the school, and the respective roles of the various informal and formal agencies involved with the school in the process of education. All are interlinked. To speak of a change in the role of the teacher is also to speak of change in the roles of parents, communities, the public communications media, churches, and a host of other agencies and professions. 'The sharing of the responsibilities for providing learning,' says one Asian commentator, 'by the several agencies—the family, the work-place, the temple, the mosque, the shrine, the community and mass media—presents a complex pattern of sharing with overlapping areas of responsibility.' [2] To change one area of responsibility is to affect all. Change is, in fact, occurring all the time, but it is not always taking place rationally or smoothly. Difficulties have been evident, the same writer remarks 'when ... the community and the family transferred certain of their earlier socializing and custodial activities to the school. When this happened, in most contexts, instead of a systematic adaptation to the situation both by the teaching cadres and teacher-educators, the widening of the teacher's role was often reflected in an increase in confusion as to what expertise the teacher needed and how and when it needed to be applied. In short, there was increasing confusion as to the teacher's extended role.'

When there is widespread belief, as seems to be the case at the present time, in the need for substantial and controlled change, and when the conviction is generally established that teachers should be in the forefront of the effort of redefining their own role, it becomes exceedingly important to do everything possible to reduce the confusion referred to.

GOALS OF CHANGE—PROBLEMS OF DEFINITION

Any attempt at clarification must begin with the definition of some basic assumptions.

To start with, it is necessary to recognize that education is a natural activity of all societies. It is the process of integrating the growing individual into the collectivity—fostering the development of powers and influencing the individual's chosen exercise of those powers in ways that are thought to favour his own survival and the collective well-being of the group in which he functions. The process of education, then, is not something that is added on to the structure of a society, a mechanism which it may or may not choose to operate. It is integral to the nature of any collectivity of living organisms. It rests upon an acquired knowledge of what is beneficial and what is harmful.

Schooling is an attempt to undertake the deliberate management of certain aspects of this process. To do so is to incur the moral obligation of ensuring that the process takes place to the greatest possible benefit of the two parties concerned—the individual and the social collectivity.

This leads us into a number of problems of definition. We face first of all the need to define the phrase 'the group in which he functions', as used in the paragraph above. A major difficulty is that people function for different purposes in groups of different sizes. For some purposes we have to see ourselves as members of a local community; for others as citizens of a nation; for others as members of the global community of mankind. Various aspects of this problem are examined in later chapters of this book. The main point to be made at present is that the events of the last thirty years have faced us with the urgent need to recognize the responsibilities of membership of the *world* community,[1] and that this presents an awesome challenge to the knowledge and competence of the teacher, as well as to educational policy makers.

Then we are confronted with the need to interpret the word 'benefit', to define the legitimate demands of the 'individual' and the

1. 'One of the most important educational tasks of our schools,' says the report of the People's Republic of Hungary to the thirty-fifth session of the International Conference on Education, 'consists of education about the requirements of international collaboration.'

'social collectivity' respectively, and to make decisions about the kind of balance that should be maintained between these possibly competing claims.

It is precisely in the definition of these demands and the assessment of a just balance between them that we become aware of the radical nature of recent change, and of what that change implies in relation to the role of the teacher. The evolution of industrial societies towards a more humane concept of social organization, the worldwide movement of decolonization, and the struggle of new nations to establish identity, social coherence and economic viability, have deeply affected the definition of the general goals of education.

Priorities, of course, vary because of differences in cultural context, and in the stage of economic and technological development of various societies. Some nations are necessarily preoccupied with the urgent task of improving the material well-being of their people, or with specific necessary goals of literacy or the improvement of agricultural or manufacturing skills. Others must give priority to social reconstruction or to the preservation of valuable social structures through a period of economic upheaval and political change. Some concerns are unique to a specific time and place, and these must be accurately identified and resolved in unique ways. It is most important, though, for educational planners to distinguish between those problems which are truly unique to a particular place and time and those which are local facets of universal problems and concerns. When we are dealing with the latter category, international communication is of the utmost importance. The experience of others is there to be examined. By selecting what might be relevant to our own situation and discarding those elements that are not transferable, we can achieve dramatic short-cuts—but only if we are prepared to recognize the extent to which we are *not* unique. The questions 'What should people learn? For what purpose?' have to be asked and answered in each local context, but underneath the local variations there lie some universal principles.

That there is a considerable degree of agreement at the level of basic philosophy, in spite of large ideological or cultural differences, is evident from a study of current statements about goals, the teacher's role and the need for change. From Upper Volta comes this statement about the impact of the school upon its students: 'We must not make of them robots who record a certain number of questions to which they furnish replies . . . but rather men in the full sense of the word—that is to say, creators and movers of society' [3]. A document of the International Bureau of Education [4] records the Peruvian commitment to 'conscientization', defined as 'an educational process whereby individuals and social groups gain a critical awareness of the historical and cultural world in which they live, shoulder their responsibilities and undertake the necessary action to transform it'. It was reported at the 1975 ICE that Unesco's Member States 'expected the school to contribute to the creation and formation of a new man and of a more just society', and coupled this expectation to that of reform 'with a view to the democratization of education' [5].

A NEW COMMITMENT—REGENERATION, NOT CONSERVATION

It would seem, therefore, that the major emphasis desired in most countries is upon effective preparation for participation in the building of a new social order, rather than the conservation of the old. This is indeed a major change, substantiating the dramatic statement by the authors of *Learning to be* that 'for the first time in history, education is now engaged in preparing men for a type of society which does not yet exist' (p. 13). It involves the adoption of the position, at first sight paradoxical, that the liberation of individuality, and therefore of creativity and inventiveness, favours the true interests of the collectivity, and calls therefore for a corresponding de-emphasis of conformity, authoritarianism and standardized examination-oriented teaching. This does not yet suggest any very specific answer to the question '*What* should people learn?', but it does begin to answer the question 'For what purpose?'. This latter question really has to be answered first, anyhow. It is when we know what we want to do that we begin to be able to decide what we need to learn in order to do it. As we shall suggest in later chapters, an important part of the 'new' role of the teacher is the responsibility for devising curricula suitable for new purposes (and the acquisition of the ability to do so).

A third question that might have been asked is 'Who should learn in the schools?'. The general commitment to the answer

'Everybody!'—to the idea that the schools should be taken out of the service of the élite and re-shaped to offer everyone the possibility of self-improvement—represents a worldwide change on a radical scale, with revolutionary implications for the role of the teacher. There are countries which have professed this answer for many years, but which have not yet grasped or accepted these implications.

The notion of preparation of the individual for entry into a fluid, regenerating society rather than for the perpetuation of existing conventions, roles and structures is also revolutionary in its impact upon the oldest of all the aspects of education, that of graduation or initiation into adult society. In two respects that impact is violent. The first is that of time. When 'integration' is seen as the induction of the individual into a fixed, well-defined environment, it is possible to establish a particular moment of readiness, and to say that what precedes it is 'education' and what follows it is 'life'. Learning is separated from living, and is considered to be a prerequisite stage with a definite terminal point. But when the integrative process is seen as a matter of preparing the individual for participation in change, the outcome of which cannot be predicted, there can be no prior establishment of a terminal point. To adopt such a goal is to accept at the same time the necessity for continuous learning, and most probably, therefore, for recurrent schooling. Learning is not, then, a prerequisite to living, but its accompaniment, a means of continuous re-adaptation to emerging responsibilities, aimed not at the acquisition of selected pieces of past knowledge, but at the mastery of techniques for interpreting and applying unpredictable new discoveries. Teaching, therefore, will have to respond to the needs for learning as they arise, rather than dominating the learner by imposing rigid, arbitrarily pre-designed patterns and programmes. This has very important consequences both for the practice of teaching and for the preparation of the teacher.

The second respect in which the impact of this change of emphasis upon traditional initiatory procedures is violent is in their actual application. A stable society develops a highly organized and complex specialization of functions, and a major purpose of initiation, in that case, is to demonstrate the specific fitness of the candidate for entry into one or other of those functions. In preparation for that moment, the educational programme will, with the passage of time, tend to develop an ever-higher degree of specialization, choosing candidates for each category of society by applying a series of preliminary ordeals. This point will be developed at greater length later; at the moment all that needs to be said is that a stable, highly-organized society tends to develop a selective, exclusive system of schooling, relying heavily on examinations which challenge the pupil in an almost antagonistic way—and will, of course, train its teachers to function in that mode. A fluid, evolving society, however, needs a school system which will prepare people for adaptability. This calls for self-assurance, for the maximum development of each individual's talents, whatever they may be (thus influencing the answer to the question '*What* should people learn?'), and for a supportive rather than an antagonistic approach.

THE NEED FOR 'SCHOOLING'

So far, we have used such terms as 'education' and 'schooling' rather imprecisely, in spite of the distinction made between the former as the general process of social integration and the latter as the deliberate management of that process. It may be useful, at this point, to examine the distinction a little more closely.

All living communities have mechanisms for regulating the behaviour of growing individuals for their own good and the general good. Man is not an exception, but he is a special case. Of all animals, man is born the least able to take care of himself. His will to move and act, to alter his state in relation to his environment, operates long before he has either the knowledge necessary to predict consequences and make prudent choices or even the physical power to ensure his survival. Since an imprudent act can endanger not only the individual but others around him, the educative process (including, necessarily, some limits to freedom of choice and some element of coercion in the interests of the collectivity) is of supreme importance in human society.

The basis of education is experience. Human beings have the advantages of consciousness, memory and language, all of which can be used to refine the lessons of experience and transfer them to others. Much of human learning, as a result, is really second hand.

Properly organized and displayed, people's experience—as stated earlier—becomes a short-cut to progress for others.

The lessons of experience are transmitted in two ways. Ways of doing useful things can be observed and imitated (perhaps to be improved later by the exercise of inventiveness). Knowledge about what it is most useful to do can be passed on symbolically—either by explicit language or mathematical expression (methods so familiar that we often forget that they are symbolic, not real) or by artistic representation (picture, mime, dance, song, music, poetry, fable). The former method transmits the ability to do things that contribute to the well-being of the community. The latter method transmits the taboos and mythology of the community—the stock of beliefs and ideas and the moral code that must be subscribed to for the maintenance of peace, order and the public good—and so develops the will to choose right action and the wisdom to see what is right.

In the isolated communities of a pre-industrial society, the educative process, whether in the positive sense of the teaching of appropriate behaviour, or in the negative sense of teaching the limits beyond which individual whim may not be allowed to go, needs no separate institutionalized framework. In such communities the orthodox mythology is coherent and all embracing, and it is scarcely possible for the growing child to engage in any activity or suffer any encounter that will not serve to communicate the knowledge and the attitudes needed for social integration. The community itself is the school and all the people are teachers, whether by precept, by example, by recitation of the proverbs and parables in which the conventional wisdom is stored, by the assignment of work or the provision of materials for play, or by the organization and performance of the artistic and religious activities that preserve, in symbolic form, the essence of experiential learning and the definition of the collective identity. Where nothing new intrudes into the life of a community, to live in that community is to be exposed to a coherent programme of orthodox learning.

Only such a society—one which has reached and which maintains such a balance between needs and resources that it can sustain itself without impairment of the environment, in which everyone has a clear, direct and unambiguous relationship with the basic concerns of survival (food, shelter, hygiene and defence), and into which no new challenge or disturbing factor intrudes—only such a society can afford to leave the educative function to be taken care of by imitation and the informal communication of taboo and mythology. Only a return to such a society could make 'de-schooling' feasible.

The moment any new or disturbing factor comes upon the scene to impair the cohesiveness of the social structure, to compel a complex division of labour, to encourage dependence on some prosthetic device more potent than the simple hand-held tool or weapon; the moment the uniformity of the cultural message transmitted to the child through his random encounters is impaired, so that the force of precedent is weakened, and the message becomes ambiguous and loses its indoctrinating authority, there is need for some formalization of orthodox doctrine, some educational policy, some formal organization of schooling. In proportion as a society needs to be organized, it has need of an organized orientation process for its young. Thus is created the specialized role of the school and the teacher.

SCHOOL AS INSTITUTION—SOME OBSTACLES TO CHANGE

As was earlier remarked, the first appearance of a separate, formalized institution consciously serving a purpose in the educative process is the initiatory ceremony, the rites of passage, in which proof is demanded by the elders of the community that the young candidate for adult status has internalized the orthodox skills, the traditional lore and the discipline of taboo to the point of readiness to enjoy the freedoms of an adult and participate in maintaining the socio-economic machine. Examiners, it seems, are invented before teachers, and the concept of the teacher as primarily an examiner dies hard.

The first transfer of teaching responsibilities to a designated institution raises the questions of which skills, which taboos, which aspects of the prevailing mythology are to be entrusted to that particular agency, how orthodoxy is to be established, how the teachers should be selected and prepared, and when and how it is to be determined that the school has done what has been asked of it. At the present moment this entire complex of questions, bearing upon the mandate of the school, is under review; this book, indeed, is mainly devoted to that exercise. It must be stressed once again, however, that the same or similar questions must be raised about the manner (institutional or otherwise) in which society is meeting its obligations to its young people in those aspects of the educational process which have *not* been entrusted to the school.

School, we have asserted, is a necessary device. Its existence, however, like that of any other institution, creates an attitude among those inside it and among those outside it. Those who participate seek a higher degree of differentiation from the rest of society. Specific goals are formulated, and internal criteria of efficiency in the pursuit of those goals are developed.

Those who work in an institutionalized activity tend to seek an increasingly precise definition of the 'proper' nature of their work, in line with the tendency of the institution to refine its goals and its criteria of efficiency. This has a narrowing effect, since the process excludes any activities which could distract the practitioner from his recognized business.

There are good and bad effects in this. The definition of professionality does tend to strengthen the identification of the practitioner with his art, and his commitment to its successful outcome. By continuous refinement of the definition of purpose, also, it promotes rational analysis of the factors leading to success, and a consequent improvement in efficiency—within its own internal criteria. It does, however, raise serious moral problems if there is too great a dissonance between internal criteria and external mandate. In some societies the reproach is being raised against the schools, with considerable justification, that they are too faithful to their own traditional goals and not responsive enough to the present learning needs of the people they should be serving. 'There is an Arab proverb,' says Joseph Ki-Zerbo, 'that says that a man is often more akin to his times than to his father.' [6] For reasons that will be explored in the next chapter, some nations are experiencing difficulty in reform because their school systems seem to be more faithful to heredity than to environment.

The main point here is that the institution may develop within itself a concept of its own special responsibilities, its own 'proper' functions, which is not the same as the set of functions that society wants to assign to it. This produces statements like the familiar assertion that 'school should only be asked to do what the school *can* do'. The principle seems logical enough, but the best answer may be to make some radical changes in the institution of the school and the role of the teacher so that the school *can* do what it is asked to do. Those whose principal concern is with the protection of the traditional institution of the school against the threat of change should not have the last word.

The practitioner within an institution, moreover, may come to attach more importance to consistency in the pursuit of his rational but artificial concept of professionality than to the diverse and possibly non-rational perceptions and needs of his client. This degree of hyper-professionalism is conspicuous in the legal profession, clearly detectable in the medical field, and a real danger in education.

There is the further risk that the professional who is committed to a narrow definition of his professionality may strongly resist any suggestion that the mandate of the institution is changing and calls for different kinds of activity. This is particularly the case if there is a past history of real or threatened exploitation, either in terms of the workload placed upon the practitioner or in terms of misuse of the institution in favour of the self-interest of dominant groups.

This intransigence is shown by educators in many situations where there is strong pressure for change in the methods and proposed purposes of education. To endorse it wholly, as proper professionalism, or to condemn it wholly, as negative unionism, are equally wrong reactions. Professional conviction and the protective exercise of collective caution are both entirely legitimate, and it is the obligation of the innovators to demonstrate that what they are offering is a better assurance of individual and collective advantage, and of protection from harm—a better means of integrating the individual into society to the greatest possible benefit of both. Nevertheless, the establishment of a working mechanism for responsible and timely change is an absolute necessity in education, imposing still another condition upon the definition of the role of the teacher.

SCHOOL AS AN INSTITUTION—THE PROBLEM OF SOCIAL RELEVANCE

It was earlier stated that schooling is the deliberate management of certain aspects of the educational process. In other words, it is a transfer of responsibility from the private domain to the public. In the transfer of functions from the private to the public sector, many problems arise from the fact that, as has been said, most functions of a community are interwoven with many other functions. When one function is isolated and institutionalized—and this is true whether we are talking about teaching, physical healing or punishment—it is extremely difficult to preserve the threads which bind it to the others. The transfer from private activity to public institution ordinarily takes place when the function under consideration has been seriously impaired by continuing to operate informally (the institutionalization of hygiene, for instance, was promoted by the failure of private methods of sewage disposal), but when the function is too narrowly defined, and the thread linking it to others is broken, further impairment may follow (public sewage disposal systems are creating serious ecological problems). Education is not exempt from this. The identification of those aspects of the educative process which it is appropriate to isolate in the institution of the school, and the means by which the threads can be preserved, is an undertaking of crucial importance in the present re-examination of the function of the school and the resultant role of the teacher.

The traditional school may be said to have four main functions. These have to be interpreted, for particular societies, in terms of specific cultures, but in one form or another they are widely subscribed to. All four are open to question, and difficult to sustain, in a time of deep social change.

First there is the *custodial function*. Parents generally look to the schools to keep their children under safe surveillance, out of sight and out of mind, for several hours of the day. This implies, however, that the school will exercise pro-parental discipline—at least for the safety of the child if not also for the comfort of the guardian— and that it will also, as a good custodian, impose and enforce some code of conduct.

As custodian, in other words, the school embodies the adult as a censor of behaviour. What happens to that function in a time of dissolution of the social consensus, when the authority of the adult as an arbiter of morals and controller of behaviour is weakened (as in so many countries today)? What becomes of pro-parental discipline when parental discipline dissolves?

Closely associated with the custodial function is that of *indoctrination*—the transmission of the prevailing set of social values, the perpetuation of the ethos of the collectivity. Most people expect the school to persuade their children to think as they do, not to challenge their convictions. How legitimate is that expectation when ethos and ethics, values and commitments, are unclear or are hotly contested between competing groups?

A third—a relatively recent addition to the processes of institutionalized education—is the *vocational function*. This too is open to serious question. How effective can vocational preparation be within the school in an era of technological and economic change, when old occupations are disappearing and new ones coming into being, and when the projection of manpower needs is a task of baffling difficulty?

The fourth function—obverse of the vocational—is the *credential*. Most people, it must be admitted, do not really go 'to' school. They go 'through' it, rather, not for the intrinsic value of the activities which it provides, but for the advantageous status conferred in the end by proof that one has participated, with supposed success, in those activities.

Credentials ensure differentiation—a better kind of work, a higher level of employment in a particular kind of work, a higher social status. Some are based on proof of the acquisition of real and relevant knowledge or skill. Some have a ritual quality, based on proof of survival of the elegantly artificial ordeals deemed proper to initiation into privileged categories of society.

But what happens when expectations of advantage prove false—when credentials lose their preferential value because they are too widely generalized, or because the social distinctions that they confer are obsolete?

When these questions arise, with the urgency with which they are now presenting themselves in so many countries, we are driven to ask whether the threads binding the school to the general fabric of society have not been broken, allowing the school to drift into irrelevance and unrealistic formalism.

These are the questions which are now, in the varying conditions of societies in different regions of the world, compelling a reassessment of the functions traditionally assigned to the school. The broad aim of education does not change; but the ways in which it is pursued must be adapted to changing circumstances. New decisions must be made about which aspects of the educative process have to be deliberately managed within the school, and how these should interact with the informal educational processes of the larger society. Because the central element in schooling is the teacher-learner relationship, the assignments given to the school will set the frame of reference within which the teacher exercises his function of promoting learning. The competence of the teacher, in turn, will be the factor that most decisively affects the possibility of carrying out the assignment given to the school.

These decisions have to be made, moreover, in terms of the real needs of people in the specific circumstances of their place and time, not in terms of artificial conventions or institutional tradition. We must, therefore, expect that the coming years will bring a much greater diversity of styles and approaches than was to be found in the past.

Despite the importance of local variation, however, there are enough common elements in human experience, and a powerful enough interaction of human societies upon each other, to permit us to make statements of general validity about the need for change and the stresses which it induces.

REFERENCES

1. Faure, E., et al. *Learning to be: the world of education today and tomorrow.* lst ed. Paris, Unesco; London, Harrap, 1972. 313 p.
2. Alles, J. Mediation in learning: the changing scene in Asia. *Prospects* (Paris, Unesco), vol. 5, no. 2, 1975, p. 239-54.
3. Ki-Zerbo, J. Education and development. In: *Education and development reconsidered: the Bellagio Conference papers.* New York, Praeger, 1974, p. 111.
4. Bizot, J. *Educational reform in Peru.* Paris, Unesco, 1975, p. 17. (International Bureau of Education, Experiments and Innovations in Education, no. 16.)
5. International Conference on Education, thirty-fifth session, 1975. *Final report.* Part I: Major trends in education. Paris, Unesco, 1975.
6. Ki-Zerbo, J. op. cit.

CHAPTER TWO

Stresses of change

Everything gets faster; everything intensifies. In diverse and frightening ways, the course of events shows us the need for more and more rapid readjustment, more and more drastic adaptation; and the consequences of failure to adjust and adapt are ever more alarming. A watershed seems to have been passed: there is no time now for evolution to follow its natural rhythm, and no limit to the damage that may occur in consequence of the forced pace.

CHANGE TAKES ON A GLOBAL DIMENSION

Changes in social organization, demanding change in the function of education, come about in response to the growth of human powers. The key powers, the anthropologists tell us, are the power to measure, to calculate, to communicate, to travel and to kill. At various times and in various places, environmental or economic pressures have given special stimulus to the development of one or other of these powers. This in turn produces a surge of change in the conditions of life of the society. The need to learn how to cope with these new conditions—to absorb the new knowledge needed for the collective advantage and for profitable exploitation of the new environment—shapes the tasks assigned by society to the schools and their teachers. The really significant change in the last few decades is that, for mankind as a whole, these powers have increased beyond all possibility of their full deployment. This planet, at any rate, offers no scope for the human race to do all that it is capable of doing (though this has not yet deterred the most powerful States from continuing to develop and apply their powers).

This is a radical change. The meaning of it is that we are compelled by the increase of human powers to look at the entire human
race as one community, and to realize that for that community there
is no other place to go. The problem now for mankind as a whole is
not to seek new fields for the deployment of enhanced powers, but
to restrain the exercise of existing power by the selective application
of a global morality. There are no more 'others' to compete with;
from now on every defeat we inflict is visited upon ourselves. It
becomes the urgent task of the schools to instill that truth and the
discipline involved in applying it.[1] 'All future teachers,' says the
report of the 1975 ICE, 'should be urged to be aware of the need for
human solidarity in a shrinking world, and for service to humanity
rather than to discriminatory nationalism; and respect for life and
ecology were prime imperatives in the formation of the teacher' [1].

This is not mere rhetoric, but reflects the deep concern already
felt by young people. Torsten Husén reports a European viewpoint:
'A questionnaire administered [in Sweden] to 1,300 pupils in grade
nine showed that problems of human dignity, of race, and of peace
and war headed the list of philosophical and ethical topics that
concerned sixteen-year-old pupils—I could not escape the reflection,' Husén adds, 'that young people now seem to be reacting in
the same way more or less universally' [2]. Global morality is a
strong concept in the minds of our children.

The school, it was suggested earlier, is the instrument through
which society develops both the ability and the will to act in ways
that promote survival and the well-being of the community. We
have to find our way to the effective performance of that role in
terms of the thesis that the only sensible definition of 'community' is
the totality of mankind.

TEACHING IN THE GLOBAL CONTEXT

The key element in instilling a global morality, and an understanding of the kind of behaviour that confers advantage in the perspectives of a global morality, is the teacher.

1. 'Answers,' said Prime Minister Manley of Jamaica in a recent speech, 'will be
found within the framework of a perceived global ethic, whether arrived at by a
moral or a pragmatic route.'

The teacher must be effectively reached, encouraged and helped to seek out and recognize the information which most powerfully supports the basic theses of the global morality. He must then learn to use it not only for specific and explicit teaching in the terms which are most likely to reach the consciousness and stir the emotions of his students, but to shape his own attitudes and influence the rituals, routine and discipline of the school.

This requires that the teacher no longer be seen as the transmitter of what is already orthodox, the purveyor of materials previously prepared in terms of established ideas, the obedient actor in a context that is not of his making, but as prophet, initiator, creator of curriculum, designer of the learning context, engaged in a sustained and deliberate effort to modify the tastes of his students (child or adult) and so, by influencing their acceptance or rejection of messages embodied in taboo and mythology, to accelerate change in the central stock of the ideas of the society. Teacher education and curriculum development are the most effective means of intensifying the deliberate effort of communication through the school, and the change in the teacher's role brought about by increase in the initiative he has been allowed is the most effective means of causing the mechanism to operate in a different, more deliberate way.

The implications of this, the difficulties and the possible dangers are, of course, enormous, and will be examined in later chapters. In stating the necessity for an adaptation of all school systems to recognize the morality inherent in the concept of a worldwide human community, however, we must in the meantime recognize the real and urgent needs of different peoples to accomplish specific changes of a less drastic kind in their own different ways. This raises again the problem of change in institutions.

OVERCOMING INSTITUTIONAL RESISTANCE

As has already been remarked, institutions once established tend to take on a life of their own, developing their own internal goals and their own internal measures of quality, efficiency and success. They develop, in other words, a powerful internal dynamic that makes them very resistant to change. Public education systems tend to be particularly obstinate in this resistance. For one thing, their original mandate was to conserve and perpetuate the principles on which the social organization was based, and as a result they tend to exhibit a hierarchical, authoritarian structure. In such a structure, it is of course easy to 'decree' change. The effect of this usually is that everyone obediently adopts a new vocabulary and a new style of reporting, and goes on doing exactly the same thing behind the screen of apparent compliance.

Social policy, especially in those States which are necessarily attempting to bring about rapid transformation in their economic orientation or to forge cohesive nationhood, needs an acceleration of educational reform. The introduction of new social policy is often accompanied by an attempt to prescribe a change in education—to short-cut the adaptive process by substituting decree for the natural cultural input.

This is almost always bound to fail. The only effective way to introduce new purposes into the school, and to secure new outputs, is to provide for change in the role of the teacher. In particular, it is essential, as the 1975 ICE pointed out, 'that conditions exist for serving teachers and future teachers to be aware of the changes in the teachers' roles and to be prepared for new roles and functions', and that 'Teachers and administrators of all categories and levels should be aware of the roles played by them in the present state and development of education. They should understand that the roles and functions are not fixed, unchangeable categories, but are evolving under the influence of changes taking place in the society and in the education system itself.' [3] This need must be recognized and provided for at the first stage of educational planning; it cannot be built on as a kind of suffix or afterthought.

At the same time, the initial planning for any social policy change, and the educational planning that must be integrated with it, should reinforce the direct effort of educational change by a widespread effort to engage the public in understanding and discussing the implications of the change. The 1975 ICE recognized this necessity in the following words:

'All appropriate forces of the society should be involved in the definition of aims and objectives of education and consequently of teacher education. In this definition of purposes and objectives, teachers should take a responsible part, together with their professional associations or groups [4].'

The converse proposition is illustrated in a report from Colombia, where a retrospective study of an unsuccessful reform states: 'What failed in Colombia was the political will to "let the educational system go ahead" as well as the mobilization of the national community for the establishment of a "new education". These are failures not only of the political authorities, but also of the professional educational leaders and, in a lesser degree, of educational professionals in general' [5].

The institution of the school (which may, in the different conditions of different countries, be seen in terms either of the individual school or of the entire school system) is, in a sense, a community of its own. As earlier remarked, it tends to develop its own internal goals and its own criteria of efficiency and quality. These may come to be at variance with the philosophy of the outer society and the mandate given to the school, and very sharply at variance with the goals of new social policy as formulated by the government of the nation. In the meantime, they will have generated a system of taboo and mythology within the community of the institution, which creates strong resistance to change.

The goals of the school may also preserve the particular interests of the group which was dominant in society at the time when the original mandate was conferred. Given the importance of the credential function of the school, it may not be easy to make the necessary adjustment to the wider-ranging needs of a larger constituency, and to abandon or modify the purpose of differentiation that was originally central to the design of all the processes of the school.

MAINTAINING A RELEVANT SCHOOL SYSTEM

The problem of maintaining an appropriate interaction between the school and other instruments of cultural adaptation—of preserving the threads which must bind the specialized institutions of education to the larger community which must still perform parts of the educative function—is discussed in detail in a later chapter of this book. In the meantime, however, it should be observed that failure to do so is creating a real danger to the well-being of young people in that it promotes scepticism about the necessity for formal schooling. It cannot be said too often that the kind of cultural and behavioural conditioning that young people are being exposed to in a random way in the society outside the school is not only counter-productive but may be positively harmful. The lore that is being transmitted is not often related to valid survival strategies for the individual—still less for the collectivity. The body of taboo and mythology that is being ingested and internalized is to a great extent formed in disregard of the lessons of objective scientific knowledge, makes far too much concession to conjecture and speculation, and is alarmingly authoritarian in its prescription of techniques of communication, codes, rituals, routines and initiatory rites.

Again it must be stated that a society which needs to be highly organized (and that is the case in today's world of shrinking resources and enormous pressures of population) also needs a highly organized process for regulation of what Eduard Lindeman described as 'the momentous and necessary adjustment which all children must soon or late attack ... accommodation to the adult world with its complex of habits, customs, mores and traditions' [6].

This is not to deny that there is, in many countries, clear evidence of the progressive isolation of the school from its context, and the consequent alienation of its clients, and of the need for a massive effort of reintegration. But the need is for improvement, not abolition; for re-schooling, not de-schooling.

Developing regions have a particular problem, in that so many of them have inherited education systems which were implanted in the first place by a colonizing power. These embodied the system of taboo and mythology that was proper to the circumstances of the metropolitan country at the time of colonization, the credential function appropriate to social ranking in that country, and a vocational function developed to meet the economic needs of the colonizers, not of the native peoples. In every respect, indeed, the colonial school systems may be said to have been instruments of exploitation, designed exclusively to maintain and promote the collective advantage of the dominant sectors of the population of the 'mother' country, and therefore, almost by definition, alien to the peoples among whom they were implanted. In their curriculum, practicality was only of the slightest importance, since practicality referred only to the minimal skill levels required for reliable supply of primary products for export. Rank and distinction, which brought with them the right to share in the authority of the colonizing power (and enjoy the comforts of reasonable working conditions and superior food), were based on mastery of the literary and theoretical 'knowledge' distilled from the past experience, the economic imperatives and the resultant cultural biases of a totally alien community. The problem is well summed up in a policy statement from Indonesia: 'To-day's general education system as inherited from the colonial period was not originally planned to: (a) produce development-oriented individuals; (b) extract and develop worthwhile values and aspirations from the Indonesian culture as the basis for to-day's cultural development' [7].

The very isolation of such an institution from the generality of its social environment, strengthened and perpetuated by the fact that its most influential practitioners and policy makers were themselves graduates from its own processes, who had got where they were by internalizing its value system, made it all the more obstinate in its resistance to change. The greater its alienation, the more radical the need for change; the more radical the change proposed, the stronger the resistance. To compound the problem, the administrative skills needed to turn an institution around, to redefine its mandate and translate it into actual procedures, were generally lacking; and the need for these skills drove the developing countries back to seek the help of the very people who were the embodiment of the old values. With the best will in the world, expatriates and foreign experts cannot imbue an education system with the sensitivity and the spirit of cultural fidelity that it needs to answer to a valid mandate. Again, we have to recognize that the creation of a teaching force which has a high level of understanding of social imperatives, a clear perception of the perspectives within which priorities have to be set, a strong cultural bond with the society it serves, and a high level of initiative in devising effective curricula and methodology, is the key to appropriate change. This implies close involvement of the teaching profession in the elaboration of educational policy.

Equations begin to emerge. For many of the world's nations, irrelevance of the school to contemporary needs is a function of dependence. Active involvement of the teaching profession in policy development is a necessary condition of true independence.

Delegates to the 1975 ICE stressed these points: 'To make educational reforms real, teachers must be involved in their conception and elaboration as well as their implementation. . . . The over-riding priority was to bring education and teaching into line with economic and social realities; otherwise it must lack innovative force. In some nations élitism and false prestige still had to be eradicated . . .' [8].

Many commentators have written eloquently on the problems of the colonial inheritance. 'Are Africans free,' asks Dragoljub Najman, 'to change the existing system of education and to try to find their own way ... without great resistance and violent criticism from those of their people who have been educated according to foreign standards and who consider those standards as being the best possible in existence?' Answering with a hopeful affirmative, he adds: 'If we want a reform to succeed ... then we must not forget those who will eventually implement the reform—the teachers.... Whether they are good or bad teachers does not matter, since they must in one way or another be associated with the reform. This is even more true when it comes to educational innovation' [9].

REGULATING CHANGE—PROBLEMS AND PRINCIPLES

Each nation must make its own analysis of where it stands in terms of its purposes and powers in relation to the environment, its present goals of development, the kinds of studies and life-skill training that have to be formalized in the school system, and the specific objectives of each. This kind of analysis is a very complex task, and it has to be continuous in order to keep the school system in touch with actual needs. The built-in tendencies to obsolescence and alienation in school systems are so strong that they will constantly tend to distort educational purposes; so they have to be constantly challenged by a continuous re-appraisal of educational policies.

Very few nations, if any, have so far found a really satisfactory way of keeping the relationship between general social and economic policies and the education system under this kind of continuous review. In fact, it is only recently that it has been recognized that educational planning at such a comprehensive level is necessary, and the need for its continuous renewal is a new and rather frightening idea.

The planning of appropriate change in education must rest upon a careful estimate of the stage reached in the transfer of responsibilities from the informal area of natural social interaction to the domain of formal public institutions, as well as of the nature of the knowledge, skills and attitudes that have to be developed. In other words, it is not enough for planners to decide what kind of social or technological changes are needed for the healthy development of the economy (though that is the first question that must be asked). It is not enough, either, to ask what increments of knowledge or skill, what development of attitudes or understandings, are needed to make these changes possible and successful. The planner must go further and ask three more questions. In the specific conditions of the society, what tasks and what objectives must be assigned to the *school* system because they cannot any longer be accomplished by informal processes of observation and imitation outside the school? Which learning tasks and objectives might, on the other hand, be more efficiently accomplished by organizing the process of observation and imitation in the community outside the school? What are the organizational implications of the redistribution of responsibilities?

But that is only the beginning of the inquiry. The fact must be faced that any significant increase in the responsibility of the school (or, for that matter, any increase in the complexity of the learning needs of a community, whether or not the school system responds) is itself a cause of social change and possible social disruption, which will have to be countered in turn by further changes in the purposes and processes of formal education. Every step forward by the society into areas where new knowledge or new understanding is needed puts a new strain on the competence of the informal educators—the parent, the elders of the community, the priests, the custodians of traditional lore and conventional wisdom. When the school undertakes to teach new knowledge or new ideas, it may seem to be competing with these traditional educators and diminishing their authority, and pulling the student away from their world. It becomes a necessary task of education to help the community to accept and understand the need for new learning—to sell itself, as it were, by making its processes and goals understood. It is part of the duty of the schools to see that, in taking over the teaching role in necessary ways, they do not teach disdain for valid tradition nor break the fragile structures of trust and understanding which are needed to keep the child in a healthy and secure relationship with family and community. The new knowledge, the new skills, have to be introduced in a setting that respects old ways and preserves their human and cultural values.

Social harmony and the personal development of individuals are closely linked. People can experience growth only when they also have a sense of security, or human continuity, of identification with a stable cultural tradition. They must also be helped to acquire a sense of personal worth, a sense of confidence in their own identity. Without that, they cannot be expected to develop any real respect for others nor to become responsible decision makers. When the school takes over any part of the education of young people, it must take conscious and deliberate responsibility for those aspects of personal development. The failure to realize this fully, or to work out satisfactory ways of coping with that responsibility, must be seen as a major cause of alienation of young people in many societies, and as a factor in the widespread increase in individual and societal neuroses.

Thus, Amadou-Mahtar M'Bow, in a foreword to Dragoljub Najman's book, speaks of the need 'to integrate both the contribution of local traditions and the most recent results of science and educational technology' and to seek 'the integration of authentic values into the new education systems' [10]. This effort of integration is a vital part of the new role of the teachers, and will be discussed in a later chapter.

To say all this is, of course, merely to re-state what was said at the beginning of the previous chapter—that it is the moral duty of the school system to bring about the integration of the individual into the collectivity in a manner that is to the maximum advantage of both.

Specific decisions will vary greatly, depending on the stage of development of particular societies. In some situations, the first imperative for the collective good may be to improve communications skills—basic or functional literacy—either as a vehicle for technical instruction or as the basis for cultural studies designed to promote awareness of a national identity. In others, familiarization with the characteristics, needs and limitations of machines may be a necessary prerequisite to the mechanization of farming or manufacture. Adjustment to new and more productive modes of rural living may be a high priority. The main point is that the decision as to goals and the evaluation of the success of the schooling process must be in terms of the stage of evolution of the particular society and the kinds of knowledge appropriate to that stage. In each society there is a particular need to disseminate some form of new learning. In the circumstances of each society there are things that could be done better in the school than outside it, if the school were adapted in appropriate ways. They are not necessarily the things traditionally assigned to the school, and to make the institution fit to handle them may mean discarding obsolete or alien procedures related to past concepts of its custodial, vocational, credential or indoctrinating functions.

Society must find ways to change its schools according to need. School, in turn, will change society, and it must learn how to do so with the minimum of discomfort and disorientation. This may mean a considerable extension of the activity of the school to include programmes designed to bridge the gap in understanding between the general public and the graduates of the new education.

PRESSURES AND PROBLEMS OF INTER-CULTURAL ENCOUNTER

It would, of course, be unrealistic to suggest that the development of educational philosophies and programmes in a particular country can be undertaken in total isolation from world trends. It was remarked earlier that every local situation must be seen not only in terms of its unique and special characteristics but also in its relationship to the general fabric of world society. The goal, as stated by an Arab educator, is to achieve 'a mature national culture, as deeply attached to its genuine values and its own specific culture as it is concerned with establishing solid links with civilization at large and the common experience of man' [11]. That fabric is changing at a vastly increasing rate. The increase in the speed of change is brought home to us when we realize that the human race, which is now so frantic in its pursuit of technological novelty, lived by hunting, fishing and gathering for 90 per cent of its history to date, and spent thousands of years adjusting to the first modest changes in the technology associated with those activities. As serious in its effects as the increase in the speed of change, however, is the increase in the geographical scope of its effects. Some nations have pushed their development to the point where they can no longer move, no longer change their economic or social policies, without in some way affecting everyone. Conversely, there is no nation that can decide to shape its own destiny without considering the reactions of others.

Every nation will necessarily either affect others or be affected by the decisions of others, day by day and year by year.

Among the most serious effects of this is the artificial acceleration of development. Peoples who spent centuries, even milennia, on the process of evolution through the early stages of their own social and technological development are now creating a world environment which has the effect of hustling other peoples through those same stages in decades. As a result, a process which was long, slow and often painful when carried out through the natural progress of evolution—in which concomitant social and philosophical change was assimilated and accommodated unconsciously through the gradual growth of appropriate taboo and mythology—has, for the developing countries, been telescoped into a few years and must be accomplished almost overnight by deliberate planning. It is often forgotten that the conscious and deliberate educational effort being made by the countries of the less-developed regions is an attempted short-cut without precedent in human history—an attempt to span several centuries of development in one leap. No such leap ever had to be attempted by the more-favoured nations. They evolved at their own pace, and certainly not without mistakes.

Even in the post-colonial era, then, the less-developed regions are experiencing a violent and abrupt modification of their environment, in one way or another, by the intrusive influence of the developed nations. ('The Africans of to-day,' says Najman, 'have their feet in the neolithic and their heads in the thermonuclear age' [12].) What is the appropriate educational response?

One part of the necessary response is an effort of 'defensive adaptation'. The causes of change have to be interpreted to reduce the sense of helplessness and alienation that abrupt change brings. The lines of human progress have to be comprehended in terms that do not outrage the values of the traditional culture. Awareness of one's own cultural identity and of the developmental imperatives for one's own people has to be sharpened, so that a healthy scepticism towards novelty, based on a realistic perception of long-term self-interest, can be developed, along with the capacity to choose what is of value and reject the frivolous. And the goal must always be to choose the lines of development that offer the best hope of independent competence and self-determination.

These purposes have to be turned into educational policies in the light of the conditions of each specific society. What is most important to remember, however, is that they can only be turned into workable policies with the active collaboration, from the outset, of a competent teaching profession, capable of designing and putting into effect the mechanisms of cultural and social linkage and communication which have not had time to develop spontaneously.

A second part of the necessary response is the rapid development of the ability to take and use what is useful in the new environment. This again will not be a valid or successful undertaking unless it is pursued in a way that is truly appropriate to local conditions. Serious mistakes have been made in development aid programmes through disregard of that elementary principle.

The impact of new technological development on a society that is already highly urbanized and technologically developed is quite different from its impact on societies that do not have these characteristics. One of the implications of this fact is that the success or failure of various devices (including various educational techniques) must not be seen as absolute. They must be studied in the setting in which they occurred and their chances of succeeding or failing in a totally different setting must be carefully considered. Examples abound of unsuccessful attempts to transplant technology—unsuccessful because those who made the attempt did not realize that what was a normal, foreseeable and not particularly radical development in one setting, succeeding because it had the strength of basic familiarity and the force of habit and cultural conformity embodied in it, would be an unnatural growth, an aberration doomed to failure, in another setting.

Technology is not just hardware, any more than education is containable in a set of administrative procedures. Time and again the installation of hardware—or of the administrative procedures proper to a technological society—has failed to produce the desired effect, because technology is a philosophy, an acquired set of attitudes and expectations, a state of mind, a system of values. Familiarity with the vagaries of machines, their need for loving care and feeding and regular maintenance; readiness to accept the discipline of schedules that machines demand; the tyrannies of timing and quantitative accounting; the dependable regularity of movement and standardization of communication that they need; regard for exactness of measurement and calculation—these things, not the machines, are the essence of technology, and if these are not assimilated the technology cannot be transferred.

Educational technology is a case in point. Educational television, for example, is a natural device in a society in which every child already watches several hours of television in his own home—a society in which television is one of the ordinary modes of communication. Educational programming must take account of the child's expectations when he faces the familiar screen, build upon the child's perceptions of the familiar medium and take account of the world view that he has already developed through his domestic viewing. To whatever extent educational television has succeeded at the school level (a limited extent at best, and dependent on the competence of the teacher as judge of its value and interpreter of its lessons) it has done so not because of its novelty but because of its familiarity. Transplanted to an area where that familiarity does not exist, it becomes an entirely different kind of instrument, and no kind of experience with its use in its original setting will be automatically valid as a guide to its employment or a means of predicting its success.

In short, unhappy experiences with educational technology have occurred where attempts were made to adopt the mechanisms without the spirit, to take devices that had succeeded because they were familiar and try to use them where they were novel and even threatening, to grasp the symbol of the technological society without its substance. The actual point of breakdown is in the classroom or in whatever place the students gather; and the specific reason for breakdown is that the cultural and communications gap, the discontinuity between the known context and the new factor, is too extreme to be mediated by the teacher. It is quite useless to ask a teacher to use a mode of teaching which requires, for its effectiveness, a cultural context or a previous level of awareness which does not exist in the society in which the teacher works.

IMPLICATIONS FOR THE TEACHER—
THE INTERPRETIVE ROLE

The key to all ordered learning is the interpretive effort of the teacher which must give meaning to the real essence of new knowledge within the framework of that which is already known and understood. In attacking the problem of adjustment to technological change, we come up against the problem of discovering what the limits may be of the possibility of doing this—the limits, that is to say, of the possible role of the teacher, as well as the immediate challenge of preparing teachers for the evident short-term demands of their changing role.

Central to the matter of response to the stress of change, and to the teacher's role in easing that stress, is the problem of cultural interpretation. If new circumstances and new experiences can be placed within the framework of existing ideas about social relationships, smooth adaptation is possible. If, on the other hand, new experience and new ideas cannot be reconciled with existing ideas about social relationships—about the nature of inter-personal encounter and the kinds of rights, obligations and resources that are involved in that encounter—a serious and painful discontinuity results. The individual or the community (for this has become a common experience of ethnic groups or entire social classes when there has been drastic change in the environment) is torn loose from the structure that conferred a sense of security and a perspective of values. The familiar, inherited system of taboo and mythology that served as an unconscious and authoritative guide to judgement and action is discredited. The known features of the landscape disappear, moral navigation becomes a matter of immense difficulty, and fear and uncertainty (often made more acute by the dominating presence of those who are familiar with and confident in the new atmosphere) provoke hostile and destructive behaviour.

Then it becomes the task of education to help in reorientation, to restore the sense of security and self-confidence and provide the basis for a rational morality, to counteract the effects of change in the roles of family or community or tribe, and to build a new understanding of the nature of the collectivity and of the rights and obligations proper to it. To do so successfully requires that the gap between old and new be made as narrow as possible—that every effort be made to preserve what can be preserved of the existing cultural identity, and to reaffirm and reinterpret it in new terms. This may involve, for example, the use of minority languages as the vehicle of instruction during early years, the deliberate revival of traditional literary and dramatic forms and of mythological themes, adapted to embody new perceptions, the encouragement of art forms through which communal identity is reassured, or even the revival and organized teaching of former principles of social organization and the design and management of human settlements—principles which may have been obscured or distorted by the intrusion of customs associated with the technological manifestations of an alien culture.

This interpretive effort is perhaps the most difficult and challenging of all the functions of the education system. Certainly, its importance has increased enormously in the recent past and will continue to increase, and this will have a very great significance for the evolution of the role of the teacher.

Success in interpretation, in mediating the encounter between the student and the new realms of knowledge or skill, will make the difference between the situation where the student understands what is expected of him and what the real importance of that expectation is with reference to his own future life and the well-being of the community—feels confident of meeting the expectation and internalizes the goals set for him—and the contrary situation where the student feels excluded by a barrier of mystery, fails to grasp the relevance of the tasks demanded of him, and develops a sense of resentment at the imposition of the dimly perceived goals of the 'establishment'.

The division often established within the school, between those who feel that they are a party to the objectives of the system and those who have not assimilated its goals and feel that they are being ignored or exploited, is still regarded with indifference in too many school systems. There is, however, a growing feeling that it violates the essential morality of public education. When it is clearly necessary for people to go through the process of formal schooling in order to be competent in the management of their lives, and when that necessity is recognized by making school attendance compulsory, there is no moral justification for anything other than equality of treatment.

The logical outcome of this, however, is the assertion that one of the major functions of the school, and of the teacher in the school, is to ensure that each and every child is enabled to succeed in mastering the learning that he or she particularly needs.

THE PURSUIT OF EQUALITY OF OPPORTUNITY

On the face of it, this is a mild and sensible statement, and it certainly expresses the goals of the informal learning process which preceded the school in society and still operates alongside it. Can we imagine, for instance, that the parent who offers practical wisdom wants anything less than complete success for the child in assimilating the lesson?

The immediate effect of a shift of attitude in this direction in the school is to introduce much more diversity of method and approach than ever before. When it was assumed that access to schooling was a privilege, so that the school, at any given stage, had no responsibility except to those who could demonstrate that they already possessed certain standard skills and competencies, or shared a common stock of ideas and knowledge, the teacher could take a great deal for granted. He could pursue a standardized curriculum by standardized methods, secure in the feeling that it was not his fault if a student deviated from the norm or was unfamiliar with the code of ideas on which communication rested, and therefore 'failed'.

But there has been a general and quite marked change in the last few years in the prevailing concept of equity in the treatment of students, and of equality of opportunity in education. At one time it was considered sufficient that, at best, all prospective students should have access to the same kind of educational process. Then it was realized that this immediately guaranteed advantage to some and handicap to others, since differences in mother tongue, in cultural background, in economic status or in home circumstances can have a decisive influence on the ability of different individuals to profit from the same opportunities. It is not sufficient, in other words, to provide equal access to equal facilities and a standardized programme unless measures are taken to ensure that everyone starts with an equal ability to comprehend and benefit from the process.

This, in turn, has been criticized as an inadequate concept of equality of opportunity. To bring everyone up to the same start line—the goal of remedial pre-school programmes in many countries—guarantees nothing. The variations in individual circumstances which cause the initial disparity do not disappear; they continue to operate, and cultural or social differences in the way of thinking, or in the choice of symbols used to communicate ideas, or mistaken assumptions about the ideas which are current and familiar in the student's home environment, may frustrate the teaching process and pre-destine students to failure.

Is it the responsibility of the school to detect such failures of communication and to seek ways to remedy them? The answer must be that it is, because the transfer of functions from private life to the institutions of the public sector has, almost everywhere, reached the stage where schooling is not just one of the ways by which people learn but the principal and necessary way. It is not an option, but a requirement, and therefore not a privilege, but a right. The school, accordingly, must not only offer an educational programme but also accept responsibility for its success and blame for its failures.

There is still a further stage, however, in the development of the idea of equality. It is the thesis that to compel the convergence of all students, regardless of their cultural or social background, towards attainment of a common goal is inappropriate and unjust. It is felt to be unjust because the goal is bound to be related to a specific philosophy, a specific cultural orientation, that will be natural to some students and unnatural to others. Those to whom the cultural bias is unfamiliar or alien will either be working under a handicap, and subject to a greater risk of eventual failure than others, or will achieve self-confidence and success at the price of renouncing their cultural identity and becoming alienated from their community of origin. This, demonstrably, has been the case for ethnic or linguistic minorities in many countries; it was long ago recognized that in very many instances the less-privileged classes in highly stratified societies suffer the effects of their cultural and linguistic deviance from the norm as well as other forms of hereditary disadvantage.

The prescription for equality, in these terms, is that the school provides goals for each student that are compatible with his or her particular orientation as an individual and as a member of a particular sub-culture within the society, and also that it offers a programme of teaching and learning that will, in effect, guarantee success in the attainment of these goals.

To meet this prescription fully is probably impossible. As an ideal, however, it serves as a useful corrective to excessive and repressive standardization, which has long been a vice of the traditional school.

The kind of compromise that must be made between the goals of equity and equality and the developmental imperatives of the society as a whole is a matter for calculation in the specific circumstances of each country. It is a calculation that should be made consciously, purposely and publicly, and, like all educational policy decisions, be subject to continuous review.

There is, nevertheless, a global trend towards a more sensitive regard for difference of every kind, towards recognition of the need to modify not only programmes but goals as well, and towards greater concern for disadvantage and learning disabilities. When this concern is extended into the area of physical, perceptual or emotional handicap (a degree of consideration that for many developing countries still lies in the realm of future ideals rather than of present possibilities), the importance of the diagnostic and remedial skills of the teacher is vastly increased. For all societies, though, it is increasingly true that effective education requires that teachers be able to sense individual differences in the perceptions of their students and to adjust the learning programme accordingly.

The development of the school, erratic but inexorable, towards responsibility for all-round learning—the pressure for it to minister to needs for survival skills, the skills of competent living, cultural awareness, moral perspective, political consciousness and responsibility, personal growth towards autonomy and an appropriate self-image, and a host of other objectives in relation to which the only justifiable outcome is success and the notion of student 'failure' is untenable—has profound implications for content, methodology, resource selection and development, the formulation of specific objectives, evaluation of progress, relationship with the community, and the modification of public attitudes. All these are matters in which the performance of the teacher is the key element, and in which the teacher must be capable of deep involvement at all stages. They imply a considerable broadening of traditional ideas about what a teacher is, and a careful study of that question in the context of the changing school and the changing society.

REFERENCES

1. International Conference on Education, thirty-fifth session, Geneva, 1975. *Final report*. Paris, Unesco, 1975. 59 p.
2. Husen, T. *Present trends and future developments in education: a european perspective*. Toronto, Ontario Institute for Studies in Education, 1973. 42 p. (Occasional papers No. 8.)
3. International Conference on Education, op. cit.
4. Ibid.
5. Benoit, A. *Changing the educational system: a Colombian case study*. Munich, Weltforum Verlag, 1974. 285 p.
6. Lindeman, E. *The meaning of adult education*. Montreal, Harvest House, 1951.
7. Indonesia. Ministry of Education and Culture. *Policy statement*. Djakarta, 1972. 16, 23 p.
8. International Conference on Education, op. cit.
9. Najman, D. *Education in Africa—what next?* Aubenas (France), Deux Mille, 1972.
10. Ibid.
11. Dayem, A.A. The changing Arab world. In: *Education on the move*. Paris, Unesco, 1975, p. 24-8.
12. Najman, D., op. cit.

CHAPTER THREE

The function of 'teaching'

Everyone is a teacher, in one sense, at one time or another. Almost every time we communicate with anyone we are trying to impart information, and we all find ourselves at some time in the position of trying to transmit a skill or persuade someone to a particular belief.

The sense in which the word 'teacher' applies in these informal situations is that of someone who, in his or her own person, possesses or embodies some knowledge, a skill or a belief, and who is usually making the judgement that it is a good thing to try to share it. This exercise of the role of teacher, however, is a matter of time, place and circumstance. The individual can make no claim to the permanent title of 'teacher', since a change of circumstances, an encounter with someone else, may at any moment reverse the roles.

No very great change occurs in this concept of the teaching function when it is first formalized in the institution of the school. The essential difference is that the community has decided that there are particular kinds of knowledge or skill that have to be continuously maintained, the learning of which cannot therefore be left to the hazard of random encounter. People who possess the knowledge or skill in question are identified and isolated, so that the process of transfer of that knowledge or skill to those who need to acquire it can be reliably organized and repeated.

In this kind of role, the usefulness of the teacher to the student begins to diminish from the first day, because it is measured by the difference in their level of knowledge. The objective set for the student is to reduce that difference to zero. Theoretically, the day will come when he knows all that the teacher knows. At that point, the teacher will have to pass him on to someone who knows more, or else to return him to his guardians with the assurance that he can do no more for him, because he has exhausted the teacher's stock of knowledge.

This assumes, though, that knowledge is finite and unchanging, and that the object of learning is to build up a store of 'possessed' learning through memorization. Real knowledge of a scientific kind, however, is not positive and finite, but elusive and ever-changing. This kind of teaching, therefore, tends to turn attention away from real knowledge and to concentrate on artificial and arbitrary kinds of scholarship. Especially, it emphasizes the mastery of the techniques of symbolic communication—language, grammar, rhetoric, numbers and the like (attractive to scholars because they can be thoroughly known)—and also stresses the traditional mythologies through which satisfyingly 'final' answers to conjecture are supplied.

Significant change in the role of the teacher begins when the rate of accumulation of new data forces upon us the realization that real knowledge is infinite and cannot be possessed; that the forms in which the human senses grasp it and the human mind codifies it are tentative and arbitrary, not absolute, and are validated only when knowledge is successfully applied to current needs; that symbolic communication has to be continuously enlarged and enriched, and even created, to accommodate new perceptions; and that skills and mythologies alike are subject to continuous modification.

BASIC CHANGE IN THE TEACHING FUNCTION —
FROM MONOPOLIST TO MEDIATOR

School systems tend to be slow in reacting to this realization. At first, attempts are made to 'modernize' the system by giving the teacher new, more specific assignments, instead of by changing his role. New packages of knowledge are prepared for delivery to students in the same old way. Persons who 'possess' knowledge about the 'disciplines' thus created are given the task of transmitting it. The emphasis tends to be laid upon the kinds of knowledge that are believed to be useful for the purpose of economic development, and also (too often, indeed) for the maintenance of social distinction and the existing social order.

The inadequacy of this response is more often felt than understood, and signs of its failure are very disappointing to those who have put so much effort into a reform which does not seem to work. 'When an education system changes in scale,' says one commentator, expressing an African viewpoint [1], 'it also changes function, though this change is not explicit. The social and cultural objectives concealed behind the academic definition of levels lose their significance, while educators and administrators deplore the deterioration of models whose structures and criteria have, unbeknown to them, changed ... they often make costly and pitiful efforts to restore levels which are now no more than shadows, outdated and out of place in to-day's circumstances.'

The scale of education systems is changing in two ways. One is forced upon us by the vast increase and importance of available scientific knowledge; the other by the recent evolution of the concept of democratization (the leitmotiv of the 1975 ICE [2]).

We have reached a stage where new knowledge is being discovered much faster than it can be adequately codified, still less 'possessed'. We are also discovering that many of our past applications of knowledge, arbitrary and over-confident, were extremely unwise, and that the separate 'disciplines' through which we tried to impose tidiness and order upon the learning process have led us into difficulties because they gave us an artificial and partial view of reality. Too often, the consequences of what we thought to be knowledgeable action have been unexpected and shocking. In such circumstances, the assumption that the possession of knowledge brings with it the power to control the future is open to serious question.

The notion of the full-time teacher as an individual who possesses a fixed stock of knowledge of a kind deemed useful is therefore less and less tenable. In the informal situation, of course, the old model continues to be valid at particular moments in time. Each of us may, at a given moment, have a need to know or be able to do something that someone else knows or is able to do and, at that particular moment, that 'someone else' exercises for us the traditional function of 'teacher'. Similar moments are always likely to occur in the formal setting of the school, also, and the competent teacher must be able to recognize their occurrence and respond adequately. But it is a mistake to see in them the essential function of a person to whom the role of teacher is assigned on a full-time institutionalized basis. The notion that a teacher is there to impart facts or demonstrate skills implies a set of social and cultural objectives that are inappropriate in face of the current explosion of knowledge and its continuous challenge to the validity of orthodox opinion, and in face of the general demand for the democratization of education.

The teacher, in his new role, makes no claim to a monopoly of knowledge; on the contrary, he realizes that knowledge is all around us, overwhelming in its diversity and oppressive in its insistent challenge to our beliefs. He realizes that to live in this age is to be always learning (which also means clearing the mind of obsolete ideas) and his task is to help people to accommodate to that fact. To convey knowledge accurately, clearly and effectively is still a vital task, but as the 1975 ICE observed, there is need 'to maintain an appropriate balance between the traditonal function of imparting authentic knowledge (a vital aspect of the teacher's role in an era when scientific knowledge is multiplying so rapidly and affecting society so deeply) and the wider social functions ...', including helping their students 'to integrate, in a coherent philosophy, the flood of fragmented, partial and often inaccurate information' which now besets them in their daily lives [3]. To be a teacher now, in short, is to be a mediator in the encounter between the individual and the mass of information, factual, conjectural and mythological which daily threatens to engulf him—an encounter in which selection and use of knowledge become more important than its absorption.

TEACHING HOW TO LIVE WITH CHANGE

But what does 'mediating' mean?

The only way that anyone can survive in any environment is by learning to extract, from the information supplied through all the senses, that which is relevant. In other words, we have to be able to control and evaluate our perceptions so that we see what kinds of decisions favour our own survival and are consistent with the imperatives of collective well-being. We have to understand what kinds of knowledge and skill will make us able to pursue our goals, having regard to our particular abilities and the changes that are likely to occur in our environment. We have to know how we can go about acquiring those kinds of knowledge and skill.

When there is rapid change in the environment, none of this is permanent. When we come upon new knowledge, therefore, we need to be able to use it to change the pattern of our previously acquired knowledge. This we cannot successfully do unless we are prepared to change our ideas about the nature of things in the face of new evidence, and so to grow both intellectually and spiritually. People cannot, however, be expected to be confidently adaptable at such a basic level unless they have the security of a stable self-image, a reasoned and realistic awareness of their own powers and their individual worth, tempered by an equal respect for the worth of others. They also need the security of seeing their own lives in the large perspectives of time and space, given meaning through knowledge and understanding of the diversity of cultures which represent the several collective identities within the over-all human community.

The function of the teacher as mediator is to help people to develop the ability to react in this way, to organize as far as possible the opportunity for them to do so, and to stimulate them to want to do so. The ideal teacher would therefore understand the way in which people at various ages and in various stages of development perceive the world around them, and the way in which these perceptions are affected by cultural or social difference and by individual variation and handicap. He would understand how thought is constructed and how the critical faculty is exercised and can be developed. He would know where particular resources of knowledge and skill are located and be able to organize access to them as and when they were needed, using the various media of communication available. He would do so, not in a random way, but selectively, rationally and constructively, so that the encounter would reinforce and promote the personal growth of the student. He would strengthen the confidence of the student in his own capabilities, and make sure in doing so that the student was learning to assess these capabilities realistically and to exercise them with due regard for the collective interest and the rights of others. He would interpret the student's perceptions in terms of past history, future probability, and the large perspectives of the global morality.

In this role, the teacher's responsibility goes far beyond the transmission of knowledge (though everything that he does depends upon his skill in identifying appropriate knowledge and ensuring that it is accessible in a usable form at the moment of need). He is concerned, above all, with teaching how knowledge can be sought, validated, assimilated and used as a basis for further learning, for forming and modifying goals and ideas, and for rational decision making. He is not so much a source or a purveyor as a guide to sources, an organizer of opportunities and an instructor in the techniques of inquiry and thought. His knowledge is not an ingredient in the student's education, to be consumed and used up, but a catalyst promoting the reactions of learning and growth as a result of the encounter between human capabilities and increasing knowledge.

'More emphasis,' says Torsten Husén in a recent paper, 'will be put on learning, not on teaching.... The focus will be shifted to the economic management of the teaching function, to a close analysis of its real import and of the purposes it is supposed to serve' [4].

THE PERSISTENCE OF OLD MODELS

It was earlier observed that the new does not drive out the old, and that memorials of past attitudes tend to be built solidly into our institutions. The old model of the teacher, and the whole complex set of attitudes and expectations that relates to that model, are extremely persistent.

Basic to that model, as has already been said, is the assumption that the teacher knows more than the student, and that the purpose of the encounter is to transfer knowledge from the one to the other. The end of the process is reached when the student knows as much as the teacher. At that point the student departs, either to begin practising what he has learned (in which case he will either refine his techniques on the basis of his own experience and capabilities, and become greater than his teacher, or practise them imperfectly and with some forgetfulness or less of skill, showing that he is lesser than his teacher), or simply to begin forgetting what he has learned (in which case he will demonstrate that what he learned was not really useful, so that his teacher was really rather silly, or that he is living at a lower intellectual level than his teacher). Or he may go on to receive another quota of knowledge or skill from a teacher who knows more than the former one (in which case he surpasses his former teacher even while he is still a student).

Whichever of these happens, status is involved, and that makes it more difficult to bring real changes to the role of the teacher. One of the most serious obstacles to the kind of change that we are advocating is the persistent idea that status is gained or preserved by knowing more than somebody else.

To say this is not to praise ignorance, nor to depreciate the value of authentic knowledge. It is very important that people should know what they are doing, and whether they are doing it well, and it is equally important (although this is a less fashionable statement) that people should be advised against professing to do that which they do not really know how to do. But it is the capability of 'doing' that is the point. If knowledge is treated as a treasure, to be laid up where neither moth nor rust can corrupt, and to be handed out in measured quantities, with regular tests to measure how much has actually been transferred without spilling, it is meaningless. It does not then matter how real or artificial, up-to-date or obsolete the knowledge is, or what it is about; it is all equally trivial, serving only as a status symbol. Knowledge is like money: it has worth only in its use as a means of doing something, or causing change. In its real, operative form it is dynamic and in constant flux.

Built into our institutions, however, and persistent as a deforming influence upon the role of the teacher, is the concept of knowledge as static, unchanging and quantitatively measurable. The diploma that attests to our past exposure to other people's learning tells us more about the number of years of study than about the quality of that study. The assessment of quality that it communicates is likely to be a measure of our ability to replicate received information in ways that are seldom appropriate in real life, rather than a prediction of our competence in *using* information to accomplish beneficial change.

When the people responsible for the policies of an institution have themselves been ranked by proof of their replicative ability, the prospects of creating an innovative institution are not good. It has to be admitted that educational development in many parts of the world is hampered by institutional structures which could scarcely be more resistant to innovation if they had been designed to be so.

In a sense, of course, they were. When a teacher is seen as the possessor of knowledge, and is dependent for his status on that definition, and when the institution which controls the level on which access is gained to adult society is one that was shaped according to those principles, the school will inevitably come to embody the worst features of the adult in relation to the child—authoritarianism, resistance to anything perceived as a threat to authority or status. In that kind of situation, the contemporary way of doing things in the adult society is insisted upon as the only proper way, and roles are assigned accordingly. In the words of one commentator, 'teachers retain what is, from the point of view of social continuity, the most important function, that of embodying and representing the model of social action that serves, or is publicly declared to serve, as the motor of society' [5]. This commitment is not favourable to innovation, and indeed must involve opposition to it. (Nor, paradoxically, is it favourable in the long run to status. The same writer points out that 'in a society in which changes in the details of social activity rapidly accumulate, and lead to rough questions about the validity of the model, teachers occupying such a role are liable to appear, not simply as traditionalists, but as comic reactionaries' [6]. Even when the pace of change was slower, however, the role of transmitting and enforcing the pattern of orthodox mental and physical behaviour has seldom been held in high esteem. The teacher in the old model of the school has historically ranked as an upper-grade domestic servant—appropriately enough, since he was performing what Paolo Freire has described as a 'domesticating' activity.)

THE PROBLEM OF SELF-PERPETUATING TRADITIONS

If the function of teacher is seen as the transmission of successive quanta of knowledge, with the outcome affecting the status of the teacher in relation to the student, two developments are likely to follow. One is that each successive teacher of a student will claim a status superior to that of his predecessor. (If a student comes to me because he has possessed himself of your entire stock of knowledge, and is now ready to surpass you, it is clear that I surpass you to begin with. Besides, I am in a position to receive the student because I have a diploma showing me to be superior to you in years to study and total quantity of knowledge ingested.) The corollary of this is a curious equation: the younger the child, the lower the status of the teacher (since everyone 'knows' that younger children have had less time to ingest knowledge than older ones, and so need less knowledgeable teachers).[1]

The second development is that, in defence, the teacher at each level may try to delay the moment when his student reaches the end of his competence, and by doing so to postpone his loss of status. One way of doing this is by striving to possess more knowledge (and preferably of a recondite nature, so that the student cannot diminish the stature of the teacher by obtaining the knowledge from some other source).[2]

Another is to make the tests of attainment more difficult, more artificially exacting. A respectable rate of student failures still counts, in many institutions, as a measure of the status of the teacher; and when status is the issue, the nature of serviceability of the knowledge purveyed becomes secondary. So does the question of what kind of competence the test or examination can truly be said to be measuring.

So, by degrees, the role of the teacher shifts to that of protector of the status of the institution and of its internal criteria of social differentiation. The teacher is an antagonist, rather than a helper, and the student is enjoined to ask, not what the school can do for him, but what he can do for the school. In reaction, and in defence of his own status and self-respect, the student may be more concerned to outwit the teacher than to learn from him. Instances can be identified, in fact, where the collective goal of the student body, developed as a response to the antagonism of the institution, is to resist the attempts of the institution to implant knowledge and at the same time to frustrate detection by 'passing' the necessary examinations.

1. The falsity of this equation has been repeatedly exposed. The report of the People's Republic of Hungary to the thirty-fifth session of the International Conference on Education notes that 'we condemn it officially and combat it where possible, but the solution still requires more time'.
2. M.I. Tuqan, in a searching study of education in developing countries, very well describes the defensive uneasiness of the teacher who is unsure of his status, and the stifling effect of this upon learning [7].

At the same time a concept of teacher specialization develops which is related more to status than to the identification of special aspects of the learning process. Traditional schooling, especially at the secondary level, tended to promote the doctrine that worth and integrity reside in the matter to be learned, not in the learner. 'Subjects' were designated and their definition narrowed and refined. Concentration of the teacher's own studies upon the more abstruse areas, in which the students might most readily be confounded, was rewarded with specialist standing.

To condemn this categorically would, of course, be quite wrong. In such areas as the sciences and languages, specialized teachers with a thorough knowledge of the discipline are obviously needed. Nevertheless, an excessive emphasis on unchanging ideas of 'academic excellence' can be a harmful distortion. Hennion, writing of the African situation, speaks of the need to 'adjust the instruments and agents of education to educational standards which are also regarded as variables, and periodically adjusted to cultural, social and economic realities' [8], and Husén comments that 'many of the activities (one is tempted to say rituals) of the school serve mainly to perpetuate the system itself by self-feeding selection procedures.... The verbal-abstract-recitation atmosphere tends to alienate the student from the world of work' [9].

It is often asserted, moreover, that mistaken and outdated considerations of status contribute strongly to the persistence in former colonies of the educational structures set up by the colonizers. Not only do the criteria of status, and the authoritarian, dominating role assigned to the teacher, harmonize very well with the colonial model as earlier described; they also reinforce the separateness of the institution of the school, and so provide strong grounds for resistance to any critical scrutiny by the public and to the kind of involvement of the community in educational policy development that is now generally held to be desirable.

IMPLICATIONS OF THE COMMITMENT TO LIBERATION

In every sense, then, the substitution of the new model of the teacher for the old is a liberating act. It liberates the teaching profession itself, because it provides the basis for a definition of specific professionality that is quite distinct from the general function of 'teaching' in the informal process of social encounter. It thus gives independent identity of a valid kind to teachers—a collective, shared identity. This, in turn, should provide the basis for valid specialization, related to the real purposes and processes of education, and so offer the satisfaction of personal and professional growth as well as the preservation of professional integrity.

It liberates the student, because it places his own development at the centre of the area of concern. Instead of seeking to subjugate the student as efficiently as possible to the interests of those who are at the moment dominant in the social order, it sets forth the goal of liberation of the intellectual and moral powers of the growing individual, and to integrate him, with full respect for his identity and recognition of his particular talents, into a growing and evolving society.

It liberates the community, because it offers to make the school the instrument of its growth, development and self-expression, instead of a screen and sorting device interposed between the home and the world.

But freedom is a heavy burden to bear, and people have too often been content to lay it aside or put it into the hands of others. An education system which is truly liberated and liberating will only remain so if it is well governed—if its mandate is kept under continuous review and actualized through democratic processes. The function of the community in this respect, and the role of the teacher as animator of democracy in school government, will be examined in a later chapter.

Some years ago a Canadian educator asserted that the goals of education must be liberation, integration and commitment: liberation from outmoded concepts, false beliefs, ignorance and negativism; integration of perceptions into a valid framework of thought and ideas; and commitment to a rational and moral purpose. He also pointed out that the process must be applied endlessly, because free societies are 'highly artificial' in that they 'rest largely upon an intellectual basis of difficult and sophisticated thought' [10]. That is particularly true at the present time, when the refinement and dissemination of the difficult, complex and subtle concepts of global morality, referred to earlier, are urgently necessary tasks. Only the resolute pursuit of free thought and free inquiry, along with a general commitment to the goals which a rational assessment of the common good identifies, can offer any hope for a tolerable future for the generality of mankind.

A formidable array of tasks and problems confronts the teacher in the management of liberation, integration and commitment. Assuming that the society has made its assessment of the over-riding imperatives of the moment, in terms of time, place, stage of development and further growth needs and capabilities; assuming that policy decisions have been made about such matters as minority cultures; assuming, in short, that policy has been worked out which ensures that the purposes of the school are real, external and liberating, oriented towards the competencies and values appropriate to the society, and not inward-looking, domesticating or self-serving: it then falls to the teacher to turn all this into programmes, into a series of events which make reality of it all in terms of the student's perceptions.

That, after all, is all that matters. If it is not achieved, nothing else counts. *How* it is to be achieved must be a major concern of all educators, since, as the 1975 ICE observed, 'we must not plunge the teacher into a welter of vague and contradictory expectations' [11].

What the teacher has to do is to arrange a series of situations in which the student, at successive ages and stages, will encounter a range of new data in such a manner that he will relate the new material to his past experiences, integrate it into his intellectual and emotional awareness in a balanced and rational way, grow in skill and understanding as a consequence, be stimulated to pursue thought and inquiry, be enabled to choose a vocation and avocations that suit his abilities and are practical in the social environment, and develop, eventually, the capability for autonomous and responsible decision making. Moreover, the teacher must be an active participant in those situations, interpreting the data in such a manner that the encounter will have the desired effect, evaluating the outcome and incorporating the results of that evaluation in planning the subsequent encounters.

NEW DEFINITIONS OF TEACHING COMPETENCE

With the shift of major emphasis from the teacher as source and purveyor of knowledge to the teacher as organizer and mediator of the learning encounter, a new set of competencies can be identified as components of the professionality of the teacher—as aspects, in other words, of the teacher's role. These competencies, for our present purpose, may be grouped under the headings of diagnosis, response, evaluation, personal relations, curriculum development, social responsibility and administration.

Diagnosis

Diagnosis involves the accurate estimation of the educational needs of the individual. It cannot, of course, be carried out in a vacuum. It has to be assumed that policy decisions have first been taken about the kinds of knowledge and skills and cultural awareness that are proper to the society at its particular stage of development, in its specific circumstances and in its particular relationship to global trends—decisions in which, as was suggested earlier, teachers will have been involved.

From those policies will have emerged some description of an ideal, which must then be turned into a goal by comparison of the ideal with the actual condition of the society. On this will be based a conceptual structure of the curriculum which is to bridge the gap between actual and ideal.

Nothing becomes real, however, until the student begins to do something under the guidance of the teacher; and at that point reality takes over completely. What the student does, and how he will perceive what he does, react to it and change through doing it, is the only educational reality. If that reality is different from the intent, then all philosophy, all theory and all planning will be vain and meaningless.

It is vital, then, that at the outset the teacher know what the student *can* do, be able to compare this accurately with what he or she is going to *have to* do, understand how the student will see and will feel about what is being asked of him, and be aware of any obstacles that may exist, whether these be in the nature of physical or perceptual handicap, emotional dysfunction or cultural orientation.

Response

Response is a matter of meeting the needs that have been identified. It will involve the selection of the media of communication which will best convey the essence of the knowledge or skill being presented, in terms of the perceptions and, the performance capabilities of the individual student. It will also involve the provision of special help or special remedy for special needs.

Effective response requires the special skills appropriate to the interpretation of various kinds of subject matter and to the teaching of key techniques—reading and writing, for example. It demands, however, understanding of the fact that these skills are validated only by evidence of achievement of the desired effect. There is a risk of placing too much emphasis on teacher 'performance', almost in a histrionic sense, and losing sight of the fact that the only purpose of teaching is to bring about successful learning. The student is not there to be confirmed in the role of student, but to achieve autonomous responsibility as a rational person. The present teaching of 'teaching techniques' too often consists of strategies for maintenance of the teacher's status, in which a passive, non-developing role is assigned to the student.

To be able to respond, therefore, the teacher has to have a deep understanding of the nature of perceptions and of the learning process at various ages and stages of personal development (not just a theoretical knowledge, but a shrewd practical awareness), comprehension of the idiom of speech and thought of the student, and a considerable degree of empathic understanding of the student's outlook and state of feeling. Response also requires a school situation which does not breed antagonism and considerable skill on the part of the teacher in dissolving antagonism. On the other hand, it excludes sentimentality and demands realistic assessment. The teacher must respond as teacher and must retain responsibility for organizing and maintaining the situation. The perception of the needs of the student for order, leadership and discipline must be as accurate as the perception of all other needs. Many attempts at school reform have failed because teachers did not perceive these needs clearly, and made their plans, instead, on the basis of a sentimental idealism about children which reflected their own cultural bias.

In other words, as was pointed out in the Commission which formed the core of the 1975 ICE, teachers may need to be 'deconditioned' in a number of ways. That they may have to be educated out of their former role perceptions and expectations—and the concepts of security, status and purpose that went with these—is self-evident. What may be less evident is that they may have to be liberated from the more subtle conditioning of their own home environment, in which even the humanitarian impulse may be deformed by the biases of their social class. A condescending sentimentality, for instance, can lead to a disastrous alienation of students. So can an immature radicalism. It has been observed by American researchers that problems may be caused by "chronic teachers" who are old hands at licit and illicit means of maintaining control ... and by "acute teachers" who arrive ... assuming that they are going to teach in permissive ... style' and are 'systematically destroyed by the children who do not understand them'; also that 'open education attracts many who find the facilitator-of-learning mantle a comfortable cloak under which to hide' [12].

Evaluation

Evaluation, to be justifiable, must be linked firmly and strongly to the public mandate of the school and show, in terms of that mandate, the evidence of growth in the student. The only thing that matters is the nature of the change that has occurred in the student—the evidence, in other words, of the correctness of diagnosis and response.

In the long run, the only evaluation that affects anyone's real commitment is his evaluation of himself. That, in turn, is greatly influenced by his self-image, which can be deeply affected by his experience, from earliest childhood, of the judgements passed upon him by others.

Evaluation, therefore, must take account of the need of each individual for self-respect, for realistic self-confidence, for recognition of genuine achievement, and for the development of a positive self-image. At the same time, the notion of honest self-evaluation must be introduced as early as possible, so that the responsibility for assessment of performance can be progressively and successfully transferred from the teacher to the student.

Evaluation, and the guidance of students in carrying out self-evaluation, both require considerable psychological skill, as well as familiarity with specialized techniques and the ability to relate specific objectives to the processes by which they are pursued.

Personal relations

The need for skill in personal relations has been touched on in the above remarks on diagnosis, response and evaluation. Nothing in education really matters except the reactions of the student, and the nature of the change that takes place in him. This reality must be seen as the discipline that ultimately, and properly, constrains the whole process of schooling. To motivate, to interpret, to win confidence, to build realistic self-esteem in the student, and to develop his capacity for self-assessment—these are the tasks in which the teacher must succeed. They call for sensitivity and skill in interpersonal communications. Often overlooked in this, but of extreme importance, is the matter of non-verbal communication through which a teacher can unwittingly convey a devastating message of cultural bias, condescension, mistrust or antagonism.

A further demand is made upon competence in personal relations by the fact that the changing role of the teacher necessarily brings him into closer association both with his teaching colleagues and with people working in allied fields—particularly those concerned with physical, mental and emotional health and in the various fields of cultural expression. Mutual comprehension of roles, expectations and the boundaries of expertise is essential, and mutual respect for capabilities and responsibilities is equally necessary.

Curriculum development

Something has already been said about curriculum development. The importance of this aspect of the teacher's role cannot be overstressed.

When the teacher was seen in the role of purveyor of a predetermined quantity of well-established knowledge, the scope of the term 'curriculum' was narrow. It implied little more than the breakdown of the subject matter into a sequence of units, each one manageable within an allotted period of time, presenting concepts and facts in a logical order. In more recent years, there was also some concern for the appropriate psychological order. The work of scholars like Piaget and Bruner focused attention on the nature of intellectual growth, and on the need to make proper allowance for the workings of the mechanisms of intellectual growth when preparing a sequence of units of study.

Now we have to take our concern further. When the school is seen as the major part of the environment in which the child becomes an adult, and when it is accepted that that environment should be supportive of healthy all-round growth, the meaning of 'curriculum' must be extended to encompass all that the child experiences. Indeed, it is probably necessary to extend it still further. In its own adaptation to its social setting, in reaching for appropriate resources of knowledge and skill in the community, and in seeking to compensate for deprivation in the child's home environment, the school both penetrates and is penetrated by the life of family and community. In fact, it must do so in order to restore, as was previously said, the threads that should link the formal and informal processes of education.

In these circumstances, the terms 'curriculum' and 'extra-curricular' become blurred; the experiences of the child in what used to be called 'extra-curricular' activities, and indeed in his domestic life, become relevant factors in the planning of teaching-learning strategies.

Social responsibility

The teacher, then, cannot limit his responsibility to delivering packages of instruction in the most efficient manner possible. He must become the creator of a series of environments favourable to the growth of the student towards desired ends, shaped to the characteristics of the student, *and* taking account of the effects of that part of the student's life which lies outside the school.

In so doing, the teacher must exercise a great deal more social responsibility than in the more sheltered setting of his former role. Diagnosis, response and curriculum design lead him into the consideration of causes which arise from social conditions. Poor learning may result from domestic discord, the manifold embarrassments of poverty, or simple hunger. The teacher must know how to recognize these causes, and must show sound judgement in responding to the resultant problems. The selection of learning resources in the community, and of real-life examples for problem-solving exercises, may involve value judgements, and the interpretation of historical and current events implies a moral posture. The active teacher cannot be neutral, but in communicating his own attitudes and so influencing the attitudes of his students to social problems he has no right to impose his own partisan convictions and biases.

PRACTICAL LIMITATIONS—SOME CRUCIAL ISSUES

This awesome array of demands upon the teacher raises many questions.

The first, of course, is the question of how much can be asked of one teacher. This arises in terms of the straight physical demands of the job in time and energy. Teachers, after all, are also persons with lives of their own, their own needs for rest and recreation, their own right to private interests and hobbies, and very often their own family commitments. Few, indeed, are the education systems which are enlightened enough, or affluent enough, to provide within the school day the time needed even for the amount of planning, thought and consultation needed in the teacher's former role; still less that which would be needed for the satisfactory exercise of the new role.

The same question also arises, however, with regard to the range of competencies involved. Even if the teacher had the time and energy necessary to do a thorough and well-prepared job of diagnosis, response and evaluation (including the very substantial amount of time that should be spent in individual counselling if these things are to be well done), as well as curriculum development, community involvement, participation in the recreational activities that are so important to the personal development of people and so inadequately provided for the vast majority; even if, as well as all this, he or she could find time to be a knowledgeable participant in the collective activities of the profession, discussing educational policies and their implications and planning appropriate action programmes; even if our superhuman teacher could survive the demands of this many-sided role, could one person be expected to be good enough at all these things?

Clearly it is going to be necessary to establish some minimum level at which all teachers are expected to be competent in all the major aspects of the teaching role, and beyond that point to provide for specialization; but it must be specialization in the competencies of teaching, especially as defined by the differing needs of students of various ages and backgrounds, not in the abstruse realms of artificial 'disciplines'.

Other questions arise which have to be answered according to the conditions in which each community organizes its education system. How far may the school be allowed to go in promoting free inquiry, a healthy scepticism towards inherited mythology and convention, and a commitment to social justice, before it incurs the risk of provoking cultural discontinuity and disorientation, social disruption and economic disorder? To what extent should the school, once seen as the prime agent for the transmission of orthodoxy and conformist thought, be permitted to be the critic of the society it serves?

In transmitting knowledge and skill, how far should the school go in adjusting to individual disability and the need for a sense of achievement? What are the limits of compromise beyond which one cannot go in protecting students from the humiliation of 'failure', without destroying the integrity of the knowledge or skill involved? In some areas of study we must say without compromise that the student must prove that he knows what he is doing before he is allowed to go on. In some others we can say that what matters is simply to be exposed to experience or to engage in activity, without measurement of an output in objective terms. What are these areas? Where do we draw the line? What is the proper balance, in each instance, between precise and exacting instruction and developmental supportive guidance? Though not the antagonist of the student, must the school not, at certain times and in certain ways, challenge him?

In its incursion into the life of the community, in its search for control over the factors influencing student growth, how far can the school go before it invades the proper domain of the parent, the family or other social agencies? When does support end and trespass begin?

These questions come up, and are answered explicitly or (much more often) by implication, each time a decision is made about curriculum. It is increasingly necessary to face them openly. In each community, the teacher should be a party to their consideration and resolution. Without an intimate understanding of their implications, and competence in the use of reasoning and the exercise of judgement, he cannot assume this role.

The search for the answers in the varying circumstances of different societies will, in turn, focus attention on the larger question of the interaction between the teacher, in his new role, and the community that is the setting for his activities.

REFERENCES

1. Hennion, R. The problem of educational expansion in Africa. In: *Education on the move*. Paris, Unesco, 1975.
2. International Conference on Education, op. cit. p. 10-11.
3. Ibid., p. 17.
4. Husén, T. Functions of the schools of the future. In: *Present trends and future developments in education: a European perspective*. The Peter Sandiford Memorial Lectures. Toronto, The Ontario Institute for Studies in Education, 1973. (Occasional papers no. 8.)
5. Macdonald, J. *The discernible teacher*. Ottawa, Canadian Teachers' Federation, 1970. p. 65.
6. Ibid., p. 65.
7. Tuqan, M.I. *Education, society and development in underdeveloped countries*. The Hague, Centre for the Study of Education in Changing Societies, 1975, p. 60-1.
8. Hennion, R., op. cit., p. 23.
9. Husén, T., op. cit., p. 163.
10. Wittenberg, A. *The prime imperatives*. Toronto, Clarke, Irwin, 1968.
11. International Conference on Education, op. cit., p. 17.
12. Sussman, L. The role of the teacher in selected innovative schools in the United States. In: Organization for Economic Co-operation and Development. *The teacher and educational change: a new role*. Vol. 1: *General report*. Paris, OECD, 1974, p. 99, 101.

CHAPTER FOUR

Interaction: school and community

It might be said that, in the process of leading the growing individual into harmonious and fruitful social living, the school has a three-way obligation. It has to be faithful to some concept of what a human individual is and might be, so that it fulfils, rather than deforms, the potential of the person. It also has to be faithful to some model of what society is or ought to be, not only because it should serve the best interests of the collectivity, but because our ideas about the 'good' society tell us what kinds of emphasis or restraint we should apply to the development of the individual. When we talk about realizing the full potential of the human being we are not entirely honest. History shows us that the range of human potential extends all the way from saint to fiend, from self-sacrifice to ruthless egoism, from compassion to sadism. We have to choose the kind of values we want to foster for the good of the whole society—and that means, in our era, for the good of the whole human community. We are, after all, not concerned merely with securing the safe passage of the individual into today's world. We are also concerned with fitting him for the task of shaping and changing the future. Education must not only develop people's ability to do things better, but also their will to do better things.

There is a third dimension, though. We are all members of the human club, but we have our homes in one specific place. The school owes some fidelity to the local community as well as to the individual and to society at the national and global levels.

It is very difficult to separate these three elements in education, and even harder to put them back together again in the right proportions. One of the things that make it difficult, as noted earlier, is the tendency of the school to make its own demands—to become a kind of miniature society of its own.

ASPECTS OF ALIENATION

It is fatally easy for people involved in running a school to see it in isolation from the outside world and to concentrate blindly on matters of internal order. Ideas develop about what a good teacher is (usually centred on the notion that a quiet room, with students engaged in listening or writing, is the sign of a good teacher) and about what a good student is (clean, neat, attentive, submissive, willing to listen and write), and school can all too easily become a place where these roles are insisted upon to the exclusion of all else. In the process, there may be real violence done both to the development of the individual (who really cannot be expected to change from model student to responsible, autonomous adult on the day of his graduation) and to the interests of the society and the community. If you learn only to be a model of good pupil behaviour, you are not learning how to be a participating member of an adult community. And certainly it is no good talking about the virtues of self-reliance, enterprise, initiative, co-operation and democratic responsibility to young people who are forbidden to exercise any of these qualities for fear they might disturb the tranquility of the school!

So a school which concentrates too much upon its own internal convenience may draw further away from its community.

Other things may contribute to this, too: the preservation of old status systems and the curriculum that goes with them; or the introduction of new educational approaches which differ from the traditional attitudes understood by parents and other adults in the community. These two opposite reasons—conservation and the challenge of change—may both have the effect of alienating the school from its community. Those who govern the school or teach in it may, in fact, feel that their job is easier when the uninitiated public and the inquisitive parent are kept at arm's length.

The school, then, has to interact responsively and responsibly with its community, and the teacher must play a positive role in that interaction. 'The sharp institutional boundaries between school and community,' says a New Zealand report, 'need to be made more permeable to allow for a two-way flow of experience and of resources. This calls for a change of attitude on both sides' [1]. In the same vein, the 1975 ICE found that 'in the context of the new nations, it was stated to be essential that the teacher be a part of the struggle of the people for a better way of life. To do so he must move out from the traditional isolation of the school, identify with the daily life and the aspirations of the people' [2].

Unfortunately, communities are seldom unified within themselves, and those elements which demand attention most loudly or most effectively are not necessarily those to which the far-sighted educator would wish to respond. All the more reason, then, to work for the widest possible involvement of all elements in the community in policy development, to promote open and continuous discussion of innovation and change needs, and to see the teacher's role in this as one to be exercised collectively, carefully and responsibly, and strengthened by preparation, planning and co-ordination.

Sometimes the frustrations created by a lack of communication with the community are on a very mundane level. It is a very common experience, for instance, for the teacher who is working to promote individualization, continuous progress and self-evaluation to meet parents who understand and ask only one thing—a numerical mark which will tell them where their son or daughter stands in relation to the rest of the class. The teacher must then be a clear interpreter of new goals and methods to an adult who may be totally unfamiliar with the basic concepts. Better still, the teacher should have taken part, in advance of the introduction of new methods, in a general effort not only to explain the new approach but to win approval and support.

Sometimes the confrontation is more subtly expressed and harder to define. The teacher may consciously or unconsciously be the advocate of a philosophy or a way of life which is alien to the local tradition. This is often the case, for example, when industrial development or the need for more efficient agriculture has raised the level of skill and knowledge required or challenged the usefulness of the existing social organization, or when the need for scientific knowledge invades the domain of traditional mythology. It may also occur when the expansion of the education system has brought a higher degree of school organization into a community which was formerly satisfied with a less-formalized, less-directive type of schooling. And it may occur with particular intensity if the teacher is making special efforts to encourage self-esteem, self-assertion and free cultural expression among children whose families have traditionally suffered racial, cultural or class prejudice. Tolerance can be a disturbing and threatening idea in a community in which a habit of discrimination is deeply ingrained.

In cases of this kind the problem may show itself in the school in the form of disrespect for the teacher, resistance to assignments, hostility and behavioural problems, or simple failure to learn (the kind of passive resistance in which students excel). The source of the trouble may be that parents and other family members, failing to understand the new ideas, fearful of a threat to their life-styles, or resentful of the challenge to inherited taboo and mythology, are competing with the school for influence over the minds of the students.

It is not always, nor inevitably, the case that a school which offers non-traditional knowledge or ideas is seen by the community as a threat. Often, indeed, it is received with enthusiasm because it seems to offer a means of escape from a history of poverty and restriction. The danger, nevertheless, is there, as was pointed out by Julius Nyerere, President of the United Republic of Tanzania, in a speech in 1974. 'Parents, politicians and workers,' said President Nyerere, 'are suspicious of, or hostile to, the educational innovations required. But the total result is that few of our schools are really an integral part of the village life. . . .'

COMMUNICATING WITH THE COMMUNITY

In a changing environment, whether the school itself is the initiator of change or attempting to respond to changing needs, the school must in the true sense become a community school. Teachers have the responsibility of explaining the perceptions and purposes of the educator to the lay community, so that parents are not confused and alienated by finding their children living and learning in a realm of new and unfamiliar ideas. They also have an obligation to learn how the adults of the community perceive the changes that are being introduced, so that they can teach with sympathetic understanding and respect for the child's cultural orientation. The co-ordinator of a United Nations project in the South Pacific reports: 'I would sometimes detect a concern in some of the questions directed to me. I had to reassure the questioners that in the project we were not saboteurs out to undermine the traditional heritages and cultural patterns' [3]. In this instance the questions were overtly raised and explicitly answered. In many cases the apprehensions of the community will not be voiced, and the teacher will have to take the initiative in offering reassurance in indirect ways.

In a general sense, teachers have to see themselves and to be seen as allies, not antagonists, of the community. This is so not only because of philosophical concern for the fidelity of the institution to its community, but for very practical reasons. As was earlier remarked, positive encouragement and coercion both have their legitimate place in getting young people to learn. Neither can really succeed unless the teacher can feel that he has the backing of the community. If the school seems to be in any way scornful of the home, or the home scornful of the school, or if either feels threatened by the other, the alliance between them will not operate, and neither encouragement nor coercion can be very hopefully attempted. The teacher, said the report of an international conference some years ago, 'must establish close relationship with the pupils' parents or their representatives and discuss with them the problems of teaching, thus constantly demonstrating that teaching is a specialized job, requiring qualifications that most parents do not possess, but that education is a collective undertaking in which parents have a part to play' [4]. It must, after all, be remembered, as was pointed out in a working paper prepared by the German Democratic Republic for the 1975 ICE, that 'education and training of the young generation is the affair of all the people. The *teacher* is the most important helper of the working people in this regard.'

In this two-way effort of interpretation, the professional teacher will often need intermediaries. There is much to be gained by recognizing and reinforcing the dignity of those people in the community who are the guardians of traditional lore. A teacher who can win their confidence and who knows how to draw upon their knowledge can strengthen the sense of identity and therefore the self-esteem of students, and an analysis of the real meaning of traditional lore can be a valuable means of relating new knowledge to inherited concepts of human worth and basic ethics. We are not necessarily wiser than our ancestors, or than the untutored adults from whose homes our pupils may come to us; only (let us hope) more scientifically knowledgeable about real causes and effects, about the real ways of making things happen. An apparent contradiction between old ideas and new knowledge may be capable of resolution through interpretation and synthesis. If we can show how ancient wisdom can be made more efficacious and more serviceable by the use of new knowledge, we have gained the best of both worlds and, if we can find a workable way of giving the traditional 'teachers' of the community an appropriate role within the formalized effort of education, we may hope to enhance and assist the role of the professional teacher.[1]

It is sad indeed to see in how many countries an imported set of educational values, and the disruption of traditional culture by urbanization, have alienated people from their own inheritance. 'There is a touch of irony,' says a Ugandan educator, 'in the way some African university graduates delight in, if not boast of, their inability to write their native tongue or join in a native dance!' [5] And the unbalancing, disabling effect of this kind of cultural discontinuity upon education is pointed out by another commentator with the remark that 'certain institutions may render the under-privileged unable to understand the sources of their cultural inequality, denying them the cultural resources of reflection and redefinition necessary to improve their social position' [6].

One of the functions of the teacher, then, in promoting a fruitful interaction between the school and the community, will be to identify sources of traditional lore and bring the people who possess that lore into the educational situation in appropriate ways—either through their physical presence or through the use of audio-visual media. Pupils, indeed, taught the skills of interviewing, can become enthusiastic collectors of local legends, proverbs, songs and so forth. In so doing, under the guidance of a sympathetic teacher, they may well find that they are motivated to improve their own abilities in writing, music, drama and art, acquire a sense of history, and learn to respect, rather than despise, their heritage.

1. A good example of this is the way in which, in China, the traditional lore of country people is drawn upon in the training of 'barefoot doctors'. Many ancient remedies, scientifically validated and refined by teachers and students, have become part of the rural doctor's armoury.

Such activity must not be random, of course, and must be related to clear learning objectives. In the process of involving those who were formerly powerful in the informal educative process, the teacher cannot and must not lay aside his own ultimate responsibility for the design and the effective implementation of the formal programme of teaching and learning. It is the teacher who is and must be accountable for the educational value of what is done, both in terms of the personal growth of the individual, the well being of the community, and the developmental needs of the society in general.

Examples of the kind of management which this calls for here are to be found in an open-air geography course in the province of Tolbukhin, Bulgaria. In the grounds of one school, for instance, a number of wild flowers are planted which indicate time by opening and closing, raising or turning their heads, and so forth, at various hours of the day. Knowledge of these peculiarities is a very old piece of traditional lore, and is both valid and practical, and the geography course sets it in the context of wide-ranging studies designed 'to guide pupils towards an understanding of the laws governing the environment and changes in it, with due regard to the needs of society' as well as to promote 'the harmonious development of the personality' [7].

The same principles apply to the learning of skills. Many countries are at a stage where valid vocational training, corresponding to the needs of the local economy, is of the highest importance. The most effective and most economical way of giving that training may be to arrange for observation and imitation outside the school, with the teacher acting as organizer and intermediary to make sure that what the students learn is what they need to learn, and that they understand the principles underlying what they are observing and doing. In taking this approach the school and the teacher would, in a very practical sense, be shifting from the role of monopolist of knowledge to that of organizer and orchestrator of learning opportunities.[1]

1. It is common practice in the USSR for a school to be taken under the special patronage of a factory or collective farm. Trade unions, management, party officials and workers' committees take part in organizing work experience for groups of students, and the practical lessons thus learned are backed up by theoretical studies and laboratory work in the school. Similarly, in China, school science classes are used as a means of solving problems actually encountered in the fields or factories.

None of this is easy to do, and the more complex the structure of the local community the less simple the teacher's task becomes. Serious conflicts, and even outright contradictions, may arise to make the achievement of harmony with the community in the development of policy and curriculum a very difficult process.

SPECIAL PROBLEMS

Most societies have suffered to some extent from social fragmentation resulting from industrialization. This effect, together with the associated consequences of cultural discontinuity and personal disorientation, is greatly accentuated by the movement of large numbers of people from rural areas to the towns and cities, a movement which up to now appears to be an inevitable result of industrial development.

In this situation, demands which seem to come upon the school from the 'community' may actually come from sectors representative of special and selfish interests within the community. The employers of labour may make quite insistent demands upon the school to modify its programmes and processes so that it will serve as a training ground and selection mechanism—they may, in fact, be quite ruthless in wanting to use the school as a means of screening out and rejecting those whose productive capacity is doubtful. They may not otherwise care whether young people are satisfactorily educated or not, and complain that any effort to encourage personal growth and cultural development is a wasteful luxury—a 'frill'.

On the other hand, the guardians of the traditional social order may be both articulate and forceful in insisting that old values and standards be maintained. This is often proclaimed in the name of morality or of what is 'good for' the child. On close examination, however, the professed morality may turn out to have more to do with the preservation of adult status and authority than with real ethics, and concern for what is supposed to be 'good for' the child may really be concern for the comfort of adults.

Against the demands of these conservative elements we may have to weigh the equally extravagant demands of their reformist or radical opponents. Organized labour unions, in their zeal to protect the worker against exploitation, may demand that the school pro-

vide a very specific indoctrination and teach the art of labour organization and confrontation. Other enthusiastic or opportunistic ad-
herents of various causes will from time to time claim to be the
authentic voice of the people and insist that the school promote their
purposes by introducing new courses, new modes of organization,
or their own particular forms of taboo and mythology.

Among these competing claims the school has to hold a balance,
plotting a course which will maintain its fidelity to the growth needs
of the individual (the needs, that is to say, of the boy or girl of
today and the man or woman of tomorrow) and to the needs of the
larger society both as it is now and as it will be or should be in the
future. The need for this twofold commitment, and its difficulties,
were very well stated in *Learning to be*, the report of the International Commission on the Development of Education. The following observations are especially pertinent: 'For the first time in history, education is now engaged in preparing man for a type of society
which does not yet exist' (p. 13). 'Education loses sight of the sort
of man it wants to turn out; nor does it for all that centre on the
child at which it is aimed' (p. 64, footnote 1, quoting the report of a
Unesco seminar on teacher training, Bouaké, Ivory Coast, March-
April 1970) [8].

It is certain that in its attempt to keep this balance the school
will be harassed, challenged and questioned. The teacher who lacks
comprehension of the kind of commitment that the school is making to the future as well as the present, or who feels that he has no
part in shaping its policies, will be at a severe disadvantage in his
inevitable encounters with the community.

The picture so far drawn may seem to present an environment
full of perils, threats and challenges. To many teachers at the
present time that is indeed how the picture appears. There is a
painful sense of betrayal when someone who has worked for years
as a conscientious and loyal servant of the collective will comes to
feel that his mandate is now, at best, confused and uncertain, that
the authority which was bestowed upon him by the public consensus, giving power to his commands and force to his prohibitions,
has failed or been withdrawn, and that he is reproached and abused
by those whom he only sought to serve.

It is all the more necessary, then, that the teacher be armed with
a strong sense of purpose and a realistic philosophy, based on a very

accurate perception of individual and social needs. Philosophies are shaped by a combination of experience and understanding, so the teacher's own education must include exposure to scientific methods of inquiry, acquaintance with the diverse factors which influence personal and social development, intensive psychological and pedagogical study, and extensive practice in varied settings.

Special problems occur when the local community is of a fairly homogeneous nature, but not in close tune with the development of the national or regional economy. There may then be very strong pressure for the school to meet immediate local needs which are at variance with those of the larger society, and even with the long-term interests of the local community itself. A farming community, for instance, may be very unhappy to see children and adolescents taken away from work on the farm to learn things that seem to have nothing to do with the prosperity of the family—even if the kinds of things the children are learning will make them more able to understand and apply a more efficient technology in farming, give them the kind of skills and knowledge which may save them from a life of poverty on uneconomic smallholdings, fit them for productive work in necessary new industries, and help them to take an effective part in democratic decision making. The children themselves may be resistant to any kind of education which seems to be irrelevant to their present way of life.

In such cases the school has to be its own missionary. The drive to educate the young must be supported by a vigorous programme of adult education to improve the general level of understanding of national and regional development needs and of the long-term benefit of improved education. Since this may be seen as a direct challenge to traditional values and vested interests, the teacher's role will require not only solid, up-to-date knowledge and commitment to policy goals, but also a high level of skill in debate and diplomacy.

The important principle here is that although the school must not be the antagonist of the local community, its proper loyalty is to the long-term interest, not necessarily the immediate local need; and the claims of the community must be reconciled with the goals of personal growth and the developmental needs of the larger society.

In short, the school has to decide upon its attitude to the various forces operating in the community with as much objectivity, rationality and long-range soundness of perspective as it should, ideally, bring to the examination of its own internal processes.

This would be a major change for an institution which has historically tended either to submit uncritically to the strongest voice in the community or to impose its own perspectives without much concern for community perceptions and needs. It is, however, a necessary change: passivity and arbitrariness must both give way to interaction.

SCHOOL AND THE ADULT POPULATION: A CHANGING RELATIONSHIP

There is a tendency to think first of interaction with parents; and certainly the role of the teacher must be seen as a partnership with the parent and the home. Neither the programmes of study in the school nor its extra-curricular activities can hope to be very effective unless they are designed to build upon or compensate for, as necessary, the conditions of the student's home life and, whichever is the main purpose, the maximum involvement of parents in discussion and implementation is desirable. But it is not only parents who have a legitimate interest. The benefits of appropriate schooling, and the harm done by poor or inappropriate schooling, fall upon all members of the community. The changing role of the teacher demands a greatly increased consciousness of the realities of community life and the dynamics of local society, and a ready willingness to discuss educational policies and strategies with all kinds of groups.

Discussion, of course, is not enough. It must not be assumed that the only role of adults in relation to the school is to make decisions about the education of children.

In a rapidly changing world, adults also become learners. The school and the teacher must, then, be prepared to offer appropriate learning opportunities to the adult community, so that the ability to find and perform remunerative work, to protect economic interest and personal rights, to organize and sustain family relationships, to safeguard health, to build a community of mutual trust and co-operation, and to fill leisure hours with satisfying activity, may be maintained and enhanced.

But childhood memories and ingrained attitudes towards institutions make many adults hostile to and suspicious of schools. Nor can adults be conscripted, like children, to learn what someone else considers to be good for them. The teacher has to find the adult in the workplace, in the natural gathering places, and in the home, and has to offer something that is seen to be of value. As in dealing with young people, too, the teacher must not hope or pretend to be the possessor and source of all knowledge. The role of the teacher of adults, like that of the teacher of children, is to see and comprehend needs, identify the sources from which the necessary knowledge and skill may be obtained, create a coherent curriculum accordingly, and provide mediation and interpretation in the terms best suited to the perceptions of the learner.

Imaginative and flexible approaches, in terms of the media of communication, the organization of subject-matter, the opportunity provided for trial and practice of new skills and knowledge, and the times and places chosen for teaching, are of the first importance in adult education.

Once again, however, the point has to be raised that, as the concepts of school and of the teacher's role broaden and deepen, two consequences follow inevitably. One is that educational design and policy making acquire more and more importance and have to be carried out with the deep involvement of teachers and the public. The second is that rational specialization within the broad category of 'teacher' is an absolute necessity.

Community interaction: demands on the teacher

Interaction, to be effective, must be selective, continuous and forceful. That the school must 'open its doors' to the community is a platitude, meaningless until decisions are made about what should be inside those doors, or let out through them, and what teachers and the people outside should do in relation to each other.

Interaction begins with the concept that the school is not a micro-society in isolation, but a special extension of the social structure, designed to intensify, and to bring clearer purpose and greater efficiency to a basic social activity. It requires, then, a co-operative effort of planning, involving the various groups which have formal or informal involvement in the upbringing of children—parents, worker and employer groups, religious agencies, health authorities and so on—with generous opportunity provided for mutual explanation and thorough discussion of roles, expectations, purposes and long-term goals. Agreement on personal and collective needs, and on the concessions to be made to general social purposes and long-range development objectives, should lead to further agreement on the nature of the major sources of knowledge and skill required, and the kind of arrangements that can best be made to secure access to these. The organization and successful conduct of this kind of consultation requires a kind of specialist expertise on the part of senior educators that is not well provided for in present training programmes.

At this point the professionality of the teacher comes into full play. On him now rests the responsibility for designing the ways in which the real activities of the community—the working world of factories, farms, boats, shops, banks, offices, law courts, hospitals; the practical world of plumbers, doctors, carpenters, priests, peasants, mechanics, wholesalers, fishermen, architects, scientists, shepherds, advertisers; the symbolic world of the theatre, television, dance and music—can best be related to the theoretical, interpretive analytical role of the school and woven into a pattern of successive encounters which will have meaning for the student and lead him progressively towards personal growth and successful social integration or reintegration.

On the teacher, too, falls the responsibility for deciding when and in what particulars he must, for the good of the student, challenge and criticize the practices observed, or the value system implicit in the structures and procedures of the community. The teacher must not only organize each episode in the encounter between the student and the world; he must decide what it is that he wishes the student to retain from those episodes. 'Community' is in danger of becoming a magic word in educational jargon, charged with emotional connotations of beauty and truth. The fact is that the only true community is a community of interest, that some of the most active and most vociferous interest groups about education have a highly selfish and injurious purpose, and that when we use the term in the wider sense of 'collectivity' we are facing the whole range of human activity, from creativity, compassion and noble aspiration to corruption, perversion, exploitation and crime. The pupil who observes the life of the community with a keen eye will see injustice, cruelty and folly as well as co-operation, kindness and efficiency, and part of the teacher's task will be to help him to exercise his judgement upon what he perceives.

What the last two chapters have tried to say is well summed up by an Egyptian commentator in a recent article. 'We need,' he says, 'to unite the school and the community; education should be mainly based on self-education and should go on continuously and at request. These are the two dimensions of time and space, as they should be for education' [9].

These are the two dimensions in which the teacher has to learn to exercise his new role. But there are other dimensions. The teacher, interacting with the community, is subject to the responsibility which rests upon the educator in all circumstances—that of selecting as well as organizing—bringing a sense of value and keen ethical discernment to the business of choice and design.

Also, in this as in all aspects of his activity, he is subject to the constraints of that most inexorable of all realities, the reality of his relationship with the student within the setting of the school.

Interaction—some examples

It is not, however, the privilege of the teacher to invent or impose the scale of values or the ethical code. Not uncommonly, the teacher's viewpoint can be brought into a sounder perspective by encounter with the community. That is one of the reasons why Chinese policy insists on periods of manual work by teachers and students. These periods of work are seen as opportunities for 're-education' of students by the workers and peasants.

There are, of course, other purposes for this determined blending of the worlds of work and school. It 'has contributed,' says one writer, 'to the gradual reduction of the threefold gulf between town and country, workers and peasants and intellectual and manual work,' and so, in the words of another commentator, helps 'to bring up students who will serve the people whole-heartedly and have the knowledge and skill to do so' [10].

There are situations, nevertheless, where the present condition of a community owes too much to ignorance, error and popular indifference, and into such situations the school has to enter with a strong leadership role. One example of this kind of action is to be found in the city of Curitiba, in Brazil. It was noted that, after almost ten years of effort to implement reform in education, the conventional schools were 'accomplishing their programs without attending to community needs', and were in fact inefficient in that the habits and attitudes they taught were not reinforced and were 'frequently contested' in the home. It was also observed that those who most needed pre-school education were the least likely to get it, and that children in poor districts, exposed to the ill effects of poor hygiene and malnutrition, were simply unable to profit from schooling and were likely to be handicapped for life, continuing the inescapable cycle of poverty and ignorance.

To counter this, fourteen community centres have been opened in which health care, education and social welfare services are provided jointly. A basic school curriculum, from kindergarten to eighth grade, is supplemented by special instruction on the importance of water, the avoidance of pollution, parasites, the prevention of infection, nutrition and immunization. Strong emphasis on direct microscopic observation and practical experiment, from the earliest stage, maintains pupil interest. Aims, concepts, activities, resources and behavioural objectives are developed in collaboration with medical and welfare workers. School meals provide protein-rich dietary supplements. Schooling is enriched with music, drama, games, mime, modelling and physical education. A vigorous programme of adult education, with the collaboration of the social welfare staff, uses various audiovisual media and encourages the formation of neighbourhood associations, but the major emphasis is on making the child 'an efficient agent of social betterment' and improving his or her chances of successful learning and healthy development. Teachers, who must have full professional qualifications, receive two months of special training before taking up work in the centres [11].

In less extreme ways, other experiments aimed at forging a stronger alliance between schools and their communities are showing an encouraging degree of success. In Vancouver, Canada, the Britannia complex, which has involved local people very directly in its planning, is attempting to integrate cultural and recreational facilities within a cluster that includes a kindergarten, an elementary school and a secondary school. A recreation centre for the older people of the community has been placed (at their request) in the centre of the school cluster, and secondary students are invited to share its facilities. The high school library is open to the community (a popular expedient in Cuba also). At present, however, there is no attempt to integrate the teaching efforts of the school and adult education staffs.

Teachers are, however, active in the Ivory Coast as animators of adult education programmes based on television transmissions. Topics range from sensible money management to agricultural practices and home repairs. The expertise brought by the teacher lies, not in the subject-matter, but in the art of interpretation, maintaining an effective link between the medium of instruction and the learner, and working with the adult groups to ensure a follow-up of systematic learning.

In Papua New Guinea new teachers are being attuned to this kind of role by assignment to community projects during their training. It is felt that adult education, with a strong practical content, must accompany school reform so that parents and children can interact to each other's advantage.

Sometimes the goals of adult and community education are more modest than those professed by the school system, and yet of considerable importance to the well-being of the community. In Fiji, for example, the benefits of the motorization of fishing canoes were reduced by the frequency of breakdown, often leading to abandonment of the motors. Lessons in small engine maintenance, provided by itinerant teachers, are proving highly effective as a remedy. In such a case, instruction may not call for the special skills of a professional teacher; in this instance, the instructors are volunteers provided by the Young Men's Christian Association (YMCA).

The major significance of many such projects in adult and community education is that they indicate the ways in which the school should be reaching out to provide a reliable and regular resource for *all* would-be learners. The school must move out of its buildings and the rigidities of traditional curriculum to find and serve the learning needs of the people. That, of course, is the message of the Chinese and Cuban reformers. If it is taken seriously, it greatly increases the importance of localized decision making and teacher initiative, and so places new and important demands on the competence and training of the teacher. Most of all, it calls for a change of attitude—for teachers to see themselves not as the aloof guardians of an austere academic tradition, but as persons whose mission it is to place knowledge at the service of people, to empower them to work for their own individual and collective betterment.

REFERENCES

1. New Zealand. Ministry of Education. *Improved learning and teaching.* Report of the working party on improving learning and teaching. Wellington, 1974.
2. International Conference on Education, op. cit.
3. Bishop, G.D. Curriculum innovation in the South Pacific. *Prospects* (Paris, Unesco), vol. 3, no. 1, spring 1973, p. 110-17.
4. Schuller, A., ed. *The role of the teacher in educational change: report on the international conference in Berlin, October 10th to November 1st, 1968.* Berlin, Pädagogisches Zentrum, 1971. [Also published in German: Weinheim/Berlin/Basel, Beltz, 1971.]
5. Bagunywa, A.M.K. The changing role of the teacher in African educational renewal. *Prospects* (Paris, Unesco), vol. 5, no. 2, 1975, p. 220-6.
6. Hake, B. The social and cultural futures in western Europe. In: Jensen, S., ed. *Possible futures of European education.* The Hague, Martinus Nijhoff, 1972.
7. Ivanov, V. Open-air geography teaching in Tolbukhin. *Prospects* (Paris, Unesco), vol. 3, no. 1, spring 1973, p. 103-9.
8. Faure, E., et al. *Learning to be: the world of education today and tomorrow.* Paris, Unesco; London, Harrap, 1972.
9. El-Koussy, A.A.H. For a self-criticism of education in the Arab countries. *Prospects* (Paris, Unesco), vol. 3, no. 1, spring 1973, p. 57-66.
10. Yong Hong. The educational revolution; and Hsin Wen. Primary and secondary education. *Prospects* (Paris, Unesco), vol. 5, no. 4, 1975, p. 484 and 486.
11. Caldas Silveira da Mota, C.; Grein dos Santos, D. *The pre-school and the schools of the less developed areas.* Report. Curitiba (Brazil), City Education Authority, 1976.

CHAPTER FIVE

Constraints of reality

In Chapters 2 and 3 we painted what may seem to be a very ambitious picture of the role of the teacher. The very broad and all-embracing role that was described is obviously in conflict with the present reality in a number of ways. It is inconsistent with the reality of the school situation in most countries. Its demands go far beyond the present ability of teacher education institutions to provide appropriate pre-service or in-service training. Its scope far exceeds the potential of the teaching force in most countries (in terms of existing levels of education, professional training, attitudes and orientation) for adaptation and re-training.

FIRST STEP: A DEFENSIBLE ORIENTATION

So we are in the familiar situation of describing an ideal which is probably incapable of realization, and then considering what practical steps might set us on a path that would take us a little closer to, rather than further away from, that ideal. A perfect education system, after all, could exist only in a perfect society. The best we can hope for in the meantime is a system that rests upon appropriate and morally defensible principles, and which, from the outset, provides real improvement in the lives of those whom it serves. What the previous chapters suggested was as follows:

1. The traditional school (which also, in its day, professed fidelity to a noble and unattainable ideal) rests upon principles which, in

this present era, are no longer appropriate nor morally defensible, and offers too little improvement in the life of its community.

2. Reform must start with the description of a necessary new orientation, without which qualitative assessment of change is not possible.

3. The new orientation should include: (a) a much broader and more generous definition of the clientele of the school; (b) a commitment to support the development of individuals to the maximum, balanced by concern for the collective identity and the collective interest (both in moral and in material terms); (c) a serious attempt to reconcile short-term local interests with the long-term interests of nations and of the entire human community; (d) recognition of the revolution in communication which overwhelms people with information and presents them with the problem of learning how to select and use that information for their individual and collective benefit; (e) awareness of the supreme importance of human relations and individual characteristics in all phases of education; (f) sensitivity to the needs, the aspirations, and the actual conditions of life of the learner, and responsiveness to change in any of these; (g) recognition of the key role of the teacher as diagnostician, motivator, co-ordinator and primary instrument of action in this enormously enlarged field; and (h) deep involvement of the teacher, and the organized participation of teachers, students, parents and representatives of the community, in the design of objectives and programmes.

To put it briefly, the change in orientation that is proposed for the education system would mean adopting the goals of democratization, individual autonomy, competence and voluntary co-operation in place of selectivity, coercion, artificiality and subjugation to the special interests of dominant groups.

The ideal, like all ideals, would remain incapable of complete realization; but it would reflect more accurately the realities of the world in which most people live their lives and strive for betterment, and it would provide an appropriate guide to the makers of educational policy.

SECOND STEP: SELECTING PRIORITIES

Where to start?

Each of us must start from where we are, with a sober assessment of realities and potentiality.

Many of the more developed countries are wrestling with the problems of equity and equality of opportunity in a school system that already professes to be universal. To explore such questions as pre-school education to remedy social disadvantage, special support for socially handicapped minorities, greater effectiveness in vocational education, student mobility in a genuinely comprehensive school, access to education for adults whose occupational training or life skills are no longer adequate in a changed environment, and the need to raise the level of skill in the management of personal and family life, would take us far beyond the scope of this book.

There is every indication, however, that 'teaching' in the future will involve dealing with a much wider age range than in the past, making a much more particularized response to the specific needs and perceptions of people whose life-styles differ very widely, drawing upon a much wider range of resources in the community, and making appropriate use of media to communicate with groups who are not gathered in the conveniently regimented classrooms of the traditional school. It will require, initially, a higher level of general education for the teacher than was customary in the past (so that he or she may better understand the many dimensions of the world the student lives in and must come to terms with), and also a higher level of understanding of human psychology, sociology and the learning process. It will also call for the systematic provision of in-service training and re-training in a range of specialized skills, in response to the needs or predilections of individual teachers and the changing demands of a responsive school system.

In many of the developing countries, the pressing need is still to lead people out of the debilitating miseries of hunger, thirst, disease and deprivation. For them, there are four necessary priorities: radical improvement of the content and methods of primary schooling, massive increase in the participation rate at that level, provision of extra-mural basic education, in an effective manner, for adults, and vocational training made real by substantial on-the-job experience.

These objectives, like those of the more urbanized, industrialized states, lie within the orientation described at the beginning of this chapter. The overriding need is to make people more competent to understand the causes of problems, and better able to devise and apply sound solutions—'to lead the rural and urban masses . . . to a greater awareness of their condition and to arouse in them the will to change it' [1]. The response to that need must bring the teacher out of the protective artificiality of the academic school, so that he can help people to find the real knowledge they need to cope with their real situation. Pre-requisite, once again, is a solid improvement in the general educational level of teachers, in the level of their understanding of the learning process, in their ability to work on their own initiative in a wider and less-structured field than formerly, and in the provision of recurrent training to upgrade their skills and develop appropriate specialization.

Common to all situations is the need for the teacher to be animated by a clear sense of purpose, rooted firmly in the realities of people's lives. The teacher, says the official report of Costa Rica to the 1975 ICE, must hold firmly to the realization that 'although education is a basic factor in development, when it does not answer to the needs of the individual nor to the demands of society it can be, rather, an obstacle to development (cultural, social, economic).' Teachers, in other words, 'should be aware of the important role they are called up to play in the community as professionals and citizens, as agents of development and change' [2].

THIRD STEP: CHANGING THE TEACHER

As is the teacher, so is the teaching.

On the competence and performance of the teacher depends the possibility of making a reality of the principles enunciated, for example, by the Republic of Cuba [3]:

'Integral education of youth, combining ideological, scientific, technical, cultural and physical training . . .

'Uniting of the school with social praxis, with production, with the economic and social development of the country . . .

'The concept of the school not only as a place to receive "instruction" but also as a centre of life in society. . . .'

It was recognized by the 1975 ICE that education, whether formal or informal, involves many people other than the professional teacher (as defined, for instance, in the German Democratic Republic: 'a graduate from a teacher training establishment who was trained under binding curricula and concluded his studies successfully'). It was recognized, further, and specified in the Recommendation adopted by the Conference, that 'the need may arise to use other professionals and specialists in the education system on a full-time or part-time basis to participate with teachers in the realization of the education programme', and that 'it important to analyse the national situation in order to identify the categories of personnel desirable in the educational process apart from regular teachers...' [4]. To organize and manage such participation, however, and to make it effective, is part of the expanded responsibility of the teacher—another factor to be considered in defining the competencies and level of skills that we must now expect the teacher to acquire and exercise. It is with the teacher, and the problems of defining and providing the competencies necessary for the exercise of his or her changing role, that this book is concerned.

Recognizing that in many countries education must still compete with other sectors for its share of a very limited supply of educated personnel, what general criteria should be applied in selecting candidates for teaching?

What kind of preliminary education, and what kind of initial training, will help to form the attitudes and develop the competence that the teacher will need to begin his or her journey into professional life?

What kind of special skills may, or should, be added to draw the teacher further into the expanded role described in previous chapters, to prepare him or her to collaborate more effectively with the other agencies and cope with the extraneous factors involved in effective learning? What kind of system of teacher education will ensure that, within the totality of the teaching force, a sufficient range of specialization evolves to meet the most urgent demands of the expanded role?

How can the present teaching force best be introduced to the requirements of the changing role of the teacher, attitudes influenced and levels of competence upgraded?

These questions will be posed, and answers offered, in the chapters which follow this. Before we move on to these specific problems, however, some further aspects of the reality within which change must be effected should be stressed.

THE CENTRAL REALITY—THE TEACHER-LEARNER ENCOUNTER

Whatever our view of the educative process, the crucial element must be seen as the encounter between someone who is teaching and someone who is learning. It has often been remarked that every attempt to reform education, even the most radical, is an attempt to improve the circumstances of that encounter. When education is formalized, whatever the form of the 'school'[1] thus created, these matters become the responsibility of the teacher. We must, then, consider the role of the teacher to be the single most important factor in the effort to change the school through deliberate policy, and we must base all policy on the nature of the realities experienced by the child and faced by the teacher—the realities of the school. This must be so whether we hope to exploit and build upon those realities or to alter their character. There is no place to start from except where we are.

Encounter is not always easy or natural, nor is its outcome always that which was intended. When two people confront each other, they do not come out of nowhere, in spiritual and cultural nakedness. Each is the end product of a long development. Each is conditioned by past experience and past learning, by emotional disposition and cultural adaptation.

It is a common error to believe that to be conditioned means to have one's responses altered. That is not the case. We all respond in basically similar ways to pain and pleasure, danger and threat. To be conditioned is to have one's *perceptions* altered, so that one reads the signals of the environment differently. What to one person may be a clear message that hurt is imminent may be screened out by someone else as irrelevant noise. A gesture that is meaningless to

1. The word 'school' is used, throughout this chapter, as a convenient term to indicate a situation in which an organized effort of teaching, with a clear concept of the intended outcome, is taking place. The emphasis is placed on the teaching of children, but the observations offered should not be read as applicable only to that limited sector.

one may communicate hate or love, esteem or contempt, to another.

When one person encounters another, a great many messages are exchanged. Some are verbal, some are non-verbal. Some are intentional, some are unconscious. Some are received as sent, some are totally lost, and some are received in mistaken form. Too much has been made of this in the very recent past, and it is not here suggested that the teacher should be obsessed with the mechanisms of communication to the extent that 'encounter' and 'awareness' are seen as ends in themselves. On the other hand, too little was made of the problem in the less recent past. It is only common sense to say that when an encounter takes place for a specific purpose, with a view to the exchange of certain kinds of messages on a specific topic and a consequent change in the state of knowledge or level of skill of one of the parties, it is important to be sure that the messages are received as sent and that irrelevant or conflicting messages are kept to the minimum. For this to happen, it is necessary that the teacher learn how to be aware (and realize the need to be aware) of the way in which the student is reading and reacting to the message that he is conveying, and also be able to understand what the student is trying to communicate.

It is also essential that conditions should exist which make a genuine encounter possible. A teacher who is overwhelmed by pressure of numbers is simply not capable of being aware of the gaps in understanding that exist.

Yet the spanning of those gaps, the fusion of the two viewpoints—that from the front of the room and that from the back—into one common effort of learning, is the starting point in the change of the school and the teacher from a censorious, selective, antagonistic role to a supportive one. If there is to be any move towards humanizing the process of education, to make it more responsive to the personal development needs of its clients, this is where it must begin.

It is not an easy undertaking. It implies a sensitive understanding on the part of the teacher of the nature of perceptions at various ages and stages of growth, of the peculiarities of vocabulary and idiom that are part of his own style of communication and the ways in which they may differ from those of his various students, and of the differences in the emotional, moral and cultural conditioning that he and they have experienced. He must know how he looks and sounds to his students, what commands their respect and what arouses suspicion or insecurity in them, and how they see them-selves and each other. He must know what kind of teaching media will be effective for particular kinds of students, and be able to devise or improvise appropriate aids. He must know what kind of additional learning resources, if any, he can reasonably expect students to have access to outside the school (a factor which is often badly misunderstood by the inexperienced teacher). He must be able to recognize situations in which the barriers to the effectiveness of the encounter are caused by factors which the school cannot deal with, and know what other agencies can be called upon for help.

REACHING THE COMMUNITY—CAUSES OF FAILURE

To be effective, the supportive effort of the school must reach beyond the classroom. The success of the teaching-learning en-counter will be enhanced in proportion to the success of the school in gaining acceptance as part of the community. For this reason, as well as for the purpose of bringing the resources of the school to bear upon 'the struggle of the people for a better way of life', the thirty-fifth session of the International Conference on Education recommended that 'the teacher should have more opportunity for involvement in extra-curricular and out-of-school activities, in guid-ing and counselling the pupils and their parents, and in organizing his pupil's leisure-time activities' [5].

Here the matter of encounter becomes even more important. In the traditional, academic school the teacher did not need to estab-lish a strong rapport either with his students or with the community. He could afford to remain aloof and unbending, guardian of the 'standards' of an artificial curriculum, and to the extent that his students succeeded in meeting those standards they also removed themselves from the reality of their community. In the words of a Chinese commentator, 'students undertook book learning only, in a vacuum as it were, remaining in complete ignorance of the lives of the workers and peasants ... In addition, they were emotionally strangers to the worker and peasant masses' [6]. The difficulty of overcoming the traditional aloofness of the school has been identi-fied as a major obstacle to the implementation of reform in the United Republic of Tanzania: 'Education is criticized as still being too academic and too removed from the reality of life for a majority of the population. It is felt that this situation stems from the strong influence which examinations still exert upon the curriculum' [7].

PROBLEMS OF THE CHANGE TO SUPPORTIVENESS

It is easy to speak lightly of the shift of the school and the teacher from a censorious and antagonistic role to a supportive one. The real obstacles in the way, however, are very substantial. To begin with, not everyone welcomes the change. There are deep-seated reasons for opposition to the very idea of the supportive school, and for justification of antagonism, rather than sympathy, as the basis of the teacher-student encounter.

Essentially, this is a reaction of fear. The law of all living things is that the young must eventually supplant the old. The presence of a young learner is an inescapable reminder of that fact. The unconscious fear that it arouses—the fear of supplanting, the fear of one's own obsolescence and eventual death—is a real and powerful factor in shaping adult attitudes in the encounter. Its counterpart on the other side, the unconscious drive of the young to displace and supplant the old, is an equally powerful factor. On the one side there is a growing impatience with authority and the restraints of past conventions; on the other, the fear of the loss of hard-won status (felt especially in a time of change, when novelty has high status and tradition is disdained). The defence of the adult is to impose more and more restraints as evidence of status, and to require the passage of severe ordeals as the price of admission to adult standing.

The encounter between teacher and student must not be made the occasion for comforting reassurance of the teacher's status, whether the student is adult or child. To the extent that it is so, it is an attack upon the self-confidence and self-esteem of the student. It will be resisted, and very quickly becomes a conflict in which both sides seek allies and develop competing survival strategies.

Such a situation is unhappily familiar. The present physical conditions of so many schools—large numbers of students, impossible for the teacher to know or respond to as individuals; strong commitment to obsolete purposes, shown by styles of organization, evaluative procedures, programmes and resource materials that defy adaptation; teaching assignments that leave little or no time for reflection, diagnosis, planning, organization of resources or consultation with colleagues—make conflict and confrontation inevitable. It is a sterile confrontation, because neither side can really win. If the teacher is defeated, chaos results and whatever the student learns in the course of his victory certainly will not lead him to fruitful personal growth or healthy integration into society. If the student is defeated, the memory of his defeat will tend to shape his future attitude towards learning and towards social integration. In the meantime, he will withdraw, at least in spirit, from the battle-field—leaving his physical presence as a kind of decoy, performing the minimal activities required by the victor, while his real self, his mind and emotions, seek fulfilment in other directions.

Even the well-meaning student, far more often than we like to think, is baffled by a school environment that is not, in his view, rational. If he is lucky, however, he will eventually realize that, though he may not fully understand what is going on and what is required of him, there are certain passwords that will cause the right things to happen. The shrewd child who has been raised in contact with the teacher's idiom finds the passwords quickly, and they open doors for him. The less perceptive child, or the child whose home background has not equipped him for the encounter with that idiom, gropes in the dark with growing anxiety, and a growing probability of frustration, defeat and hostility. M. Tuqan quotes a report on the learning of new mathematics among the Kpelle of Liberia: 'He (the student) is forced to repeat aloud collections of words that, from his point of view, make no sense. He knows that he must please the teacher in order to survive, but he finds what he is taught incomprehensible' [8].

As the student grows older, he understands the process better—perhaps too well. Even if he knows the passwords he may not want to use them, because to do so may involve denial of the heritage of his particular race or cultural group, submission at the cost of identity and self-respect; or he may simply, because he is an adolescent, rebel against the threat of being described on his record as 'co-operative'.

At the best of times, communication between adults and young people has a potential for difficulty and apparent mutual threat. In traditional societies, where social disruption has not occurred and the extended family system is strong, the difficulty may be slight. In societies that have experienced upheaval and the destruction of old forms of communal organization, it is intense.

NEED FOR APPROPRIATE MODES OF ADMINISTRATION

An over-arching, authoritarian administrative structure which appears to the student to down-grade him and deny him status or identity will not help the teacher to stimulate interest in learning. It must be realized, as was pointed out by some of the national representatives at the thirty-fifth session of the International Conference on Education in 1975[1] that administration—the organization of situations, the management of resources, the determination of objectives and the evaluation of outcome—is inherent in the teaching function. The over-all style of administration must reflect the style of teaching; otherwise it will negate the efforts of the teacher. In consequence, just as administration in specific situations is part of the individual role of the teacher, participation in the administration of the school as a whole must also be part of the teachers' collective role.

A statement of this kind is likely to be contested from two directions. In societies where the tradition of hierarchy in the governance of education is still strong, the school tends to perpetuate the assumption that the institution embodies righteousness, and the student real or potential error. Teachers hover somewhere between the two, and despotic control is the rule. In societies where major political power lies in the managerial stratum of an industrial hierarchy, or with the proprietors of business and industry, there is constant pressure to deform the school by imposing a management-labour model upon its administration.

Neither of these aberrations can resist the pressure of reality for very long. In the former case, the claim to despotic authority derives from the monopoly of access to knowledge, and is being rapidly undermined as sources of knowledge other than the school become available.

---

1. As, for example, in the statement made to the Commission of the Conference by the delegate of the Netherlands: 'It will be necessary to strengthen the collective influence which the teaching staff have within their institutions'; and in similar statements by the German Democratic Republic and others.

In the latter case, the inappropriateness of the industrial model, with its basic assumption that only the proprietor cares about the over-all purpose of the enterprise, and that there is an automatic opposition of interests between the management (which seeks high quantitative productivity for a minimal wage bill) and the workers (who want high wages for minimal effort) must eventually be seen by all concerned.

PRACTICAL DIFFICULTIES AND POSSIBLE REMEDIES

The school is there to facilitate effective and appropriate learning, in whatever sense that phrase must be interpreted to bring about successful integration of the individual into a healthy social collectivity. No other institution has that responsibility. There is no excuse for any practice or any administrative procedure that serves any other purpose, or for imitation of the practices or procedures of any different kind of institution.

As the educational level of teachers improves, they themselves are becoming more aware of this, and of the conditions that are necessary for the exercise of their evolving role. As a result, they are becoming increasingly intolerant of artificial divisions between the functions of teaching and administration, and especially of any attempt to give priority to administrative convenience over the requirements of the teaching-learning endeavour.

Nothing can really close the gaps in the school and unify the effort of the institution except, on the one side, the genuine motivation of the student and, on the other side, genuine trust in that motivation.

To say that, of course, is simply to re-state the fact that the essence of education is found in the inter-personal, human encounter between teacher and learner, and that the success of the effort of education depends on overcoming the barriers to accurate, trustful intercommunication.

EXTENDING THE TEACHER'S CAPACITIES

The biggest single barrier is the lack of time for direct encounter, which in turn is a function of numbers. The number of students with whom the teacher must communicate is directly related to the effectiveness of communication, and also to the level of stress upon the teacher. The importance of the stress factor, incidentally, is often underestimated. Quite apart from the teacher's claim to humane consideration, stress reduces his or her sensitivity to the needs of students and also the capability for appropriately flexible response. Moreover, the need to enforce docility and submissive behaviour (the alternative, when large numbers of children or adolescents are gathered together, being noisy and intolerable chaos) runs directly counter to the imperatives of an educational situation.

These considerations engage us in a search for ways of extending and concentrating the powers of the teacher.

One approach, mentioned earlier, is to insist upon the fact that teaching is a collective effort. This means identifying the kinds of specialization that make sense in terms of the real, essential activities of the school and of the multitude of factors, described in previous chapters, which influence the outcome of the educational enterprise. It also means the structuring of teams of specialist teachers in an appropriate relationship with each other, and especially a team approach to the design of curriculum and programme. This is of the highest importance. The development of school-based curriculum, created jointly by teachers in a team relationship, with support from suitably trained specialists, is one of the most necessary and most urgent of all reforms.

A second requirement is the involvement, in a close and cooperative relationship with the teacher, of specialists in other professions—those concerned with physical, mental and emotional health, with remedial psychology and with various techniques of communication.

A third is the transfer of non-teaching functions, where possible, to aides or paraprofessionals. The definition of 'non-teaching' is, however, of crucial importance. Any transfer which would make it more difficult for the teacher to understand the student's individuality, or to detect personal problems and learning disabilities, does much more harm than good. An aide is not, and cannot be, a substitute for a teacher—only a substitute for the use of the teacher's time in activities which are not an integral part of the teaching-learning situation.

A fourth possibility lies in the use of appropriate technology. Great caution must be used in this, however.

It is certain that in the technical process of instruction, which is in many ways the least demanding and least noble of the teacher's functions (false status considerations to the contrary), technological devices have a great deal to offer, provided that their mode of operation is in harmony with the ways in which children learn. Computer-assisted instruction, in particular, with its promise of an almost infinite multiplicity of responses to the inquiries and the tentative efforts of the student, may eventually free the teacher to be a teacher. (At the same time it will create new and demanding functions for specialists in curriculum design and the psychology of learning.) Their proponents, however, must be firmly told what these devices cannot do. As one specialist in this field remarked, a computer cannot distinguish among the many eloquent inflections affecting the meaning that a pupil is trying to convey by saying 'yes'.

There is a particular danger in the use of technology, too, in that it has a tendency to institutionalize itself—to develop purposes and criteria of quality derived from the nature of the technology rather than from the goals of the user. Educational television, for example, which always runs the risk of failure through encouragement of passivity in the student, has fallen into that trap in many instances because its decision makers were more concerned with developing a 'good' television system, with impressive programmes rivalling those of the entertainment world, than with improving their own understanding of the fruitful use of the television medium as a learning resource in the context of student needs and in the physical situation in which the students find themselves. 'Teacher-proof' packages of study materials have suffered the same fate. In all such instances, the basic error is the attempt to exclude the exercise of human judgement in specific situations—ignoring the fact that the exercise of judgement is at the heart of the teacher's role.

None of these expedients can succeed except to the extent that teachers are competent to use them—to participate in team activities of curriculum design and teaching, to assign appropriate tasks to various helpers and direct their work, to co-operate with professionals in allied fields and to use technological devices with authority and discernment. This point is well summed up by a writer on world problems in basic education: 'The evidence on the use of the new media, such as television and radio, is that they do not reduce the need for teachers. They improve quality and cost-effectiveness *provided they are accompanied by* teacher training' [9].

Nevertheless, when all the necessary cautionary remarks have been made, it must be recognized that the capability of such devices as computers, satellites and television to diffuse a multiplicity of messages over vast distances offers almost the only hope of rapid solution, in the short term, of the most pressing problems of the developing regions. Such rapid progress has been made in making these devices portable, robust, resistant to climatic factors, and simple to operate, and in reducing the cost of their use, that there is reason to hope that within the next decade they may be effectively available for regular use in educational programmes at a basic level. If that is so, *and provided that* a cadre of competent people has by then been properly trained for the exploitation and maintenance of such systems, there will then be a real possibility of easing the appalling burden that so often rests upon the shoulders of the under-trained local teacher, of bringing him the chance of fast and effective up-grading, and of making relevant knowledge directly available to the general mass of the population, both juvenile and adult. It cannot be too often repeated, though, that an early priority in the application of technology to widespread learning must be the training of teachers to become, themselves, the interpreters and monitors of educational programmes at the level of the learner.

Many things are already very clear about the emerging role of the teacher, and about the kind of setting in which that role must be exercised. Educational theory has made enormous advances in recent years, but these advances are often negated by public misunderstanding and the persistence of inappropriate practices. A necessary part of the role of the teacher is to work for the creation of conditions in which the essential functions of teaching can be properly undertaken. The common contradiction between theory and practice can only be bridged when a satisfactory level of teacher competence has been reached and when the professional understanding that is a part of that competence is admitted as a major influence in the shaping of policy.

Good schools must be shaped around the exercise of good teaching, which in turn rests upon an accurate assessment of student needs. This goal cannot be achieved as long as situations exist in which good teachers are baffled by administrative artificialities, overwhelmed by pressures of time and numbers and by unreasonable and unrealistic assignments, and driven back to survival strategies based on the memory of their own school days, or in which enlightened and imaginative administrators and policy-makers are frustrated by the low level of competence of the teaching force. At present, the encounter between future imperatives and present realities is often a sterile and frustating confrontation. When the general availability of enlightened and competent teachers, and their involvement in the design of policies and procedures, restores unity of purpose—and appropriate purpose—to the institution of the school, there begins to be a hope for harmony in the purposes and viewpoints of the teacher and the learner. That is the beginning of success in the teacher-student encounter, where the deliberate activity of education begins and ends.

What has been argued in this chapter is that the transformation of the teacher from the role of assessor of the outcome of a terminal process to that of animator of an open-ended, supportive undertaking can only be accomplished by an appropriate re-orientation of the entire school system, taking account of the human and social realities in which the teacher works. Crucial to this effort of re-orientation—and the major concern of the present authors—is the inauguration of an adequate and appropriate system of teacher education, one which will prepare the teacher for the basic realities of his task, lay a groundwork for further development of his competence in one or other of the special aspects of his changing role, provide for a gradual entry into full responsibility, and offer continuing resources of help, support, inspiration and professional development.

The following chapters will examine the problems which cluster around the attempt to develop such a system of teacher education, and some of the ways in which, in a variety of settings, those problems may be attacked.

REFERENCES

1. International Conference on Education, op. cit. p. 29.
2. Ibid., p. 22.
3. Cuba. Ministry of Education *Cuba: organización de la educación 1973-1975*. Report of the Republic of Cuba to the thirty-fifth International Conference on Education, Geneva, September 1975. Havana, Viceministerio de Economia y Servicios Generales-Mined, 1975, p. 144-5. [In Spanish, French and English.]
4. International Conference on Education, op. cit. p. 22.
5. Ibid., p. 22.
6. Yong Hong. The educational revolution. *Prospects* (Paris, Unesco), vol. 5, no. 4, 1975, p. 482.
7. Wanjohi, G.J. Tanzania: socialism and education for self-reliance—seven years after the Arusha Declaration. *The Kenya teacher* (Nairobi), no. 20, May 1976, p. 34-8.
8. Tuqan, M.T., op. cit.
9. Phillips, H.M. *Basic education—a world challenge*. London, Wiley, 1975.

Learning to teach: priorities for action

by James F. Porter

Principal of the Bulmershe College of Higher Education, United Kingdom.

Introduction

Socially, politically and economically the world is changing at a dramatic rate, and it is certainly not possible to foresee any diminution in the pace of change over the next decade. As the world has changed so has the school, and so has what we mean by teaching and by learning. In the first part of this book we have tried to describe the nature of the change and its implications for the role of the teacher. Faced with the massive problems and deep divisions which are evident at all international gatherings, it would not have been surprising if delegates at the thirty-fifth session of the International Conference on Education had cast serious doubt upon the capacity of teachers and schools to cope with the task of inducting and guiding the young. On the contrary, however, the conference reaffirmed the centrality of education as the most important single means of a country coming to terms with the demands of the contemporary situation. Such a view, however, assumed a major redefinition of the role of the school and of the teacher. As indicated in the final report, 'Social relevance and the democratic ethic both required that the teacher reached beyond mere instruction to become a guide to his pupils and effective mediator between the young person and the confusion of the environment'.

In the second part of this book we are seeking to confront a number of central issues. Following our definition of the changing role of the teacher, is it possible to define certain universal objectives for teacher training? What are the implications for the enormously wide differences of demand for teachers and of the available supply of appropriately educated manpower? Many countries have high hopes that their education systems will enable them to achieve economic prosperity and a range of social and political goals. Are such hopes justified? Can the new social function of education be achieved through modification and development of what is already there, or is it necessary to propose a radical reappraisal of educational institutions and their relationships both with each other and with the wider society?

There are many factors influencing policy with regard to teacher education and training: philosophical and social dimensions are among the most important. However, the iron law of supply and demand is particularly influential in order to be able to understand what can actually be achieved in various regions of the world. Thus, it is necessary to review the demographic and economic factors which must precede any discussion of teacher education and training.

TEACHER DEMAND AND SUPPLY

In preparation for the thirty-fifth session of the International Conference on Education, the Unesco Secretariat provided a detailed and comprehensive survey of the issues, including those relating to teacher supply and demand. What emerges is a great discrepancy between developed and developing countries.[1] Even when these discrepancies are 'averaged out' on a regional basis, the differences are still acute. Not only is this the case with pupil/teacher ratios in both primary and secondary education, but also a more crushing fact is that the developed countries have universal primary and secondary education whereas the position in the developing countries is of a substantial proportion of the population being denied access to primary education and the majority denied access to secondary education. All this is in spite of a massive increase in the number of teachers in developing regions between 1960 and 1970: from 4.2 million teachers to 7.8 million. As Tables 1, 2 and 3

1. All regions with a gross reproduction rate below 2.0 are considered as developed regions, while regions with a rate of 2.0 or above are considered as developing regions. The developing regions include Africa, Latin America (with the exception of temperate South (America) and Asia, with the exception of Japan and of the East Asia mainland region (which had to be excluded as these data were not available for the People's Republic of China).

TABLE 1. Teacher requirements in primary and secondary education maintaining the 1970 pupil/teacher ratio (thousands)

	Primary education				Secondary education			
	No. of teachers		% increase 1970-85	Average annual growth rate 1970-85[1]	No. of teachers		% increase 1970-85	Average annual growth rate 1970-85[1]
	1970	1985			1970	1985		
World	11658	15630	34	6.0	6892	11629	69	7.5
Developed regions	6302	7060	12	4.8	4469	5825	30	5.8
Developing regions	5356	8284	55	7.0	2423	5280	118	9.3
Africa	843	1275	51	6.8	231	582	152	10.4
Asia	3770	5837	55	7.0	2029	3606	78	7.9
Latin America	1353	2014	49	6.7	794	1917	141	10.1

[1] +4 per cent for replacement.

Note: It will be found that the sum of three continents exceeds the developing regions' figure because some countries in these continents are classified as developed regions (e.g. Japan).

TABLE 2. Required number of primary school-teachers to reach universal primary education in 1985 (thousands)

	Children aged 6-12 years 1985	Required number of teachers 1985	% increase in number of teachers 1970-85	Average annual growth rate 1970-85[1]
Developing regions	504767	13642	155	10.4
Africa	101094	2527	200	11.6
Asia	344851	9320	147	10.2
Latin America	78954	2467	82	8.1

[1] +4% for replacement.

TABLE 3. Number of primary school-teachers per 1,000 persons in the labour force

			1985	
	1960	1970	Projecting enrolments at 1960-70 rate	Reaching full primary education
Developed regions	11.3	12.9	12.4	—
Developing regions	5.4	8.1	8.8	14.4
Africa	4.5	6.4	6.8	13.5
Asia	5.8	7.5	8.3	13.3
Latin America	11.2	15.3	15.5	19.0

illustrate, in the recent past and in the immediate future inequalities within the world are acute in this field, as in many others. Thus, in a number of developed countries it is possible to maintain an adequate supply of teachers with an actually *reduced* supply of newly trained teachers because of the slowing down, and in some cases the reversal, of demographic growth in such countries, e.g. Federal Republic of Germany, Sweden, United Kingdom, United States, etc. By contrast, the developing regions will have to increase their efforts to produce both primary and secondary teachers beyond the peak efforts of the 1960–70 decade.

The main issue is that by 1985, even with a linear projection, the developing regions would not be providing anything near to universal primary education. Of the 6–11 age group, Africa would have admitted 44 per cent, Asia 67 per cent and Latin America 75 per cent. The corresponding proportions for the enrolment of the 12–17 age group would be: Africa 30 per cent, Asia 36 per cent and Latin America 55 per cent. The widely accepted goal of full primary education in developing countries, continuing with traditional modes of organizing schools and using teachers, would mean doubling or even trebling the output of trained teachers. In addition, such an objective would increase education's share of the total labour force in countries where there is already sharp competition for well-educated manpower.

The challenge to developing countries is seen most clearly, for example, in the United Republic of Cameroon, where the attendance rates for children in the 6–13-year-old population are below 60 per cent and where higher education was only established at the end of the 1960s. Seventy-two per cent of the teachers in 1970 had got no further than the level for which they were preparing their pupils. In Indonesia there were about 425,000 primary teachers in 1973, and in the next five years there is a need for nearly another 200,000, which is well beyond the capacity of the present annual output of training institutions. Both of these countries have interesting and imaginative plans for educational development which will be referred to at various times during this section. However, all developing countries face a similar kind of challenge and an urgent need to respond.

Overlaying the problems arising from the massive growth of population in the developing countries and the consequent need for even more teachers is the severe economic plight of many of them. For the world as a whole, expenditure on teachers' salaries forms two-thirds of public expenditure on education. (Related solely to recurrent expenditure, the fraction is much higher, being about four-fifths.) Many developing countries, in order to attract well-educated manpower into teaching, have improved salaries and conditions of service during the past decade and thus will find further growth even more expensive.

Such gross demographic and economic differences between parts of the world must necessarily have a substantial influence upon particular governments' decisions about priorities: in particular, the realities of the situation must be noted by those who seek educational reform and who work within education systems. There is a great danger that, if the gap between the myth of what education could ideally achieve and the reality of what is actually happening becomes too great, then the confidence which governments still have in education may be seriously diminished.

As well as the global differences, there are, of course, the problems which relate to the internal deployment of teachers and difficulties of relating supply to the changing needs of the schools and the fulfilment of national policies. Again and again developing countries point out that the massive need lies in the rural areas within which often 70–80 per cent of their population lives. However, the trend towards gradual industrialization from a basically agrarian economy has tended to attract educated manpower into the urban areas, while at the same time educational priority is being given to the rural population (for example, in Egypt, India, Indonesia, Nigeria, and many others). Along with the pursuit of greater democratization of education, developing countries have also been interested in expanding educational provision so that it reaches those who have been previously disadvantaged. This in itself is more expensive than providing it in areas of high population density or in a restricted mode. Democratization, therefore, is seen not only in quantitative but also in qualitative terms, with the consequent implication for levels of expenditure.

With the growing political and economic commitment to education, governments naturally look for results. Thus, governments are increasingly expecting education to give students the economic and technological skills required to compete in the modern world. On the other hand, they also expect it to produce citizens who can be creative, co-operative and committed members of society, able to sustain a happy and productive family and community life. Even the most idealistic (or unrealistic?) educational administrator does not really expect any individual teacher to be able to provide all the outcomes discussed in Part I of this book or in the wide-ranging discussions at the International Conference on Education (ICE). On the other hand, the thirty-fifth session of the conference did underline the increasing importance of the teacher's role in contemporary society. While delegates were aware of the importance of the media and of educational technologies, as well as of the significance of other workers involved in the development of children, there was a powerful reaffirmation of the overriding importance of the teacher–pupil relationship. This relationship was seen as being far more complex and demanding than had previously been the case. The implications of this extended and more diversified role for the teacher impelled the conference to take a new view of the process of teacher education and training. Thus, teacher education was seen as a continuous process, beginning with a phase of initial training and continuing throughout the teacher's professional life through regular and sustained periods of in-service training, thus maintaining the view that a teacher must also remain a learner. A recent national report on teacher education and training expressed it in the following way, 'No teacher can, in a relatively short or even in an unrealistically long period at the beginning of his career, be equipped for all the responsibilities he is going to face. This familiar truth has been given a disturbingly sharper edge in a world of rapidly developing social and cultural change' [1]. Although the support for such a view was universal at the thirty-fifth ICE, the phrases 'initial' and 'in-service education' mask very great differences between countries in what is required and, indeed, what is possible.

NATIONAL PLANS FOR TEACHER EDUCATION

The purpose of the following chapters is to provide a framework for action. There are tens of millions of children waiting to be helped to live in a bewilderingly complex world and, even more urgently, to be equipped to understand and assist in the shaping of their own countries in a dangerous universe. The teachers to be trained now will influence the shape of society well into the twenty-first century. However, although a teacher must serve certain universal needs of individual pupils, the schools must also reflect cultural, economic and political goals for each society. There is evidence to suggest that many States have well articulated plans for schools, but often vague and ill-defined arrangements for the initial and continuing education of teachers. All countries are therefore requested to give urgent consideration to the task of defining a national strategy for teacher education in the context of their plans for school and post-school education.

It is urged that all Member States of Unesco should develop plans in close consultation with all partners to the enterprise: teachers' associations, national and local administrators, teacher trainers and independent educators of standing. In addition, close consultations should be held with those whose objectives are very similar to many of those now involved in education; these include representatives of parents, social and community workers, those engaged in the mass media and those with a concern for the direction of economic affairs. Questions which may be raised will concern the identification of responsibility for the education and training of teachers at national, local and institutional level, clarification of the role of the teacher, and the content and organization of courses in initial training. Particular attention should also be paid to the relationship between preparation for teaching and for other professions concerned with the social and personal well-being of the young, as well as the relationship between training institutions, the school and the community.

Many of the themes that are developed in this book have had their origin in the conference organized by the International Bureau of Education. One of the most unusual aspects of the discussions on the role of the teacher and the priorities for training was the demonstration of an intensely high level of agreement on many of the major issues. The chapters which follow, however, necessarily provide a limited range of response to what is one of the most complex and challenging issues with which Unesco is concerned. The next three chapters attempt to deal specifically with the personal education and with the initial and in-service training of teachers. The final chapter gives a detailed illustration of the way in which these three stages can be put together in a particular country in order to achieve a radical reform of the total education system. Different systems will require different strategies, and other cultures need other reforms, but there are grounds for believing that teacher education can indeed be the catalyst which many countries seek.

REFERENCES

1. United Kingdom. Department of Education and Science. *Teacher education and training.* A report by a Committee of Inquiry under the chairmanship of Lord James of Rusholme. London, HMSO, 1972. 127 p.

CHAPTER SIX

The personal education of the teacher

INTRODUCTION

A teacher is considered as the man or woman with full professional responsibilities for the education of children and young people who are in attendance at school. It must be recognized, however, that the teacher is only one of the adults with whom the child comes into constructive contact. Later, emphasis will be placed upon the importance of interprofessional training for those who are concerned more specifically with social and community work, health, planning and other roles which have a specifically community and education orientation. As has already been indicated, the role of the teacher is increasingly being broadened to include a variety of social, economic and leadership functions which must be carried out in co-operation with others. Similarly, many social, community and medical workers are directly involved in pedagogy.

The increasing democratization of education, which is a worldwide movement, should ensure an increasingly common base of education at the school level for all members of society—at least up to the completion of the primary stage. Whatever other political and economic arguments there may be for the common school, the professional arguments are overwhelming: if one wants the education system to be genuinely influential, the new role of the teacher requires him to argue from a common base of experience and understanding and to have the capacity to empathize with those with whom he is working. Although in many countries the family is losing many of its traditional functions in the culturalization of the young, there must be sufficient common educational experience between parents and those who are assuming surrogate roles in the education and social services. The teacher needs to be strongly committed to the highest development of each individual child and also be sensitive to the social and economic context within which the child must operate. This sensitivity can best be achieved if all citizens are part of the mainstream of education during their most formative years.

Even before school, however, many of the basic characteristics of the future teacher are being shaped. Everyone knows that some of the most able and creative individuals find it impossible to work successfully as teachers. Teaching, particularly in present times, requires certain personal characteristics which must initially be developed within a secure and supportive infancy and early childhood. Again and again in this book we shall see that, like the seasons, education is strongly cyclical in character. Thus, the quality of a country's support of parents and families, its encouragement of pre-school education and the establishment of policies that give priority to families with children, provide the essential store of stable and balanced children that will be needed to carry the heavy burdens of teaching and allied professional work when they achieve maturity.

When the teacher was primarily regarded as a 'knowledge giver' a certain degree of separateness or social distance from children was regarded as essential. However, when, as in the Philippines, he is seen as a 'social integrator, attitude changer and community worker', he needs to display personal skills which no amount of training alone can create. Thus, the first major implication of the changed role of the teacher is that no amount of training alone can guarantee success within some of the critical dimensions of the teacher's new responsibilities. Teaching is now, and will increasingly be, a deep and searching personal challenge for the man or woman who takes on such a role. The teacher is no longer able to shelter behind his superior knowledge or to step onto a raised desk and look down with authority upon the bent heads of the children. Democratization is not only a process which affects education systems: it enters the classroom and the intimate relationships between the teachers and the taught. Thus, if those who seek to train and employ teachers wish to be able to choose those with the necessary potential for commitment, sensitivity and understanding, deliberate policies of family support and a strong common school system are essential. Carefully planned social and economic support systems are particularly necessary at a time of rapid change.

It is obvious that many countries are actively pursuing policies which do aim to provide such a common base of support and schooling for all members of society. In Ghana the government has proposed that the length of basic, formal education should be nine years and that this should be free and compulsory. At the same time there is strong encouragement of kindergarten education to provide opportunities for over-all personal development and to pre-dispose a child to the learning processes which will be involved in formal schooling. Ghana, like all other countries, still perceives primary education as enabling the child to have numeracy and lit-eracy, but again, as is generally the case, puts increasing emphasis upon the development of inquiry and creative skills, upon socializa-tion and development of attitudes.

The general theme of the development of universal primary edu-cation is fundamentally a quantitative interpretation of the concept of democratization and an important step in the direction of equal-ization between the developing regions of the world and those which are already at an advanced stage of development. A significant number of developing countries, however, are increasingly concerned to bring about a more rapid improvement in the quality of education. Thus, in Indonesia considerable effort has gone into such projects as the development schools. In Malang and Padang good purpose-built accommodation is provided for the teaching of all the sciences. These centres provide high-level facilities for students from junior and senior high schools.

Such an emphasis upon qualitative differentiation within the basic school system is less frequent than in post-school education and teacher training, but it is here that we come across one of the first major decisions with regard to priorities. In developed regions the problem with regard to priorities is almost entirely concerned with the length of school life. In developing countries, because of the enormous gap between educational policies and economic resources, the decision is whether to spread those inadequate resources thinly over as large a part of the population as possible or to engage in positive discrimination for certain sectors of the population. This decision in developing countries is not merely a matter for post-school education but for even the most basic primary provision. The Indonesian Minister of Education described the difficulty dramatically when he said it was clear that, in the near future,

Indonesia could no longer solve its quantitative problems in education, by which he meant to underline a brutal fact—Indonesia (like most countries in South-East Asia) cannot expect to train enough teachers or build enough schools to meet the present and the future increase in the number of school-eligible children [1]. Thus, while endorsing the over-all aim of comprehensive schooling in all countries of the world, one must relate this to other imperatives: for example, an inadequate resource base may prevent proper provision of teachers and materials and impose upon the school a narrow instructional and custodial role. A number of examples of excellent practice *within* each country are far more important influences upon educational practice than whole armies of experts and theoretical treatises.

Such examples of innovation are not only effective because they grow from the culture of the particular country but also because they inspire confidence and provide essential field experience for future educators. In concluding this section on the social and educational context from which teachers should emerge, it is recommended, therefore, that, although universal education in childhood must be seen as a fundamental objective of all countries, it should not in the short run prevent positive discrimination being used in order to encourage innovation and experiment, which in the long run should inform and enrich the total educational provision. In this area it is obvious that the main funding agencies have a particular role to encourage and facilitate creative experiment. For example, one of the most significant improvements made in the preparation of teachers relates to selective support to schools that are in close association with training institutions.

POST-SCHOOL EDUCATION

Given the establishment of a sound and responsive system of basic education, it is likely that the potential teacher will emerge from a broad social background and will enter into some form of full-time post-school education. In developed countries this will be universal and normally in an institution of higher education. Thus, in the United States all teachers will have pursued a four-year degree course; in the German Democratic Republic all teachers will have

had four years of higher education and professional training following completion of schooling. The position in developing countries,
however, will vary widely. As in developed countries, some teachers
will have pursued a degree programme and training, but others will
complete their secondary education and go straight into a teaching
appointment. Such wide variations occur not only between countries but also within each country. Again, as indicated in the last
chapter, priorities have to be established. Put in its simplest form,
the question is: Should all potential teachers have a period of personal education beyond school and before taking up formal responsibilities as teachers? The answer must be in the affirmative. While
such a reform may take longer in some countries, it should be the
acknowledged objective of all governments. In a highly traditional
society and in a slowly changing world, the concept of apprenticeship for teaching, whereby the new teacher merely practises the
skills handed down to him by his predecessor, is an acceptable one.
Nothing, however, could be further from the truth of the contemporary situation.

While common experience of the school system in his own society is an essential prerequisite for a future teacher, it is also of
considerable importance that the teacher should have a period when
he is able to make a critical and informed assessment of the school
and the social context within which it operates. This capacity for
objective assessment, including an evaluation of his own schooling,
will be of great significance in enabling the future teacher to assess
his own success and to be alive to the need for change within the
formal system of education. Ideally, the stage between schooling
and training should not only provide the opportunity for reflection
and for intellectual and personal development, combined with the
acquirement of a capacity for independent study—emphasis should
increasingly be put upon the need for relevant experience. Thus,
there is a powerful argument for a break between school and post-
school education or between the personal education stage and the
training stage. It would be of particular value for a potential teacher to have had some work experience characteristic of the economy
within which the school is situated. This could mean industrial or
commercial experience in a highly urbanized society, or agricultural
work in a rural economy. There are no examples where previous
work experience is made compulsory for entry to teacher training,

although an increasing number of countries are giving priority to students who have had such a break and are deliberately recruiting from mature students with appropriate experience. For example, in Japan in 1973 the Educational Personnel Certification Law was revised so as to establish a new teacher certification for people who have acquired specialized abilities through their professional careers and self-training, and also to attract people from among wider sections of society for the teaching profession. It should be emphasized that the need for a post-school stage of personal education and opportunity for work experience relates to the changed role of the teacher in which he is more dependent upon his own personal resources than on a body of accepted knowledge.

It is important to look at the transitional stage between schooling and training to see what kind of higher education and experience would be most appropriate for a potential teacher. It should be emphasized from the beginning that teachers at this stage should not be seen as a special category. They should essentially share in the wider provision of post-school education. However, personal education does have a particular function with reference to teaching, where, in spite of the rejection of the concept of the immutability of knowledge and the importance of the development of social and personal skills, it is still assumed that the teacher should be an educated person with a sound level of scholarship, an inquiring and critical mind and a sound grasp of certain well-defined areas of knowledge. It is interesting to note that many ministries of education are also ministries of culture, and schools have a direct responsibility to maintain cultural traditions and to encourage personal development through the creative arts and the humanities. However, during this stage the teacher should not see such studies merely in relation to his preparation as a teacher, but study them alongside others as a personally challenging stage of development.

As indicated at the thirty-fifth session of the International Conference on Education, higher education is becoming an education for the people, whereas hitherto it was élitist. Higher education increasingly should not be understood as being exclusively university education. Trends towards diversifying higher education are apparent in many Member States. What is plain is that democratization of the school system and the growth towards comprehensive secondary school systems are producing a 'wave effect' which is transforming the student population in higher education institutions.

Thus, a teacher should be a well-educated person requiring some post-school education in order to give him the necessary personal perspective both upon his profession and upon society. It is possible, however, to fulfil such a requirement in two major ways: firstly, through a consecutive form of training in which the higher education stage precedes the teacher training stage; the second is a concurrent style of training in which a personal education element interacts with professional training. Both styles are widely pursued in both developed and developing countries. Both have been found from experience to have merit, but there has been an unfortunate tendency to polarize the two approaches and to debate the merits and disadvantages of each in a way which seems to assume that there is some ideal method which can be translated into any situation.

However, as indicated earlier, the truth of the matter is that a teacher is being prepared from the moment he interacts with another human being, through his childhood, through his schooling, through the range of his experiences and through his own individual perceptions of the world. Teaching is not a highly exclusive and acquired skill like playing the piano or printing a dress; the successful teacher calls upon personal qualities which can only be developed over a lifetime and thus there is a sense in which all his preparation is 'concurrent'.

The point has already been made that the potential teacher should be brought to confront difficult intellectual problems and attempt to master difficult skills as an individual and as an adult alongside other individuals with different career intentions. In the next chapter it will be argued that the best preparation of a teacher is to be involved critically and sensitively in the process of teaching. The potential teacher at the personal education stage should put substantial emphasis upon his own role as a learner. The question then becomes whether there are certain forms of learning which have particular relevance to his future role as a teacher. A further question is whether current systems of higher education are particularly attuned to assist in the personal education of those who will have a responsibility to carry society through a period of unprecedented change and stress.

While in many countries there is a good deal of experiment in higher education, it is clear that much of it is still highly selective, conservative and slow to adjust to new social and political realities. A reformed system of higher education is an essential prerequisite to creative development of teacher training. Encouraging examples of such reforms are becoming more numerous and reflect an international movement to a more broadly based and relevant system of higher education.

The issues are well put by a Unesco mission to the Sudan in 1974. The mission stated that the Government of the Sudan had been perceptive and courageous in facing the fact that the function and structure of its system of higher education was not well adapted to national requirements. However, the mission went on to say that the problem could not be solved 'until the fundamental problem, which is political, has been decided'. The political problem is 'whether the education system exists to support a protected university-trained élite, or whether the system exists to advance the general standard of education and, with it, to raise the standard of living'. The mission noted particular problems in the present system of education, e.g.: it segregates education from community and work; it is hierarchical and divisive between levels and kinds of education; it is terminal, i.e. most education is completed before work begins; it is closed and inflexible with little opportunity for return or mobility or transfer; it is largely controlled by examinations—hence undervalues non-formal and non-credit education. In its place the mission proposed a preferred system as a guide for planning which was: integrated with other forms of experience, especially work; oriented towards learning rather than examinations; open with regard to access between institutions and levels; flexible, with ease of return after a period in employment; recurrent or interrupted, i.e. interspersed with periods of employment; adapted to changing needs with much more emphasis on non-formal and non-credit courses.

Similar needs for reform are widely expressed elsewhere: for example, in Sri Lanka a single university with five campuses was organized in 1972, and a sixth has recently been added. Reorganization of the university was aimed to realign higher education programmes to conform to the development needs of the country and to eliminate wastage through duplication and under-utilization of existing facilities. In India an effort is being made to restructure the present courses of study in the universities and colleges in order to make them more relevant to development needs, improving the employability of students and enabling them to acquire greater experience in practical work.

In developed countries democratization of higher education and its full utilization for national purposes has accelerated over recent years. Thus, the Netherlands Ministry of Education has produced a comprehensive study of future policy in education, including higher education. It argues that higher education must not only be for those who are continuing their studies immediately after leaving high school but will be for mature students, including those who are alternating work with study and those who wish to make up later the chances of higher education they missed earlier. The principle should be that any who wish to be admitted to higher education and are suited for it should have the opportunity. Students should be able to transfer with ease from one field of learning to another, and higher education will have to offer a large number of courses—general education courses in addition to vocational training courses, courses for teaching of skills in addition to methodologically oriented courses, courses run individually in addition to standardized and collective courses. In order to enable progress to be made, the Netherlands proposed to introduce a new kind of higher education institute in addition to the universities. They would be the growth sector *par excellence* and must widen the objectives of higher education.

One of the most clearly articulated plans for reform of higher education was described by the Ministry of Education in Finland in 1974, in which they argue that the central qualitative principles for degree reform are as follows:

1. Problem-centred orientation. The general basis for teaching and for the choice and arrangement of teaching material should be *actual problems of society*.[1]
2. Scientific orientation. Teaching and studying ought to be more closely connected with research than is the case today.
3. Multidisciplinary orientation. Problem-centred orientation assumes that, both in teaching and studying, matters are considered from the point of view of many disciplines—an approach widely different from the prevailing system.

1. Author's italics.

4. Vocational orientation. Particularly in the humanities and social sciences, degrees should more clearly than hitherto be directed to a scientific, social or vocational task or complex of tasks.
5. General abilities. Education should emphasize general scientific and methodological abilities. Instead of aiming at narrow specialization, education should give a readiness to acquire the special abilities required by specific occupational tasks and a readiness to apply and utilize the knowledge acquired.

The content for new degrees would be planned in terms of educational programmes. The programmes should have been planned and produced by one or several teaching units. They should be goal-oriented entities which offer the student the opportunity to weight his studies flexibly within the themes and goals of the programme. The ministry goes on to stress that reforms in higher education should be closely related to reforms in secondary education and to the regional development of higher education. The ministry has financed an extensive research project entitled 'The university and the environment' at the University of Joensuu, the purpose of which is to study the mutual interaction between the university and the surrounding areas and the economic, social and cultural effects produced by the university in the region [2].

The rhetoric of educationalists is often very different from the reality of institutions. However, if the broad sweep of reform of higher education which is indicated by the expressed policies of many governments is realized, then higher education institutions would be most appropriate places for teachers to pursue the formal stage of their own personal education.

On the other hand, many countries still prepare teachers in colleges which are isolated from the mainstream of higher education. While this may have been an appropriate model for a traditional society with highly specific objectives for its teachers and well-known skills to be achieved, in the present situation monotechnic institutions have certain major disadvantages: (a) their existence tends to isolate the teacher from men and women with different interests and career intentions, thus narrowing their perspective and their experience of other adults; (b) they tend to limit the recruitment of potential teachers to those who have made a choice while still attending school themselves; (c) they make change of career intention more difficult for the trainee teacher; and (d), perhaps most importantly, they reduce the resources available for the higher education of potential teachers and lead to the maintenance of a separate and sometimes substandard set of institutions which are constantly at the mercy of changes in the trends of supply and demand. Thus, at times of rapid expansion, like those being experienced in developing countries, the colleges are often under great pressure and tend to 'survive by hurrying'. However, at a time of rapidly falling demand, such as in the United Kingdom at present, colleges with excellent resources are having to be closed and staff made redundant. Thus, from many points of view there is great advantage in teachers being educated within diversified institutions which provide education for a number of careers in addition to that of teaching.

This does not necessarily mean that they should be educated in enormous universities or in vast polytechnics. One of the most serious aspects of the democratization of higher education is the assumption that quantitative growth of higher education automatically implies the establishment of higher education institutions with very large numbers of students. It has now become very apparent that multiversities and higher education complexes can become depersonalized and can inhibit learning. With particular reference to teacher education, the evidence of Thailand to the thirty-fifth session of the ICE noted that 'Campuses of teacher education institutions are becoming larger and larger. Hence the students often feel lost in the ever-expanding campuses and demand personal relations. Teachers must therefore learn to be human, and the professional education of teachers must be humanized by concern for the individual student in the larger collectivity of student population.' They note the importance of the need for students to learn group process skills and affective attitudes and behaviours.

A number of institutional models are obviously possible.

Teacher education may be a part of large universities or colleges. In such cases, however, it inevitably tends to be a minor element in the institution. All countries should have some colleges which have a central concern for teacher training while not seeing it as their only concern. Colleges of higher education, which provide up to half their places for teacher education students and then offer a range of general education and vocational courses, are being developed in the United Kingdom and in Australia.

Scope for institutions particularly interested in interprofessional training of teachers, social and community workers, health officers and trade unionists to work together will also provide an interesting institutional variation. A characteristic which is most important is that they should be open institutions with part-time students, adults from the community and with strong and active links with the region in which they are placed. The community should look to them for resources, and for access to their libraries and facilities. Their interest in research should be particularly in the fields of applied research and inquiry. Their aim should be the fullest development of the potential of each individual student. Therefore, courses will have to be a great deal more flexible than is general at present, and admission procedures much more open, so that it will be the responsibility of the institution to ensure that appropriate courses and resources are available for the purposive student. Thus, various learning modes must be evolved with an emphasis upon individualized learning and upon the student as an active participator in establishing the problems to be solved as well as in attempting to solve them.

When reviewing the particular characteristics to be looked for in an appropriate course of higher education for teachers and many others who will be entering careers in the public service, it is obvious that the curriculum must have a concern for breadth and depth. A highly specialized single-subject course would normally not be appropriate preparation. Essentially the student should be encouraged to become an active learner, and his higher education should put him into a learning network rather than a teaching funnel. There should be an emphasis upon experience and upon access to a variety of forms of evidence, and to a wide range of different learning and teaching methods. The approach to almost any part of the student's course should be illuminated by an awareness of the relationship to other areas of knowledge and to the social, political, economic, cultural and technological conditions of contemporary society.

Many higher education teachers may design elegant courses which regard knowledge as something that should be kept in a cool, dry place. It should be emphasized, however, that the most effective form of learning for many of the students in higher education, including those who wish to become teachers, is one that confronts difficult and complex questions of urgent concern at a personal, national and international level. This point was put clearly by a recent policy statement of the Department of Education and Science in the United Kingdom: 'The Government have sympathy with the sincere desire on the part of a growing number of students to be given more help in acquiring—and discovering how to apply— knowledge and skills related more directly to the decisions that will face them in their careers and in the world of personal and social action. This is what is meant by "relevance". The wider the span of student motivation, the greater the need to match it with a wide and flexible choice of course. This is being achieved increasingly by a system of units and credits devised in such a way as to ease transfer from one course or institution to another—which should help students to retrieve false starts and make more possible the develop- ment of recurrent education' [3].

It is to be hoped that many of the themes to be considered by higher education systems will relate to those of particular interest to Unesco and to leaders in the world community, particularly in the field of education. At a time when many higher education systems are coming under heavy criticism, it is all the more important that they should be seen to be concerned with helping men and women to understand and deal constructively with the problem of interper- sonal relations, of massive variations in standards of living both within and between societies, and the threat to both the human and the physical environment. Many of the issues such as pollution, overpopulation, increased appeal to the use of force, and the grow- ing alienation of ordinary men and women from political processes cannot be solved merely through conferences, political action or individual leadership, however inspired. Among other strategies which must be employed, the role of higher education devoted to a rational, humane and intensive consideration of the issues must be seen as an important one. Such an approach to higher education curricula could then have an important influence on the curricula offered in schools. This is particularly the case in countries where the teacher is given opportunities to exercise his own influence upon the curriculum and the teaching methods to be employed.

Increasing emphasis is now being placed upon the operation of choice within higher education. This includes not only the choice to follow certain programmes of study but also the opportunity to move in and out of education throughout one's working life. Strong support for the idea of lifelong education has been apparent in international organizations and in many Member States of Unesco over the last two decades. Such a movement is of particular importance for potential teachers. The need to recruit mature men and women with a variety of backgrounds and interests is one of particular concern for those professions dealing with human relations and social problems. Students should be able to leave with credit from higher education institutions at various stages and not merely, as has been indicated above, at the completion of a particular qualification such as a first degree. Experiments in short cycle higher education and the opportunity to take particular courses of training in a variety of ways later in life are essential ingredients of any society's post-school education system.

PERSONAL EDUCATION AND TRAINING FOR TEACHING

Having discussed the developing context of higher education, it is important to raise the question of the relationship between the personal education of potential teachers and their actual training. Of three main styles for the preparation of teachers followed in different countries, the first approach is that in which no specific training is offered before the teacher assumes professional responsibilities for work with children. This is the case in some developing countries where a secondary school student moves straight into the teacher role on completion of his secondary education. This is also the case in developed countries where graduates, having successfully completed their first degree, also are automatically qualified as teachers. Whatever the short-run advantages of such an approach, it simply cannot be accepted as an appropriate form of preparation for teaching.

The second style is one in which there is a specific course of training following on after the completion of the personal education stage. Again this may be immediately after secondary school or after completion of a first degree. In most cases such training lasts for a year and involves a certain amount of theoretical study in education, the content of school curricula and in certain applications of the social sciences.

The third approach is one which is firmly based upon a post-school education stage and which gives the potential teacher the opportunity to choose courses which are both relevant to his personal education and to his future role as a teacher. In most cases the concentration upon specific training comes after a student's involvement in wider ranging studies chosen from a variety of disciplines. Given that the curriculum of higher education is fundamentally reformed in the way discussed above, both the second and third approaches can provide a highly suitable base for the programme of initial training for teaching which is now discussed in the next chapter.

REFERENCES

1. Indonesia. Office of Educational Development (BPP), Ministry of Education and Culture. *Educational innovation in Indonesia.* Paris, Unesco: International Bureau of Education, 1975. 50 p., bibl. (Experiments and innovations in education, 13.) [Also published in French and in Spanish.]
2. Finland. Ministry of Education. *Educational development in Finland 1973-1975.* Helsinki, 1975. 126 p. (Reference publications, 7.)
3. United Kingdom. *Education: a framework for expansion.* White Paper presented to Parliament by the Secretary of State for Education and Science by Command of Her Majesty. London, HMSO, 1972. 49 p.

CHAPTER SEVEN

Initial training

Before specific training for teaching begins it is assumed that the student who enters the training stage will have achieved a certain level of personal maturity and is a successful learner with a good standard of education based upon the wide range of courses which were described in the previous chapter. The role of the teacher is now so wide-ranging and diverse that it is not possible to lay down highly specific requirements at the stage of admission into the training programme. However, care should be taken to establish that the potential teacher has a balanced personality, is well motivated towards teaching and further learning and has a high standard of intellectual capability. It must be admitted, however, that the problem of selecting suitable entrants to teacher training has received relatively little study. Practice varies widely and, where there is a shortage of teachers, most of those who are academically qualified can obtain entry to a training programme. However, the changed role of the teacher does make heavier demands upon personal qualities and requires certain basic attitudes which require institutions to think more carefully about their admission procedures. Teacher training should not be seen merely as a substitute for higher education. It is to be hoped that most teachers will be recruited from those who are already engaged upon a course of higher education or who have completed it. Attention to admission procedures can also help to ensure an appropriate balance in the supply of teachers in a particular country.

Much more substantial research and guidance are necessary in the important field of deciding which members of a society are most appropriate to become the nation's teachers.

TEACHER TRAINING PROGRAMMES

The two major styles of teacher preparation can be called 'directed teacher education', where the student is on a coherent programme of teacher training from the beginning of his post-school education, and 'open teacher education', where post-school education is less directed and may lead to a variety of outcomes. All countries have adopted either one or both of the above styles, but, because of the immense pressure for teachers illustrated in Chapter 6, most developing countries have been forced to adopt a third strategy to meet the urgent demand arising from the democratization of education in their countries. While cases will still persist of young men and women going into school and working completely untrained, the most common trend described at the 1975 ICE was towards what might be called 'on the job' or school-based training. Characteristically the student on completion of his secondary schooling, or less frequently after a period of post-school education, has a short period of preparation in college and is then placed in a school which becomes his place of personal learning as well as his base for teacher training. This approach is superficially similar to the pupil-teacher system adopted in many developed countries in the nineteenth century and may be characterized as 'school-based training'.

These three styles of teacher education will now be reviewed. It must be noted, however, that all have certain features in common, that each country develops its own particular version of the basic style and that the examples given are inevitably examples of variation based upon the different needs of the culture concerned.

DIRECTED TEACHER EDUCATION

The advantages of the direct style are powerful enough to have become the major style of teacher education in the world. The country is able to recruit students who will be committed to training for teaching and to operate manpower planning for the profession. In particular, however, it enables teacher educators to construct a course in which every aspect can be related to professional needs;

there can be careful orchestration of theory and practice throughout the programme, and the whole college has a unity of purpose which can express itself as a professional ethic; resources can be appropriate to the task and, because they are single-purpose, colleges tend to be small and relatively intimate communities. The widespread distribution and the size of the colleges also tend to enable links with schools to be established more easily.

The disadvantages in a direct teacher education programme based upon a discrete set of institutions relate to the very coherence and separateness which are often used to justify such a structure. Teacher education exists to prepare teachers in the most effective way to meet the demands of schooling. The assumption in direct teacher education is that all aspects of the student's studies and experience are geared towards his work as a teacher. This, however, assumes that the college teachers have a concept of a school in mind, with a particular curriculum, types of children and range of problems. The evidence of Part I of this book, however, indicates plainly that a school is not a fixed entity, and that the role of the teacher is undergoing massive and persistent change. Even where it is possible to offer certain clear guidelines, the college teacher, who has often been away from the classroom for many years, may not be the best of guides. Directed teacher education was established at a time when the overt tasks of schooling were simple and aimed towards enabling children to have basic competence in handling the skills of literacy and numeracy. However, the generalizations around which many programmes are now built do not stand up to the harsh realities of actual work in the schools. The gap between the image presented to the student in college and the actuality of the work of the beginning teacher is often unbridgeable. This is particularly so in a long, college-based and heavily theoretical programme. The fact that the majority of these programmes are offered in relatively small, coherent educational communities tends to seal the students and staff off from the schools and encourage the pursuit of an idealistic but often unworkable professional ethic. The fact that all the students are pursuing courses leading to the same work reduces the challenge and variety which are so important for critical awareness.

Three other problems arise from the institutional context for directed teacher education. Most students are admitted to a teachers' college when they are in their last year at school: inevitably many of them have a relatively immature attitude to teaching. At interview many of them will say that they have 'always wanted to be a teacher'. Such students may, in fact, never really 'leave school'. They will thus tend to cling to the image of the school in which they have been successful rather than face the implications of social and educational changes which teachers in future will have to contend with. Once in the college, the student has extremely limited opportunities for choice; if he wishes to change his career orientation, he must do so by leaving it and going somewhere else, with inevitable difficulties and sense of failure. Colleges, being small and seen only in the light of teacher education, will often have resources which are substandard when compared with those of large, diversified higher education institutions. They will thus be able to offer only a limited range of courses, which will tend to reflect the *present* curriculum in the schools rather than look towards new areas of knowledge and understanding, which are becoming increasingly important. Many teachers' colleges are also organized around training students for a specific age-range, compounding the difficulty of student-teachers arriving at an understanding not only of other activities in society but also of the total school system. Finally, from an economic point of view, the allocation of buildings and resources exclusive to a single occupation makes such resources dependent upon the flow of demand for such an occupational group. Thus, in the 1960s in the United Kingdom, and in many other developed countries, there was a major expansion of staff and plant to meet a major demand for teachers. Only a decade later colleges are being closed because the lower birth-rate has ensured a major reduction in demand for teachers. Where teacher education is an important element within diversified institutions it is much easier to regulate the supply of teachers and to redeploy staff and resources in order to fulfil other educational needs.

Many countries have clearly used the directed teacher education system with considerable effectiveness and managed to emphasize its advantages and minimize its disadvantages. Features of it are bound to persist in any reformed system in the future. However, in its present form it does not represent a genuinely comprehensive response to the challenge of the changing role of the teacher.

OPEN TEACHER EDUCATION

The advantages of the open teacher education system are that students have the opportunity to make a personal selection of the courses they wish to follow and to pursue their own learning to an advanced stage. They will go to a higher education institution which offers them scope and the opportunity for choice and for change among vocational objectives. Facilities and resources will be broadly based, and the potential teacher should be able to choose from a diversity of courses based upon the social sciences. Although the student may be committed to teaching, he will be able to test out his commitment and to take courses which will enable him to achieve a fuller perspective on such matters as the psychology of child development or the sociology of the school. When the student, after an initial period, enters on to the specific training programme, his commitment will be a more mature one based upon knowledge acquired as an adult. It will ensure that students mix with a variety of other people with different career intentions and those who might be deeply critical of the school system as they have experienced it. Research is more likely to have been developed within a larger and diversified higher education institution, and such research may well contribute importantly to the student's ultimate views on teaching. Research and inquiry in such fields as psychology and sociology obviously have a direct bearing upon the teacher's task. Similarly, access to the latest thought in subject areas such as mathematics, science and the arts will ultimately enrich the contribution which the potential teacher can make to the school curriculum in such areas. Teacher education will be genuinely part of higher education, thus giving the teacher greater flexibility both during his initial higher education and also later, when, as with many of his fellows, he may need to change his job two or three times.

There has been a tendency over the last ten years for an increasing number of countries in both the developed and the developing regions to put initial training into the university or to give teacher training parity with the universities: for example, in Norway, the Teacher Training Act of 1973 points in the direction of a system in which teacher training colleges become post-secondary institutions on a parity with the universities and other institutions of higher education. In Australia, the teacher's colleges are now being developed as autonomous colleges of advanced education, and many are diversifying their programmes to include courses in fields other than education. A greater proportion of teachers are thus being educated in multi-faculty institutions, with a consequent broadening of their course options.

The disadvantages of an open teacher education system are that the courses themselves may lack specificity and fail to focus on the teacher's role; objectives of their programmes may be diffuse, and the students may choose inappropriate and irrelevant courses; it may also be difficult for the higher education institution to enable the teacher training students to achieve a unified professional view and to give them a sustained commitment to the school system. It is certainly true in many countries that *existing* higher education institutions, particularly universities, have failed to give a central place to teacher education, and much innovation has taken place outside the university context.

SCHOOL-BASED TEACHER EDUCATION

Faced with the crushing problem of constantly accelerating demand for teachers, a number of developing countries have established a variety of strategies, all of which relate to a harsh reality: human beings only pass through their childhood once, millions of children need to be helped to learn and, therefore, the schools need the presence of the maximum number of responsible adults. Thus, although teacher training is also pursued according to the systems discussed above, it is also necessary to provide some training support for those who are already in the schools. In all cases, such schemes represent a pragmatic response to a pressing and persistent problem. Few generalizations can be made, but the following examples provide a range of alternative strategies.

Thus, in the Sudan, the political leadership, supported and encouraged by international development agencies and buoyed up by the hopes of the people, sees a bright future. Significantly, the rising youth, aged from 15 to 25, represents at least a quarter and perhaps as much as a third of the population, and they go beyond the government in taking a brilliant future for granted. However, the government lives in the harsh present, confined by the constraints of present poverty and an inadequate and outdated education system. The expansion of their schools, particularly at primary level, has far outstripped the supply of trained teachers, so that the Ministry of Education has had to recruit increasing numbers of higher secondary school-leavers as primary school-teachers. This has resulted in the accumulation of large numbers of underqualified or unqualified primary school-teachers. The need for training has become urgent and vital. The withdrawal of these untrained teachers from their schools for training imposes a problem of their replacement by others.

In 1972 it was decided to establish an educational training institute, which employs a multi-media approach to training teachers 'on the job'. The development was made possible by Unicef with support from UNRWA (United Nations Relief und Works Agency) and Unesco. The trainee, who is a teacher and a student at the same time, undergoes a two-year basic professional training. The methodology of training integrates traditional, direct methods of training (class visits, full-time summer courses, demonstration lessons, etc.) with relatively new methods, such as the study of written assignments, closed-circuit cable television (CCTV) demonstration programmes and other audio-visual methods, as well as the use of the library, so that the two methods form one whole. The institute has its main centre at Khartoum, the training curriculum is set on the study assignment, and CCTV programmes, summer vacation courses, programmes, follow-up schemes and so on are prepared. There are sub-centres in sixteen main towns in the Sudan, and the training radiates to the neighbouring schools of the trainees. The total number of enrolments is approximately 2,000. Preliminary results are very encouraging as shown by examinations, technical supervisors' reports and primary school headmasters' responses.

In Iran there is again considerable use of high school graduates in schools, and this country has developed teacher-training-by-distance learning techniques: the School of Correspondence was established in 1970 for teachers to exploit the correspondence method and other multiple-training media. The programme is aimed at teachers working in the villages in remote districts of the country, for updating, for developing more efficient implementation of national programmes, and also providing higher education opportunities for young teachers who are unable to attend universities.

Instructional materials have been developed and the materials refined and reviewed by a compilation committee, and the students' work is evaluated each month. Supplementary materials, such as cassettes and reference books, are sent to the students. Residential training through preparatory classes, regional classes during week-ends, ten-day vacation classes, and four-to-six-week summer classes are provided to remove the deficiencies arising from non-attendance at regular classes.

For practice teaching the students are required to perform an analytical survey of the curriculum and texts on subjects taught by them in their respective classrooms, and to transmit their work-papers for comments. They are also required to do demonstration teaching during summer classes. The programme has enabled teachers to acquire a junior college teaching certificate upon completion of seventy units within three years, and a B.A. or B.Sc. degree with an additional seventy units over two additional years. The government considers the programme productive because of the large number of teachers who can he helped without being alienated from their work as teachers in villages and. remote districts. It has tended also to generate creativity and self-reliance among teachers.

Other countries have adopted similar strategies, so in Nepal a field-oriented sequence has been developed in the primary teacher training programme. In Trinidad it was estimated that only one in six of the country's secondary school-teachers had received post-graduate training; the University of the West Indies at St. Augustine now offers a diploma to the untrained teachers. The teachers attend regularly at the university throughout the year and are visited in the schools by a curriculum tutor. Major components in the course are themes in education, curriculum studies and assignments.

In Qatar, evening programmes are being provided, and in Iraq a special unit for training serving primary teachers with a multi-media approach was set up in 1973.

The significance of all the above programmes and other national variations relates to the fact that training is dominated by the 'student's' experience as a beginning teacher. Inevitably his training must relate constantly to his activity as an educator. The most significant influences on him are bound to be the children with whom he works, his colleagues and the community in which the school is set. The advantages of such a system relate to the fact that the 'student' is in the situation for which he is being 'trained'; he is able to make his day-to-day experiences the material of his training; he is able to articulate problems which have actually arisen in his own work, and seek help in solving them from the training that he is undergoing. The psychology of learning is not an abstract matter but actually relates to helping an individual child in his own class to learn to read or to acquire a specific skill. In addition, a student who is also at the same time a teacher is likely to be more challenging to the teacher educator and will be better motivated if he finds his training actually helps him to achieve greater success within school. Teacher educators who visit the teacher in school get more realistic feedback than is usually available in the much more artificial and protected system of practice teaching. An overriding advantage for countries that have adopted the system is that it enables them to move faster along the road towards the democratization of education and universal schooling than would otherwise be the case. Although only a percentage of the adults in the school are qualified teachers, it is possible to organize a team which can take responsibility under experienced leadership.

The disadvantages of the system are, however, serious. Throwing someone into deep water sometimes enables them to swim, although they may not develop a particularly good style; others, however, simply drown. Putting untrained personnel with children is clearly a dangerous procedure because, although the school can be an agency for change, development and improvement, it can also be a place of boredom, inefficiency and retrenchment. Many of the untrained teachers will not even have had any post-school education and will therefore be personally ill-equiped as well as professionally unprepared. The difficulties for such 'teachers' in achieving understanding of the complex role of the teacher and the potential of schooling will be immense. While the model of the pupil-apprentice may have been appropriate for a heavily traditional society, it is inadequate for the modern situation. However, the developing countries, which have attempted at least to combine a response to the urgent educational needs of the schools with a carefully articulated programme of school-based training, may well be making one of the most important contributions to the future style of teacher education and training.

As has been indicated, all the above styles contain some advantages and some disadvantages. There is no simple right and wrong about initial teacher training. As was said in the national report from Indonesia, 'Teacher training may be regarded as one of the most sensitive and interactive parts of the education system, coming often as a nodal point between school, community and higher education'. So many influences are brought to bear upon teacher education that it must inevitably be contingent: it must serve the schools, and the schools must serve the political, social and economic needs of the country, and help children to realize their individual potential. Any country reviewing its procedures for teacher education needs to be aware of the dimensions of time, place and circumstance. There is no universal prescription. However, the implications of the changed role of the teacher do suggest a framework that may help those concerned to arrive at an assessment of the priorities for action.

THE CYCLES OF TEACHER EDUCATION

It is possible to consider the education and training of teachers in three major cycles. In Chapter 7 there is a discussion of the personal education of the potential teacher. In the present chapter we have been discussing different approaches to his initial training, and in the next chapter attention will be turned to the continuing or in-service education of teachers. These are the three cycles that have been identified in various ways in most of the countries represented at the 1975 ICE. The term 'cycle' was first used to describe the phases in *Teacher education and training*, the report by a Committee of Inquiry appointed by the Secretary of State for Education and Science in the United Kingdom under the chairmanship of Lord James of Rusholme in 1972 [1]. It is now appropriate to summarize what it is expected to achieve from the first two cycles, the first cycle being personal education and the second cycle being initial training.

The first cycle—personal education

As indicated, the democratization of education and increasing comprehensivization at the school stage are now having substantial effects upon the curriculum of higher education. It is to be hoped that various reforms and developments will accelerate over the next decade and that some of the greatly enlarged number of students emerging from the higher education system will wish to choose teaching as a career and will be better qualified to do so than their predecessors.

A good deal has already been said about the need for a more relevant and appropriate higher education curriculum. When considering the potential teacher, however, it should be increasingly possible to require a student, before he begins the second cycle or actual teacher training, to have reached a good standard of personal education both in range and in depth. In particular, the teacher educators will be looking for a background of knowledge and understanding in applications of psychology, social psychology and sociology.

Among the range of courses on offer to higher education students, those in such fields as child development, psychology of learning, the sociology of the school and the economics of education would be of particular relevance. As such courses in education and in applied areas become more widely available in the general higher education curriculum, students entering teacher training courses could be required to have followed them with success. This implies a reorganization of the higher education curriculum so that there is more genuine choice for students and there is a commitment to breadth and a movement away from single subject degrees at the immediate post-school stage.

While the conventional higher education stage for many students, particularly in developed countries, will be a first degree, the first cycle could be a good deal shorter than the time normally spent on degree study. The aim should clearly be a minimum of at least a year with the emphasis upon personal education after school, but many students may find a period longer than two years inappropriate when they wish to be getting on with the second cycle and their more specific teacher training programme. Thus, although the style of postgraduate training, where the first cycle is a degree (e.g. B.A. or B.Sc.) and the second cycle is a postgraduate qualification, will tend to persist and enables well-qualified men and women to enter teaching after graduation, it should not be the common route into teaching. A more appropriate style, preserving some of the advantages of the three systems discussed above, would be one in which there was a co-ordinated qualification containing a first cycle of relevant personal education of one or two years, after which a student could then opt into the second cycle and then obtain a degree which also qualifies him to teach.

The second cycle—initial teacher training

As has already been said repeatedly, crushing demands are being made upon individuals who become teachers, and these were spelt out by many of the countries contributing to the 1975 ICE. Thus, in the Philippines, the country is looking towards teachers who can be social integrators, attitude changers and community workers, who can understand the positive cognitive and affective processes and who can develop them instead of inhibiting their growth— individuals who can assume multiple roles with regard to rural transformation, health and nutrition, and the development of employable skills in the rural setting. They should also understand their community as a social structure, its economy and patterns of behaviour. They should be able to contribute to non-formal educational activities and can help to accelerate the acquisition of basic literary and communication skills and the development of values. All other countries have their expectations.

One of the overriding problems of current initial teacher training is that in various ways the courses often attempt to produce a 'complete teacher' who, from the moment of assuming responsibility in the school, can express a high level of competence in all the various areas demanded of him. Although, when questioned, teacher educators argue that the time they have available makes such a goal unrealistic and that they have few ways of evaluating the success of their work, they are reluctant to leave out anything which might be useful in helping the teacher to achieve success in any aspect of his multiple role. In the directed teacher education system this leads to a heavily overloaded compulsory curriculum and pressure to extend the period of training from two to three and then to four years. In the open teacher education system, the lack of a clear link between the personal education stage and the training stage means that superficial and ill-digested theory is mixed with practice over an extremely limited period, rarely extending over more than a year.

However, the fundamental reason why initial training attempts to do too much, and therefore often fails to do anything really well, relates to the fact that in most countries teacher education is a two-cycle operation. There is rarely any guarantee that there will be a third cycle when the teacher will have the opportunity to continue his personal and professional improvement, and to develop skills which essentially require maturity and experience before they can be properly achieved. Few courses of initial training accept the limited objective of preparing a competent beginning teacher. Most feel the pressure to achieve the broader aim of preparing a proficient educator who may well never have any formal opportunity of teacher education after receiving his initial qualification.

Essential to the structure of initial training, which is proposed for the second cycle, is an assumption that the universal international support for the third cycle of continuing education for teachers, which was expressed by the 1975 ICE, will be adopted by all countries who cherish the qualitative as well as the quantitative aspects of the democratization of their education systems. Given that the third cycle will be implemented, the second can be conveniently divided into two stages.

Second cycle—first part

The first will be college-based, which should increasingly mean based in a school of education and professional training in a diversified institution. The institution may be a university, a polytechnic or originally a teachers' training college. The whole of the second cycle should be sharply focused upon the skills and understanding which it is necessary for a beginning teacher to establish. Thus, although the first stage will be college-based, contact with schools should be regular and substantial from the beginning. Students will come from a wide variety of backgrounds, but all will have a sound personal education and increasing knowledge of social sciences applied to educational problems.

From the beginning of the second cycle, teacher educators should be aiming to answer problems which the students articulate on the basis of their experience in school. Courses in curriculum studies, teaching methods, assessment and evaluation should all be based upon regular and sustained experience with children. Teacher educators should work closely with practising teachers and should themselves be regularly in contact with children and seen to be successful in working with them. Students in this first stage should have the opportunity of working with individual children and with small groups. They should be able to see many examples of good teaching and be involved in close analysis of the teaching situation through modern techniques such as micro-teaching and simulation.

The teacher educators will need to be clear about their objectives, and the student will need to know how he is to assess his success in achieving them. In some cases this may lead to institutions adopting such refined techniques as those developed in the United States under the heading of 'performance education' where a list of teacher competencies is established. In this the student-teacher is to achieve skills of diagnosis, evaluation, organizing the classroom, setting goals and objectives, planning, communicating with children, instructing them, of managing the school situation and of evaluating the feedback. However refined the objectives, the over-all aim within a limited time is to prepare the student for the second stage of his second cycle. This second stage may be called 'induction' and is essentially the student's first year as a teacher. It is strongly recommended that he should not be regarded as fully qualified until he has completed his first year in the school although he may well receive his academic award and his licence to teach at the end of the final college-based stage.

Second cycle—second part

The second part of the second cycle resembles in many ways the practice referred to above as school-based teacher education adopted by many developing countries. If, however, this is built into the system of initial teacher training, the beginning teacher will require both in-school and out-of-school support during this final phase of his initial training. At the end of this year he will be regarded as fully qualified and competent, having completed his 'internship', aware of the realities and complexities of the teacher's role, and is then prepared to take advantage of the third cycle.

It is not appropriate to go into detail with regard to this stage of the second cycle, but there do appear to be two imperatives. The most important institution at this stage of initial training is the school to which the beginning teacher is appointed. Traditionally, a large number of schools have trained the beginner 'on the job' either because the training programme was ignored or did not exist. However, any country which respects the educational process will want to ensure that its teachers are properly prepared for the complex and demanding task which is described in Part I of this book.

All schools that receive new teachers have to play a training role. They should be given certain basic resources in order to do so. Firstly, they need to be staffed in a way that enables a student-teacher to have some release from his teaching responsibilities, preferably for the equivalent of one day each week. Such time will vary and will be heavily dependent upon the total supply of teachers. Secondly, each school must have a teacher-tutor, who is responsible for any student-teachers working in the school as well as the beginning teacher, and is also likely to have a role with regard to the third cycle. Therefore, each individual school needs a specific programme of activities and support for its new teachers which are agreed either on a national or a regional basis. Given such provision within the school, the beginning teacher is well placed to get the regular, daily, direct and sustained help which will have the greatest impression upon his own personal professional style and approach to his work. Here the student in the final stage of his training is dealing with the totality of the teacher's situation, not only seeing children at various times in the school day and school year, but learning about their interests and needs beyond the range of the school curriculum, often coming into contact with parents and other members of the community. He is rather in the same position as the intern in a hospital and, as well as the teacher-tutor, all his fellow-teachers have a responsibility to support and advise him.

Many of the most important questions in teaching are universal questions of great depth and permanence that reflect the undoubted fact that education is a process rather than a product. What and when to teach? How to help children to learn? What is truth? How to co-operate? How to settle disputes? What is the difference between having authority and being authoritarian? Almost every school day will bring up at least one or more of such questions. It is anticipated that giving schools clear responsibilities for professional training will also encourage them to become centres of inquiry.

Such a style and approach is increasingly important as societies all over the world move from traditional modes of thought to an era of rapid change and near revolution.

The teacher-tutor has a particularly critical function at this stage of teacher training. Ideally he should be an experienced teacher with a good knowledge of the school and have undergone a training programme to prepare him for his work as a teacher-tutor. This training course will have informed him about the kind of higher education programme the student-teacher is likely to have pursued, will have attuned him to the different approaches in neighbouring schools, and informed him of the latest developments in the field of curriculum and teaching methods. He will particularly need to be sensitive to counselling and casework methods and should be a gifted teacher, able to assist a student-teacher and the beginning teacher through example as well as through discussion and guidance. Thus a teacher-tutor needs to know how to help, to diagnose and to prescribe, to observe but not to impose. He also needs to have the capacity to learn from the student-teacher and to organize the student-teacher's own learning, both inside and outside school. Thus he will put a student into contact with the head and advisers, and assist him to organize his non-teaching time. It is important that the teacher-tutor should have the status and rewards demanded by his exacting task. His preparation may be regarded as one of the first tasks of an expanded system of in-service training.

While the role of the school is obviously critical in ensuring the success of the initial stage of teacher training, it is highly desirable that there should be some continuity of external support. This will take much longer to achieve in many countries, particularly where there is an urgent problem of teacher supply. However, there are various ways in which external support can be given. Many developing countries have been ingenious in the arrangements they have already made.

One approach is through the establishment of field centres or teachers' centres. While the school deals with the daily and urgent problems of work with children and professional duties such as the detailed preparation and use of school resources, a professional centre will enable the student-teacher to meet other colleagues who are beginning their professional lives, and also meet a different group of experienced teachers and advisers who can give attention

to the teacher's need for more long-term planning and more sophisticated aids and resources. A centre could also give the teacher a
wider perspective than that provided by a single school; the
young teacher will hear of other experiences, share problems,
begin to establish his priorities, and sort out more general
problems from those which may be specific only to a particular
school or classroom. The social support of other colleagues may
be very significant at this stage, particularly for a student-
teacher who is experiencing stress in a school operating in difficult
circumstances.

The centres in certain countries, such as some in the United
Kingdom and Canada, have established curriculum teams. While
these are always led by experienced teachers, they often contain
beginning teachers who bring more recent knowledge from their
higher education courses but require an understanding of what is
possible in professional terms from their more experienced colleagues. A centre, as well as providing a rich resources bank that can
be made available to any individual school, can also provide the
resource of centre staff, who may work for a sustained period in a
school in order to establish a new curriculum or assist a school to
try out new ideas or teaching methods. The centre itself may be
located in a large school or attached to a college or, where finance is
available, may be an independent building located appropriately for
a network of schools. The schools served will, of course, cover a
wide age range, and this again will give the beginning teacher a
wider view of the education system than he would gain from the
deep but restricted experience of one school.

Although in one important sense the beginning teacher will have
'left' college, the function of such an institution is still important.
Such research as has been done indicates strongly that the beginning
teacher identifies most strongly with his fellow colleagues in the
context of the school. He is quick to challenge and criticize the
theoretical model that he may have become aware of during the
latter part of his course of teacher education based upon college or
university. The same change occurs in all other professions, including engineering, medicine and law, but in teacher education the
change is made more acute by the fact that many colleges fail to
take any serious responsibility for their students once they leave.
Also college tutors are rarely 'visible' within the schools either

teaching or involved in curriculum development or school community projects and other activities.

The massive growth of in-service training for teachers that is
proposed in the next chapter should transform the colleges which
have responsibility for teacher education in that they will be centres
for experienced teachers and therefore contain many resources that
will also be helpful to the beginning teacher. Such colleges should
in the future spend as much time, if not more, upon the continuing
education of teachers than they do upon work with initial trainees.
Many college tutors should hold joint appointments between school
and college. Centres for regional curriculum development and
national curriculum development will naturally be located in such
colleges, as will curriculum research groups and inquiries into such
matters as assessment, learning styles, teaching methods and various
courses contracted for by schools and local authorities.

Again, drawing on the experience of many developing countries
and their school-based training, the college year should be planned
to enable the beginning teacher in the second phase of his initial
training to have a period of residence or sustained attachment for
two or three weeks in a college. Course conferences could be
planned by groups of teacher-tutors working with colleagues from
professional centres and from the teacher education faculty in the
college. Advanced resources would be available in the college's
resource centre, and practical projects could be carried through and
further developed in the final stage of the first year of teaching.
Opportunities should also be provided for the beginning teacher to
establish a programme of independent learning and he should also
be given guidance as to ways in which his own higher education
could interact with his new responsibilities as a teacher.

If the first period of teaching is to be regarded as the essential
last step in the initial training of the teacher, an assessment will have
to be made of the beginning teacher in order to enable him to be
recommended as fully registered. Different countries would clearly
make different arrangements for such assessment: in some cases it
would be done by the administration represented by an inspector or
adviser who stands outside the school; often it would be done in
close co-operation with the head of the school and the teacher-tutor
and, where appropriate, the college. While fraught with many difficulties, it may be that the new arrangements might lead to the

profession itself setting up a teachers' council to take responsibility for registering all its members and also for regulating their professional standards.

CONCLUSION

Throughout the whole of the second cycle the approach should be supportive and developmental. Most beginning teachers bring strong advantages into the teaching situation: they are nearer in age to the children than many experienced teachers; they bring enthusiasm, freshness and newly acquired knowledge into the schools; they tend to have strong social interests and are often skilled in establishing good informal relationships both with children and with other groups; they are often more sensitive than their older colleagues to the pattern of social change, and more open to the apparent unconventionality of pupils' attitudes and responses. The first consolidated experience as a teacher—the 'induction'—should not only be to provide the teacher with certain basic skills but it can also be a highly sensitive instrument in relation to national and regional policies. Thus it can be used to assist in crisis situations or to support certain drives—for example, towards literacy in rural areas or towards integration in urban areas. All Member States of Unesco should attempt to list the range of professional skills that they would expect beginning teachers to have acquired before final registration at the end of their period of initial training. The priorities in different countries and for different age ranges will vary, but the analysis of role contained in this book will suggest that they are likely to include:

1. The establishment of a professional ethic;
2. The acquirement of responsibility for a class;
3. The capacity to organize learning for children of different levels of initial performance;
4. The ability to prepare a sound educational programme, to carry it through, to assess and evaluate its success;
5. A knowledge of learning methods and of the technology of education;
6. The capacity to find information, to use sources and resources both for the children and for self-education, and to maintain a

fruitful and secure relationship with the children and with colleagues.

The level at which the above skills will be achieved will vary, but all
should be seen to be developed by the phase of initial training; all
should have been confronted and a measure of success should have
been achieved in each one.

This chapter has attempted to describe the existing system and
to propose one way in which resources that already exist can be
orchestrated to provide sound basic education and training for
teaching. Schools, higher education institutions and colleges exist in
all countries. What is vital is that the resources they provide,
however limited, should be deployed to the best advantage. In the
cyclical approach there is the implication that substantial periods of
time will be spent at each phase: thus, ideally, two or three years
might be spent on the personal education stage, a year on the interacting theoretical and practical work of the first stage of the
second cycle, and a year in a supported school situation before
registration. Again one would hope for a network of adequately
staffed schools, professional centres and colleges all working together.
Time and resources are, however, extremely limited in many
countries, and the demands are urgent and persistent. Each country
must therefore balance its priorities. Time available may be greatly
reduced at each of the stages, and the level of support may often be
rudimentary. However, any design for the future organization of
teacher education should provide for long-term objectives as well as
a strategy for immediate action. The most significant aspect of the
cyclical approach to teacher education is that, whatever it is decided
to do at the initial stage, it should certainly not be regarded as the
final stage. Having been received into full membership of the teaching profession, the stage should be set for the real task of continuing
education, built upon growing experience with children and with the
work of the schools. This is the task for a national system of in-
service education and training. Schools, colleges and other intermediary institutions will all have their roles to play in this stage, a third
cycle, which expresses most clearly the duality of the educator's
function—that of teacher and of learner.

REFERENCE

1. United Kingdom. Department of Education and Science. *Teacher education and training.* Report of Committee of Inquiry into Teacher Training. London, HMSO, 1972. 128 p.

NOTES

Examples of admission requirements referred to on the first page of this chapter:

1. The admission requirements for teacher training indicated by Austria provide one model: these include the final leaving certificate of a general or technical and vocational secondary school *(Matura)* and the proof of artistic and physical qualifications which is furnished in the form of an aptitude test before an examination board. The personality and character traits of the prospective teacher are at present not yet examined as to aptitude qualifications. Most potential teachers are, however, interviewed for entry by someone experienced in the field of teacher education. In some cases practising teachers are also associated with the interview, and this is a desirable trend.

2. Particular attention has been paid to the matter of selection in New Zealand where the number of applicants greatly exceeds the number of places available. A standard has been devised which can be applied by different committees who use the same criteria and a common rating scale. In addition, the procedure has been used to check the attitudes and suitability of a particular group of applicants as follows: in addition to the normal interview, selection procedures include: (a) a teaching experience with a group of children; (b) a one-to-one interview with an interviewer not on the original panel; (c) a written response to a film sequence depicting a teaching situation.

    The applicant's success in dealing with these three situations is carefully evaluated and an assessment given for each element as well as an over-all assessment. It is intended to carry out follow-up studies during the college course and in subsequent teaching.

3. In the United States admission to teacher training is largely open, as a student merely registers at a university on graduation and there is an ideological commitment from many educators to an open recruitment procedure. However, there is a general need throughout the country to recruit more minority and bilingual teachers. Screening devices using

traditional prior education standards tend to eliminate many of the candidates among those most sought at this time. In New York City 80 per cent of the Puerto Rican pupils do not complete high school and are thus not eligible for inclusion in conventional teacher education programmes. Mexican Americans and American Indians in the South West are in a similar situation. Foundations and the federal government have encouraged more flexibility and experimentation in this field, and the major emphasis on recruitment in supported programmes has been to expand minority populations in the profession.

CHAPTER EIGHT

Continuing teacher education

'For teachers now entering the school system it should be accepted that teacher education is, in fact, a continuous or recurrent process of which pre-service education is only the initial phase.'[1]

Support for the above concept was both enthusiastic and universal. The vital importance of establishing a system of continuing education or a 'third cycle' has been referred to a number of times. The new complexity of the teacher's role, and the inability of initial teacher training to provide all the knowledge and skills which a future teacher may need, provide an adequate theoretical justification. Theory, however, is one thing and practice is another. The difficulties are illustrated by a meeting in May 1975 of the Regional Planning Workshop of the Asian Programme of Educational Innovation for Development (APEID). It was pointed out that most of the countries in Asia have a runaway population growth and a high dependency ratio as a result of having a population structure that is overwhelmingly young and which is concentrated in deprived areas with low productivity. Uneven and slow economic progress and excessive population growth are combined with severe shortages of food, social services, electric power, water supply and qualified manpower, as well as inadequacies in infrastructure—all of which are essential to national development. Most of the developing countries are pursuing development programmes under adverse conditions, such as resource constraints in terms of funds, qualified personnel and other requirements. In addition, some are former colonies of western nations which have left a legacy

---

1. Conclusion from the *Final report* of the 1975 ICE.

of uneven development and a foreign education system which is often ill-adapted to new national needs. The story could be repeated for Africa and other parts of the developing world.

In the face of change, all countries agree that education which concentrates merely upon the conventional period of compulsory schooling and ignores the rest of a citizen's life is quite inappropriate for these modern times. It is also apparent that continuing education for all must be a distant ideal in societies where even primary education is denied for a substantial section of the population. Thus, priorities have to be established. When these have been decided, it will be cruelly obvious that many worthwhile and available schemes will not operate during the lifetime of those now entering schools around the world. It is all the more important, therefore, that priorities are established according to publicly debated and widely approved criteria. The case for the continuing education of teachers must be made in such a context.

However, one important measure of priority must be the effect that educational input will have upon the social and economic welfare of the country. Will the advantages remain with the individual receiving the support or will others profit? What will be the multiplier effect of the input? Another measure is the degree of efficiency and effectiveness that can be expected from a particular educational drive. How far will a target audience be able to profit? Have they the personal capacity to understand and the institutional support to make immediate use of the education and training they receive? Can the results be evaluated? Does the educational programme demonstrate improvements in confidence, successful performance and group effectiveness in economically and socially valued skills? Can results be seen in the immediate and specific achievement of objectives as well as in more long-term improvements?

Given that the answers to the above questions are positive, what is the cost to the society, and particularly the education system, of providing continuing education? Is there a sound and relevant body of knowledge to be communicated? Are there appropriate and available educators to communicate it, and do the necessary institutional networks and range of physical resources exist to carry out the programme?

The corridors of international organizations and national ministries are littered with good intentions that never get beyond the committee room. Lifelong education is likely to become another such good intention unless a beginning is made in an organized way with the most critical occupational group. When tested against the measures of priority raised in the previous paragraph, it must be said that teachers do justify a high priority for the establishment of systematic and continuing education aimed at their particular occupational group. Its effects are likely to be significant in the short run and dramatic in the long term. Teachers already have a sound educational base, and they can absorb educational input at a high level. The multiplier effect is guaranteed because teachers are in touch with the most impressionable members of society and have a responsibility for the only section of society increasingly required to be educated full time. Teachers are also the most expensive element within the school system and should be utilized as effectively as possible.

Such arguments, therefore, may be held to sustain the basic structure of a cyclical approach to teacher education, with in-service education or the third cycle playing a key part in professionalization and enabling the school to respond to change. The interaction between initial and in-service training is already being introduced in a number of national systems. As indicated earlier, it is only by seeing personal education and initial training as part of the continuous development of teachers that the scope and objectives of personal education and initial training can be appropriately articulated. A well-organized and effective system of in-service education and training is an essential concomitant of the style of initial training already discussed. Personal education, which stresses qualities of independent learning, choice and the acquirement of relevant knowledge, will encourage the future teacher to want to practise such skills in his work as a professional. Initial training, described above, with its increasing emphasis upon the school base and induction, will only be successful if it is a bridge into a professional life which is illuminated by regular periods of in-service education and training. Indeed, demands for a longer and more sophisticated period of initial training are likely to continue and be justified if countries delay the introduction of a national system of in-service education. However, it is becoming increasingly obvious that longer and more complex periods of initial training would not enable teachers to cope more effectively with the serious and recurrent problems referred to in earlier chapters.

The power and influence of those who would seek to de-school society are growing, and their arguments are sustained by the dangerous and widening gap between many who teach in the schools and those who come ostensibly to learn but stay to disrupt. It is impossible to ignore the fact that the initial education and training of teachers will always have difficulty in adjusting itself to the pressures which have reshaped societies and which are continuing to reshape the motivations and attitudes of the youngest and thus most vulnerable members of the population. While a relevant and contemporary course of higher education followed by a sound, practical period of initial training are essential prerequisites for the reform of teacher education, the fundamental reform relates to a shift of priorities within teacher education itself, away from increasing complexity and length in initial training and into a well-articulated and compulsory system of continuing teacher education. Following such a shift, there is then a concentration at the point where it can be most effective. Practical support, ideas and the results of research and inquiry will then be available for the teachers who are dealing with urgent problems that may not have been articulated or even anticipated at the initial phase. Even if the student-teacher could intellectually grasp professional problems, the experience of teaching is essential if he is to acquire an emotional and personal perspective which will enable him to make sound professional judgements. Thus every country is urged to establish such a system without delay. The rest of this chapter is mainly concerned with suggesting a possible framework for action.

THE PATTERN OF IN-SERVICE EDUCATION AND TRAINING

One approach is to base in-service education and training largely upon the institutions which serve initial training; indeed, this is a growing trend, emphasizing the interaction between initial and in-service training. Initial trainers have for too long been denied access to the failures and successes of their own initial training schemes. They have thus been denied an important opportunity to evaluate and refine initial training. The presence of recently qualified teachers inside colleges, bringing early problems which have not been confronted by their initial training, provides essential 'reality testing' for the trainer. Further, the consideration of real and on-going problems from local schools serves to illustrate that initial train-ing must always be generalized, and points up the dangers of 'argu-ment by analogy' which is characteristic of many training pro-grammes. Until this training system can show a concerted objective and intellectually demanding attack upon actual cases which need attention, teachers will continue to question the theoretical context of their initial training, the contribution of the social sciences and the role-models presented by the teacher training establishment. However important a knowledge of the psychology of learning may be to the teacher, many can only *perceive* its importance when faced with an actual learning problem.

Sometimes the goals of trainers and administrators are too lim-ited; very often they are unrealistically grandiose. In a 'World profile on issues in education' published by the International Bureau of Education in 1972, it is pointed out that 'teachers are human beings with limitations and ask the question, "Why should school administrators give orders to the teachers as though the teachers were James Bond actors?" What teachers would like to have is a little justice, a little freedom, a little shared feeling of belonging. A sense of isolation could be detrimental to our system.' Another teacher, commenting in a discussion on a proposed innova-tion, asked whether 'even granting his teaching competence, his knowledgeability in the psychology of individual differences, would he be capable of giving forty odd pupils the individual attention and remedial instruction that might be required? How about the teacher in remote Barrios handling a class of two or three or even of four grades? Would he be able to pay proper attention to each pupil in such a multi-grade and multi-age group? Would the teacher have the time and energy to plot the growth-rate of each pupil, adminis-ter the right dosage of remedial instruction to slower ones? Has there been sufficient frank discussion among experts on the question "just how much time to do his job and how much energy does the teacher possess?" Finally, as a teacher we pay a lot of attention to individual differences between children, but when is there time to turn our attentions to the physique, kinetic resources and psycho-logical reserves of a teacher who has to cope with a contemporary adolescent?'

All teacher training is a dialogue between theory and practice, between aspiration and achievement. Without the third cycle it is in danger of being all theory and aspiration and little achievement.

In-service training, however, does not merely get its direction and structure from a relationship with initial training. It may be necessary to develop different structures, and Member States of Unesco, while all acknowledging the central importance of in-service training, have adopted different strategies depending upon their state of development and the nature of their problems. One of the many differences relates, of course, to the current state of teacher supply. In more developed regions with a static or declining birthrate the central problem may be to refresh and update an aging, conservative teaching force. In less-developed regions with a rapidly growing population the urgency of the need for new teachers may inevitably shorten the period of initial training and require the use of in-service training, task forces, the use of mass media and well-designed programmes for individual learning, such as the multi-media approach in Iran or the Sudan. In all countries, however, four levels of operation may be defined: in-service education functions in response to national, regional, institutional and personal needs.

National

Nationally there are going to be important requirements which central governments will need to see operated throughout the system. This will relate not only to minimum standards but also to the development of plans for improvement, such as the three and five-year plans to eradicate illiteracy in the Libyan Arab Republic, and the programmes of improvement to science teaching in India with Unicef assistance. Many governments are particularly concerned about rural education and the improvement of agriculture. As pointed out by APEID, promotion of rural transformation is vital. The majority of the people in developing countries live in rural areas and, while producing food for the urban sector, they are simultaneously exploited by being deprived of the minimum conditions for decent living. A large part of the work of promoting social change is the crucial one of educating rural people, children, youth and adults, to identify their most pressing problems and actively participate in resolving them.

Thus in Malaysia there is national commitment to a kind of agricultural education that did not exist before. Here in-service training has been central. Intensive programmes are offered to teachers during the school holidays to help them implement the new agricultural science syllabus for secondary schools which includes both practical experience as well as basic theory. There is a mobile in-service education unit in which teachers attend weekend courses at selected in-service centres in their respective areas. Mobile in-service training was started as a pilot project in Johore, and the aim was to determine whether effective training could be carried out by having small groups of about twenty-five teachers assemble for week-end sessions. Five locations were selected, and lecturers from the teacher training college met with those teachers at one of those locations every weekend for five weeks. A second round of instruction was held, and lecturers again met with teachers in each of the five centres. The course content was directed at the immediate needs of the teachers; areas of need were identified, and such topics as lesson planning, teaching methods, budgeting and technical subject-matter were discussed. The project was productive, indigenous and sensitive to national needs. It was expected that 155 agricultural science teachers in the secondary schools from Johore state would be reached by these in-service courses twice each year. The project is highly feasible, since 'on the spot' training eliminates taking the teachers away from their job locations; the project is problem-oriented and adopts a systematic approach towards supplying trained teachers in agricultural science in secondary schools. The expansion of the project to other states in Malaysia is being envisaged, as well as the involvement of the Agricultural University in the training of lecturers and teacher educators. Many other examples of nationally stimulated action projects could be quoted.

In most countries the ultimate responsibility for the organization and financing of in-service education appears to rest with the Ministry of Education. In such countries as Bulgaria, Hungary, the Ukrainian S.S.R. and the U.S.S.R. full government responsibility has always been a feature of their education system in collaboration with teachers' organizations and the teachers themselves. In such countries there is a clear commitment to the establishment of comprehensive systems of in-service education.

Elsewhere acceptance of the need for further education as a government responsibility is increasing. This trend is evidenced among various countries, in particular, Australia, Egypt, Ethiopia, Finland, France, Kuwait, Nigeria, Norway, Sierra Leone, Sweden, Switzerland and the United Kingdom. Of particular importance and significance is the fact that in Finland the Teacher Education Act (1971) defines teacher education as consisting of both pre-service (initial) and in-service (further) education, both of which are considered to be of equal importance and may in future be nationally integrated to form an organic whole. However, although finance is normally centralized, implementation usually takes place at regional or even at local level, with central government exercising its influence mainly through the amount of financial support that is provided from central funds. An example of development through various states is given by Australia, where special assistance has been made available to the state education departments to expand in-service education and for the establishment and operation of teacher education centres to be governed by management committees formed mainly of practising teachers.

It is obvious, therefore, that national initiatives in in-service education require substantial co-operation between national and regional agencies and also among local administrators, training institutions, schools and teachers. Where particular national initiatives have been pursued, they have been related to specific developments, such as the action project referred to in Malaysia and the establishment of major institutes or services, such as the In-service Educational Training Institute in Khartoum, Sudan, the multimedia service in Iraq or the long-standing support for distinguished international centres, such as the Pedagogical Institute in Moscow, U.S.S.R., or the Ontario Institute for Studies in Education in Canada.

Regional

It is at the regional level that the main drive for in-service education and training is developed and sustained. A key factor in in-service training is the responsiveness to critical educational needs expressed in a local or institutional context. Each major region will have particular economic, cultural, linguistic and other features that come together in a unique pattern and in relation to a specific force of teachers with particular needs. While it is to be hoped that there will always be the opportunity for a proportion of teachers to have full-time and substantial release during their teaching lives, the majority of teachers at any one time will be experiencing short periods of release while still continuing with their major task as teachers.

Thus, in the U.S.S.R., as in other socialist countries, it is accepted that all teachers must have a residential period of in-service training for approximately five to six weeks every five years but, in addition, there are shorter courses (three to fifteen days), seminars and conferences in between. In Sweden five study days per year for in-service training are compulsory for all teachers, and the recent committee of the National Board of Education has proposed that during the first six years of service teachers should attend in-service training courses totalling six weeks, divided in normal instances into three training periods. Other countries—for example, Qatar and Kuwait—concentrate on evening courses. The nature of such training requires that centres should often be readily accessible to the teachers. This has led to a worldwide movement of establishing teachers' centres, some based on schools, others on colleges and a few 'custom-built'. One of the most comprehensive developments of teachers' centres can be seen in the United Kingdom.

Many regions also have teams of specialists who work with teachers' associations, schools and individual teachers.

Institutional

Although it is essential that in-service education should be expressed regionally, it is still the case that the purpose of much in-service education and training is to have a specific effect upon the education that children receive. If in-service education of teachers is to have a high priority, its influence has got to get beyond the personal cultivation of individual teachers, beyond the aspirations of teacher trainers and the curriculum innovations of would-be reformers. The effect of in-service education and training has, above all, to enter through the doors of the school and into the minds of children. It must enable individual children to realise their potential in a way that would otherwise have been denied them. It is there to enrich the learning environments provided by schools, to enable teachers to deal more effectively with the increasing range and complexity of the problems that they face, and to help society come a little nearer to achieving the goals that it sets for itself.

As was pointed out in Chapter 5, the crucial element in education must be seen as the encounter between someone who is teaching and someone who is learning. For genuine transfer to take place it is necessary for the teacher to be very keenly aware of the way in which the student is reading and reacting to the message that the teacher is conveying. It is also important for the teacher to be able to understand what the student is trying to communicate. We have argued for a shift of the school and the teacher from a too sharply judgemental role to a supportive one. The obstacles in the way to this are, as has been pointed out, very substantial. That is why a large part of in-service education and training should be aimed to change schools from within and should assist teachers to improve practice within specific situations. The implications of this for strategies of in-service education and training are profound: in particular, it requires a change of emphasis from provision of *courses* to the selective allocation of *resources* to schools which are attempting to solve particular problems.

Individual

Finally, in-service education and training has to meet the perceived needs of the individual teacher. Just as it would be ineffective in the schools if it failed to deal with important problems in a practical way, similarly it would remain a fringe activity if it was seen by teachers as merely a means of earning qualifications in order to take them out of the classroom or, at the other extreme, a series of simple skills required to operate a 'teacher-proof' package supplied by some 'higher' authority. A major safeguard is to enable the teachers to participate much more fully in helping to design various courses, to influence the allocation of resources and the teaching styles that are adopted.

Certainly, as a result of teacher participation, the emphases in different parts of the world will clearly vary. Where a system of in-service education exists some lay emphasis upon the continuing self-education of teachers, and the report from the Ukraine illustrates this clearly. In others, teacher participation, combined with the emphasis upon the school, is producing more school-based or school-centred in-service education, as reported by Australia, New Zealand, the United Kingdom and others. This shift arises from a view that the teacher himself should be an active partner in his own in-service education—not only the recipient of courses organized for him. The wide recognition of teachers' centres in the United Kingdom and the United States, and their more recent development in Australia and New Zealand, Trinidad and Tobago, as well as elsewhere, provide an opportunity for teachers to meet and work together on common problems and represent a significant measure in encouraging teachers' development by the profession itself. Such developments, as well as others like the teacher advisory centres in Kenya, should also enable regional authorities and schools to call more fully on the professional advice and help that teachers' organizations will be prepared to give.

The implications of a four-tier pattern of in-service education and training at national, regional, institutional and personal level argue a need for a structure which enables the various tiers to interact fruitfully with each other.

In-service education should be seen as providing *access* to resources for individual teachers and schools and to provide *programmes* to meet particular professional needs. Access to resources would include not only materials but also the services of consultants and specialists and the interchange of teachers to work in such areas as curriculum development, new learning methods and educational technology. Programmes should be established to widen the scope of professional experience of all teachers by enabling them to visit other schools, talk with other teachers, visit other regions and countries, and obtain a wider perspective on the activity of teaching.

Vital to all programmes of in-service education and training is a commitment to the provision of a minimum number of days in which in-service activities would take place. While accepting that such a commitment would be difficult to achieve in many countries, it is vital that the qualitative as well as the quantitative aspects of the teaching force are considered and held in balance by all countries who wish to see an over-all improvement in their education systems. In-service education must have the provision of time and resources. This point was made in a Unesco recommendation concerning the status of teachers in 1966 which urged that 'authorities in consultation with teachers' organizations should promote the establishment of a wide system of in-service education free to all teachers'. It is to be hoped that in the future teachers' contracts for service will require them to take advantage of the opportunities for in-service education and training offered to them. Such a requirement could never be more than a minimum. Some choice should be left to the teacher to decide which is the most appropriate and useful kind of in-service experience.

THE INSTITUTIONAL FRAMEWORK

National pedagogical centres

The institutional framework should generally reflect the different levels of in-service education and training referred to above. Thus there is an increasing tendency for countries to establish one or more 'national pedagogical centres' that will concentrate on research, initial and in-service training, resource development and support in the area of teacher education and allied professions. Examples of such a trend can be seen in the Democratic Republic of the Sudan, where the In-service Educational Training Institute has its main centre in Khartoum, long-established centres such as the Pedagogical Institute in Moscow, the Scientific Research Institute at Samodumov in the People's Republic of Bulgaria, and the intention of the Ministry of Education in Iraq to establish a national centre for educational innovation and reform. It is important that such centres should not be remote research establishments but, as argued in the report of the U.S.S.R. Ministry of Education, there should be 'closer links between pedagogical higher education institutions and schools ... directed towards giving concrete practical assistance to educational bodies and teaching staffs in improving the instructional and educational process in schools, organizing courses for teachers, studying and disseminating advanced experience in teaching, organizing optional studies and elaborating immediate problems'.

Thus the centre should be action-based and concerned with the day-to-day experience of teachers and children. It should have training responsibilities as well as a major function in research and consultancy. In a number of countries it is seen as responding to requests for information and service at all levels. Ministries should be able to test out policy and investigate the feasibility of various plans, as done, for example, at the Ministry of Education in Ontario Province through the Ontario Institute for Studies in Education, or the pioneering Institut de pédagogie appliquée à vocation rurale (Institute of Rurally Oriented Applied Education) in the United Republic of Cameroon. Trainers and administrators would look to the centres for courses and for guidance. On the other hand, individual schools and teachers should be able to call up resources and have problems considered.

The danger of recreating pedagogical centres as élite and separate establishments remote from contemporary issues is a real one. Two important safeguards might be the strong emphasis upon service to the education system as a whole and, secondly, the establishment of the centres with a small permanent staff and a large 'contract' staff. Most of the 'contract' staff could be provided by schools and colleges for limited periods, after which they would return to the field. The national centres could also serve as the country's main 'window on the world' and contact point with international organizations. They would also act as an important base of intercommunication between adjacent public services.

Operating at national level, they could help to interrelate the various functions of social policy, which are often arbitrarily divided on administrative grounds among various ministries. The tendency for governments to be organized in separate bureaucracies is often reflected down to the regional and institutional level, with administrators and workers carrying out apparently independent policies. In some areas this characteristic of modern administration is not particularly harmful. However, it is a truism that many educational problems also have social, economic and cultural dimensions. Solutions may only be possible through the fullest co-operation among different public services. Particularly important in this context are social and welfare services, agriculture, planning, employment, youth work and various agencies of social control. The essential interrelationship of such problems should certainly be apparent to national centres, and thus their research and inquiry should be relevant and problem-centred.

Research topics will naturally arise in a variety of ways, but some part of the institution's work should concentrate on issues of importance to society at a particular point in time: for example, in the German Democratic Republic the main object of educational research at present is qualitatively to improve the general polytechnical schools and also to deal with the scientific problems, whose solution would help to achieve an optimum personality development for all children according to educational goals. An interesting associated development in the G.D.R. has been the establishment of a number of experimental schools where it is possible to study and to test the results of scientific research. Reference will be made in the last chapter to the pioneering work of the IPAR in the United Republic of Cameroon.

In addition to research, the national centres should be innovating in approaches to teaching. In view of the breadth of their potential research task, many of them could give the lead in the development of interprofessional training between teaching and the areas of social work, including community work, case-work, medical and paramedical services, industrial training and management. Such training activity would enable researchers to maintain creative contact with workers concerned with making judgements and taking action in relation to the issues that should form the subjects of many of the research projects.

Regional provision

As well as institutions at national level, there will, of course, need to be institutional provision at the regional level. Ideally a combination of two institutions could meet major needs. First, at regional level, the college or university responsible for initial training should be required to take responsibility for in-service education and training. Thus a school or faculty should be given responsibility, and substantial staff and resources should be committed to the development of a regional in-service education and training strategy. It is at such a regional centre that the essential interaction between initial and in-service training will be seen most clearly. Links between the regional and national centres should be strong, so that research is readily assimilated into the teaching and the courses in the regional college.[1] Schools and teachers in a region should have access to the facilities and resources of all higher education establishments. If training along the lines of the second cycle has been established, colleges will already have a close contact with schools through the more school-based approach to initial training. They will thus be appropriate centres for teachers and other workers in the region to meet together informally and formally to discuss common problems and influence each other in the way in which their various roles are defined. A particular concern for major regional colleges will be to provide courses for credit leading to higher degrees and awards. A regional college will also be well placed to engage in evaluation and assessment of curriculum developments and teaching methods within schools. It should develop its own work and research evaluation and innovation, as well as supporting such developments in the teachers' centres and the schools.

Depending upon the size of the region, it may be possible to have a comprehensive coverage of in-service education and training with only one regional college. There will always, however, be a need for a number of teachers' centres serving much more limited areas or neighbourhoods. The teachers' centre is a social invention grounded on the assumption that improvement in education can occur if teachers' attitudes, skills and knowledge are improved. Courses for practising teachers staffed by their colleagues, tutors from the regional college and local advisers provide teachers with an opportunity to explore new techniques, improvise equipment for the classroom and exchange ideas in workshop situations. Subject groups are formed to enable teachers to meet and discuss such topics as recent educational developments and subject specialisms, important publications or television and radio series for school use. Opportunities are frequently provided for teachers to participate in national and local curriculum development projects.

It has been found important in these teachers' centres that the centre should have a social purpose which enables teachers to come together in an informal and unauthoritarian way, so that young teachers can talk frankly and freely to each other and also to more

1. The term 'regional college' is employed for any initial and in-service teacher training institution, whether it be a teacher training college, a diversified higher education institution, a special pedagogical institute or the appropriate faculty of a university.

experienced colleagues outside the more formal context of the school. Centres should be essentially operated in a democratic way by the teachers themselves, and this is also good ground on which to meet administrators and specialists whose purpose in a teachers' centre should be to help and support the teachers in their various activities. These may often call upon other personnel who lie outside the teaching profession and whose goodwill and assistance are vital to the solution of various problems, for example, the vocational relevance of aspects of the secondary curriculum, family support for innovations in the primary school, the problem of anti-social behaviour within the school and in the community, the development of a major literacy drive aimed not only at children but also at adults. Teachers' associations will often find teachers' centres useful places in which to meet and, certainly, the fullest co-operation between teachers' associations and the regional authorities will be necessary if such centres are to inform and develop the teacher's professionalism at times that will often lie outside the normal teaching day. Opportunities for part-time release to work at the teachers' centre or to attend meetings there will be another important ingredient in a successful teachers' centre policy.

The school

As indicated earlier, the ultimate success of a major drive towards the increase of provision of in-service education and training must relate to changes and development that take place within the schools. All strategies should see the school as having a major role itself within the in-service system. The school must be attuned to the situation in which teachers themselves accept a new emphasis upon their own learning, upon their own urgent need to be continuously trained in order to provide effective learning within the school. This becomes increasingly obvious as the gap between a teacher's initial training and his experience of teaching grows wider. Even in the earliest days of a teacher's career, however, he is likely to meet problems that were not confronted during his initial training. Some teacher trainers will have had limited or long-redundant experience of schools and, even with the introduction of induction into the initial training period, a particular school may fail to throw up the problems that a teacher meets in a new situation. Thus the school from the beginning must welcome the newcomer not only with friendliness and encouragement but also with specific and constructive professional support.

Such support can be formalized in the role of the teacher-tutor already discussed with reference to the second cycle. His job would be to support all forms of in-service training and staff development. He would be the link between the school, the teachers' centre and, in most cases, be in regular communication with the regional college. He will be up to date and well trained for his task; he will be influential in seeing that the school year and, indeed, the school day are organized in such a way that teachers are able to share problems and come together to achieve solutions; he will also be concerned to see that an individual teacher is not alone but is a member of a team of teachers, all of whom may be experiencing various kinds of difficulty but whose combined skills are likely to achieve greater success if they are pooled and made accessible to each other. He could also be the person who calls up more formal support and action from the teachers' centre, the regional college and the national pedagogical centre. Finally, he should have an organizing role with regard to the use of time which is made available for professional development, so that the school can carefully plan its use of the days in order to evaluate and improve the education that is offered to the children. Within this framework of provision of in-service education and training, the teacher as an individual should be better able to meet the demands made upon him by his employers and also achieve personal and professional objectives.

EXTENDED FUNCTIONS OF IN-SERVICE EDUCATION

The basic organization and function of in-service education have been described. However, in-service education will also have a number of specialized functions which become more important at a time of rapid change.

Taking a longer view of their personal and professional functions, teachers may begin to see themselves more clearly as change-agents working alongside other change-agents in public services concerned with the environment, with health and with the community. Among the more specialized functions of a developed system of in-service education and training will be that of preparing for and enabling teachers to change roles within the education service, to move into administrative positions, to retrain those entering teaching from other jobs, to develop inter-professional programmes and to deal with shared problems, and to sustain research and innovation. The role of the teacher is now extremely broad and complex. It would not be possible for any one individual to span the whole range of skill and expertise required either at any one time or through the whole of his professional life. During the phase of initial training it is essential to have a strong, well-defined, but limited concept of the role of the teacher to enable the beginner to work with security and with conviction in his initial role as a general teacher. Basic in-service education will enable him to develop his special strengths and to make good any limitations in his own professional education.

A specialist function of in-service education and training is to enable the teacher to go into one or more of the special roles that are required of teachers in the rapidly changing world of the school. Thus, training programmes for experienced teachers must be readily available for those who wish to educate special groups of children such as those whose educational development is limited because of physical or mental handicap, emotional maladjustment or limitations in the social and economic environment. In many large schools in certain developed societies the role of counsellor is becoming increasingly recognized, as is the teacher with special skills in guidance. As has already been indicated, the success of the second cycle of initial training and the basic activities of in-service education require teachers to take on specialist roles as teacher-tutors, and all such roles need to be built upon a base of sound experience within the mainstream of the profession. Ongoing programmes to enable such a role-change to take place will therefore be necessary.

It is also going to be important in the future for teachers to move in and out of the school environment, so they should move easily and effectively into such fields as community and youth work, recreational and vocational training, interprofessional centres as advisers and consultants, and into teacher education. Taking on such roles should be seen as still being essentially part of a single educational service. Salary levels and conditions of service should enable workers to move smoothly between such various roles. In-service education will be needed to provide the necessary training, introduction and refreshment.

A particularly important part of role-changing is the assumption of greater responsibility for the operation of the school as a whole through headships and deputy headships. Many assume such roles on the basis of successful service as teachers, although this is no guarantee of success when very different responsibilities are carried as the head of an institution. It should be regarded as essential for all heads and deputies to have received sound and up-to-date help with regard to their role within educational institutions, so that they are aware of the potential limitations of the head's role and get guidance as to the most effective way of functioning. Such programmes cannot provide teachers with a ready-made personality, but they can enable them to use personal qualities more effectively. All in-service programmes connected with role-change should, of course, use a range of techniques, such as micro-teaching and simulation. These may often be introduced to the teacher at the initial stage, but they can be much more profitably developed in the specific field of role-change with more experienced professionals.

INTERPROFESSIONAL TRAINING

A number of countries have attempted to develop common courses of initial training for those working in teaching, community and social work, health and allied fields. Even more countries now expect the teacher to take on a wider role which moves into areas which were previously the concern of others. Schemes of interprofessional training have had limited success, partly because the different functions performed by professional groups relate to the identification of roles which lead to the establishment of very differently balanced skills. Overlap tends to occur mainly at the stage of some commonality of personal education. It is possible that the most fruitful stage for genuine interprofessional training is at the time when all the various professionals are aware of the interconnection between their different activities. Thus, a child with learning difficulties in a primary school may be receiving medical care and his family may be supported by a welfare worker. There may be high absenteeism from a rural school because of difficulty of access for children in ill health caused through inadequate hygiene. The need in such cases to come together in the best interests of the child is an obvious one.

Opportunities for case conferences, for the exploration of joint activities and a sensitizing of one professional group to another would be part of the specialist functions of institutions offering in-service facilities. In this sphere, emphasis should be on the maximum opportunity for informal contact and consultancies bringing the administrators and workers together in productive and anxiety-free settings to explore common aims. Indeed, much of the work of interprofessional in-service education should be seen as providing opportunities for flexibly structured, but purposeful, co-operative activity. A regional college or a teachers' centre would be a very appropriate base for the various workers to come together.

RESEARCH AND INNOVATION

Interesting and unusual programmes of innovation which are manu-factured outside tend to become unrecognizable when they have been reshaped to get through the doors of the school. The message is clear: although much basic research must be done by those who are full-time workers in the disciplines applied to educational ques-tions, innovations in curriculum, teaching methods and in ap-proaches to learning must be developed in the closest contact with the schools. The pressure for research is there because basically so little is still known about the teaching and learning situation, and what is known is difficult to apply. Thus, every region should have strong teams of researchers and teachers working together on pro-grammes of research which should often be regional versions of national or international efforts. Such research should feed the courses of in-service training, so that the latest knowledge of ways in which children learn, of the effectiveness of different methods of teaching, of the acquirement of language skills, mathematical concepts and many other matters can be quickly absorbed into the work of the school.

Innovation, however, often flies on in advance of research or may appear to contradict that which has been done because a par-ticular set of circumstances suddenly co-exist at a particular time in a school. One of the most creative activities of in-service education is to bring research and innovation into a fruitful relationship which enables both to be more effective without inhibiting either. Some innovations require a sustained period of growth and development. Too close an examination at too early a stage may ask the right questions but at the wrong time and use inappropriate measures of success. Indeed, one of the problems of innovatory activity in education is that research at an early stage will tend to exaggerate the success of innovations because, at the beginning of any new development, there is powerful energy leading to success and a high level of commitment from the innovators. This ceases to be so apparent as the innovation becomes absorbed into the 'normal' practices of the school. Research should not only be concerned with innovation but also with the effectiveness of current practices and ways in which they can be improved and sustained.

Work in the field of research and innovation may be seen as part of in-service education, as it stresses the role of the teacher as a researcher and underlines his activity as a learner while he is involved in the teaching situation. It should give him the time and the skills to evaluate his own work, that of his colleagues and of the children with whom he is engaged. It also enlarges the meaning of the term 'educator' and adds to the bank of ideas and information that is available to those teachers who will follow him or who have access to the institutions in which he is operating. While much of the innovation will be carried on at school and professional centre level, it must be moderated and supported by colleges and by national centres which will store and communicate findings to the profession, both through courses and through the development of materials and information.

A number of other areas of specialist development in in-service training will be seen as more important by Member States. The critical exercise is to decide on the priorities, and to see the whole of the in-service function as providing both the base and the developing front of the education service. Many of the resources needed for in-service education and training are already available within the education service itself, either at school level or within higher education. What is needed is a clear sense of priorities and a set of objectives to tap the resources and to redistribute them where necessary. The teacher occupies a unique position within the process of education and socialization. The implications of this position will be considered in the final chapter.

CHAPTER NINE

Teacher education: the essential interface

It has been demonstrated that no consideration of the education and training of teachers can be complete unless it takes note of the personal preparation which an individual receives in his home and his community, in his schooling, his post-school education and in the cycles of his initial and, hopefully, in-service training. In this process many aspects of a society contribute to the training of teachers. Those with a formal concern for the education and training of teachers represent an essential interface between the dominant trends of their national systems of education—in particular, the trend, on the one hand, for quantitative growth in response to the cry for universal education and, on the other, the urgent national need for high quality education in order to achieve success in the modern world.

In most developed countries universal education of an acceptable quality can at present be provided. In developing countries high quality must be at the expense of the rate of expansion of education for all: thus a developing country has a hard decision to make. It is the kind of decision that cannot be left only to the educators. It is a political and economic decision of great significance.

Similarly, education is poised between the forces of continuity and of change. It is preparing young adults to work as change-agents in institutions that are often conservative and value continuity and tradition. Many countries know what it is now necessary to do to achieve a more equable, secure and prosperous society. The objectives are often clear, but the means of achieving the desirable changes are far less apparent. Teacher education is a field in which this dilemma is often experienced most sharply.

As the role of the teacher is seen to be increasingly wide-ranging and complex, the business of the education and training of teachers must spread into allied fields and be concerned with interprofessional training covering a much broader range of those people who are instrumental in changing others' lives and in carrying out national policies. This recognizes the interaction of roles within any given community of which a child is a member. The interaction can be co-operative and mutually supportive, or it can be conflicting and destructive. As in most human affairs, research and inquiry are of limited value in enabling practitioners to arrive at effective decisions. Thus, an emphasis upon interprofessional training enabling the various workers in the 'helping professions' to study and share experiences together is likely to provide a better base for the vital co-operation they will need when they are carrying out their different functions in the education and social services. Teacher education could well take the lead in recognizing that the abandonment of the narrow concept of the role of the teacher inevitably requires a new definition of the role of education and its interaction with the social and economic development of the country concerned. It is important, however, that readers of this book should be able to see the opportunities of moving forward in the context of existing educational provision. Thus, there is an emphasis in this chapter upon two detailed examples of actual practice.

The essential interface which is represented in all systems of teacher education is that between theory and practice, between the ideal and the actual, between the myth and the reality. The constant criticism of teacher education carried out within colleges is that it emphasizes an ideal condition and myths about learning which are difficult to realize in the hard world of the school and in the often even more difficult social context within which the school exists. We see that the major emphasis of progressive teacher education policies around the world is to bring theory and practice into much closer interaction, to give realism to ideals and to focus increasingly upon the actual world of the school and the community. This has often caused the second and third cycles of teacher education and training to be merged together: thus 'initial' training takes place *after* the student takes on the role and status of a teacher in school. It is the arrangement for support and development that exists in that situation which is then identified as 'training'. The dangers of the abandonment of the cyclical approach have been discussed. In developed countries each stage of the cycle can be substantial and formative; in developing countries the tendency will inevitably be for them to reduce the length of the cycles or omit one or even two of them.

Faced with a developing world crisis in education of unparalleled proportions, it is timely to attempt to affirm the priority that would seem to be most important at a time of crushing demand and limited resources. Two examples will now be given in some detail from developing countries. The first is a modest institutional initiative within the well-known context of post-graduate training. The second is a comprehensive and far-reaching attempt at an educational innovation, illustrating the interaction of teacher education, national policy and processes of change within the school and the community.

INITIAL TRAINING: INTERFACE BETWEEN THEORY
AND PRACTICE—NIGERIA

Nigeria has a larger population than any other country in Africa: about 80 million people of different origins, cultures and religions live in its 357,000 square miles (924,000 square kilometres). There has been an extremely rapid growth of primary and secondary education in the last twenty years, with primary enrolment almost doubling and secondary enrolment increased by more than ten times. Thus the problem faced in Nigeria is one which is common in many developing countries: increased demand for teachers places a strain on teacher training resources, so that education authorities are presented with the dilemma of choosing between quantity and quality. Faced with this problem at the initial training level, they become reluctant to invest in in-service training. The approach to the problem developed at Ahmadu Bello University in Nigeria goes a long way to meet this dilemma. In-service training is combined with teaching in such a way that the teachers' services are not lost while they are following the course. Thus, in 1972 a three-part course was introduced: phase one, an initial ten weeks of professional preparation in the university; phase two, a year's full-time

teaching in schools during which students are supervised but retain
the status and conditions of service of regular teachers; phase three,
a second ten-week course at the university leading to certification
fifteen months after first enrolment. Candidates are required to pass
in three separate components: theory, practical teaching, and a
research study based on an investigation carried out during the year
in schools and presented during the residential course in phase
three.

The first semester, therefore, gives students a basic grounding in
methods of teaching, foundations of education and research methodology with an emphasis upon preparing them for the year's work
to follow. The semester during phase three reviews the experience
of the year with a view to helping the student to apply lessons he
has learned in his next phase of teaching. The residential courses
have experimented with various methodologies but with an emphasis upon seminars, workshops, including a self-instructional one on
audio-visual aids. Some of the vacation courses are combined with
those being offered to serving teachers.

The research project carried out during the year in school has to
be manageable, challenging and useful to the student and to the
area in which he works. After experience the institute has compiled
a list of topics which seem to satisfy all three criteria. The student is
encouraged to have a local supervisor as well as one from the
university. During the professional year students give a full record
of their preparations and of work done. These and the teaching
itself are monitored from three sources: through the school head,
through a local tutor identified by the institute, and at relatively
infrequent intervals by an institute tutor. The advantages of the
new pattern are that it maximizes the use of resources, including
university facilities during vacation time; it provides opportunities
for improvement of qualifications without interruption of earnings;
it provides enriched opportunities for linking theoretical and practical aspects of training; it provides a more professional atmosphere
and context for training.

The sandwich course at Ahmadu Bello presents a strong case for
reconsidering whether the one-year post-graduate teacher training is
a justified investment in developing countries. There is an obvious
danger that such programmes may be mounted because they are
expedient and relatively cheap. At Ahmadu Bello, although the

programme is obviously expedient, it is clear that it has marked professional advantages, and it has emphasized how a basis of on-the-job experience backed by sound theory, which constitutes the core of so much effective professional training for other careers, is equally appropriate for the career of teaching.

The example from Ahmadu Bello University is inevitably limited and strongly influenced by its context in Nigeria. However, it illustrates an approach which maintains the concepts of cycles of teacher education and training, while responding also to the urgent need for the school to have teachers teaching as well as training. In ideal situations it may be better for the student to have a slower entry into full responsibility for teaching and more regular opportunity to relate theory and practice, and to see examples of work done in other schools and with other methods. However, we do not live in an ideal world and, if the young teachers who have been through the new course initiated at the Ahmadu Bello University retain the view that to teach is to learn, then they will soon want to see a third cycle fully established.

TEACHER TRAINING AND EDUCATIONAL INNOVATION —THE UNITED REPUBLIC OF CAMEROON

The case-study which follows concerns one African country—the United Republic of Cameroon. Although concerning one African country, many of the features must be regarded as typical of a large number of developing countries in the world. Any form of managed change must be preceded by consciousness of a particular set of problems and a sense of urgency concerning their solution.

In the Cameroons in the middle 1960s there was a widespread feeling that education was passing through a crisis. Political leaders were first to be conscious of it as far back as 1962. The Congress of the U.N.C. (Union Nationale Camerounaise) raised the problem in public and discussed it at length. The first criticism was that elementary and also secondary education were extremely expensive. The small number of children completing their primary education, and the even smaller proportion obtaining the primary school certificate (*Certificat d'études primaires*—C.E.P.), was deplored by all. The small number of school-leavers who were able to integrate themselves without difficulty and to take an effective part in society was another symptom of the low cost-benefit ratio of education. The intolerable paradox of the education system was, therefore, that, while being very costly and training only an élite, it had not trained that élite properly either to achieve personal fulfilment or to play their due role in national development. Quantitative studies and statistical surveys only confirmed what many already suspected.

By 1967 there was a general feeling in Cameroon that education was suffering from serious deficiencies both in its conception and in the methods used. All this was in spite of the fact that there had been a considerable increase in school enrolments during the 1960s and that expenditure on education had already reached 20 per cent of the national budget. The average rate of primary school enrolment was 60 per cent, but nearly 50 per cent of the pupils enrolled initially would have dropped out after three years. Of those who remained to the end, only a third obtained their primary certificate. Out of every thousand pupils enrolled in primary school, only five would pass their *baccalaureate*.

Agreement on the causes of the poor cost-benefit ratio appeared to be as general as the feeling of dissatisfaction. No one ever disputed the importance of factors external to the school system— social and health factors, in particular. The pupil's family could not help him to retain and consolidate what he learned at school; he was often weakened by malnutrition, the fatigue caused by travelling long distances, by parasites and malaria. The government was aware of the problems, which it was trying to solve insofar as economic growth permitted it to develop its social policy.

The factors specifically connected with the school were just as numerous and important, and just as indisputable. The large number of pupils per class was and still is an obstacle to effective teaching: over half have more than fifty pupils, and numbers are highest in the first grades, which often have over a hundred pupils. Problems of overcrowding are aggravated by the inadequacies of the premises and the primitive nature or absence of furniture. Age disparities also impede efficiency: primary schools accept too many children who do not belong to the age-group for which the course was designed. A substantial minority are over 14 years old. The situation worsens steadily from the beginners' class to the final class, when many pupils are as much as three years behind the official age.

Most importantly, however, from the point of view of this book, it was generally accepted long before 1967 that the main reason for the poor performance of the education system was the insufficient training of the vast majority of primary school-teachers. It was therefore natural that an analysis of the nature and consequences of this conviction, as firmly held as it was widespread, should make it possible to identify the start of the process of innovation and begin to analyse that process.

Therefore, the prelude to the innovation was the acceptance of the first reason that 'if children are being poorly educated, the cause must first of all be sought in the educators themselves and their training improved or reformed'. This, as is argued by Raymond Lallez, means that, whenever a need for change begins to be felt, it leads to a call for the reform of teacher training. The same reasoning leads to the conclusion that the better the primary education the easier it will be to improve secondary education. Thus, to be effective, the improvement of education must begin with the teachers or trainee teachers working in primary schools.

There were, however, two interpretations of the inadequacy of teacher training: the first saw teachers as being underqualified with a low level of general knowledge and culture, and also suggested that they had insufficient skill in communicating knowledge or culture to pupils. This kind of deficiency obviously existed in the United Republic of Cameroon, and there was no difficulty in reaching agreement on this point. Table 4 shows that 72 per cent of the

TABLE 4. Composition of primary teaching staff in East Cameroon, 1970

Categories	Qualifications	No. of teachers	Percentage
Primary teachers	Baccalaureate	247	1.8
Assistant primary teachers	BE or BEPC[1]	1 926	14.4
General teachers	CAFMEG[2]	1 560	11.6
Instructors	Certificate of Primary Studies	9 674	72.2

[1] BEPC: *Brevet d'études du premier cycle* (Certificate of lower secondary studies).

[2] CAFMEG: *Certificat d'aptitude aux fonctions de maître d'enseignement général* (Certificate of proficiency as teacher of general subjects).

teachers responsible for preparing pupils for the C.E.P. had got no further than this level themselves, and only 16 per cent of practising teachers could be considered as properly qualified. The situation in West Cameroon was similar.

Without rejecting this first interpretation—the inadequacy of teacher training—one might also advance other reasons for the poor results of education and, hence, suggest other remedies. Thus, the second interpretation considered that the poor standard of primary education was due to the unsuitability or incorrect orientation of the education given—unsuited not only to the pupils receiving it, to their circumstances, their way of life and their outlook, but also to the social and economic needs of their country which was supporting them and to whose life and development they must in turn make a contribution. This hypothesis does not affect the general conclusion that teachers were not properly qualified to give the kind of education they had to give, and that their own training should therefore be reconsidered and sanctioned, but the same words now have a different meaning: 'inadequate qualifications' no longer means inadequate knowledge and insufficient ability to transmit knowledge, but the training itself—its methods, content and, above all, its objectives—is now being called into question. This questioning of objectives, in fact, calls for radical changes in methods, attitudes and curricula.

As has been noted in other places, genuine innovation is only possible if new objectives are defined. Adopting the hypothesis of merely improving the level of qualifications of teachers would not have led to a genuinely new approach. Adopting the second assumption, however, meant that the improvement of teachers' training and of their qualification is directly and fundamentally linked with basic changes which go beyond the framework of training. This calls for a wider context of reform which enlarges the established framework of existing curricula and institutions. The essential point is that an improvement in established qualifications only consolidates existing systems. What is needed, however, is an improvement in which education and development are more closely linked, and a reform which emphasizes the adjustment of education to economic and social conditions within the country.

The more specific tasks for primary education were seen as,

firstly, to give those who were to continue their studies a proper preparation for secondary education, and to prepare the rest—the overwhelming majority—to integrate with their environment and to promote development therein. As both the society and economy in the United Republic of Cameroon are basically rural, the idea emerged of a new type of training college which would train teachers to play a key part within a specifically rural context. Thus, the idea of the ENIR (Ecole normale d'instituteurs de plein exercise à vocation rurale—Rurally Oriented Primary Teacher Training Institute) was born. ENIR was to train a new type of primary school-teacher and would also help to promote economic and social development. The course would consist of three years study and would lead up to an examination and a diploma—*Brevet supérieur de capacité* (Higher Certificate of Proficiency).

Those who requested aid from the United Nations Development Programme (UNDP) suggested that the education system, particularly primary education, was ill adapted to the reality of life in the country. First of all, it cut the school off from the natural and human environment, which was usually rural, thus making school work abstract, difficult, boring and lifeless, teaching subjects which could only be absorbed by dint of mindless repetition and inevitably laying tremendous stress on memorization. This situation also reduced contact between the school world and that of adults. Education was only valued to the extent that it was increasingly regarded—though quite wrongly—as a means of social advancement, but one which took the pupil outside his own environment. In this way it was indeed the second form of maladjustment: primary education was a very inadequate preparation either for secondary education or for children who were not continuing their studies and would need to fit into an essentially rural environment, work on it, master it, transform and develop it.

In order to eliminate both forms of maladjustment, the old type of school and the traditional teacher had to be replaced by a rural school and a rural teacher. 'Ruralization' thus defined became the key concept in the desired form of innovation. 'The role of the new school and the rural teacher to be trained at the new training institute will be a vital one in the dissemination of the practical information and the simple techniques necessary for all those concerned to take an active part in economic development at the level which will affect them most directly, that of the village.'[1]   The request to UNDP goes on to argue that the rural primary school must be 'a centre of influence in the community'.   Education must give children the basic skills which will enable them to understand the world in which they live; they must put basic skills of reading, writing and counting to good use; children must be encouraged to apply their skills and faculties to the surroundings in which they live and move.

However, if the natural resources of the country were to be fully exploited, the whole population, not only the children, should possess the basic skills of reading, writing and arithmetic.   The teacher will have to use methods suitable for the education of adults, and be able to place his education within the context of daily life and work. As the text of the request goes on: 'This dual responsibility will involve diversified and integrated but not unconnected or parallel activities: integration will be achieved as the inhabitants of the village, children and adults, pass through the same process'.

On the basis of a document prepared by Unesco, a national commission on curricula was set up in the United Republic of Cameroon to determine objectives for the preparation of rural primary school-teachers in order to carry out the tasks for the new primary education.   Above the teaching of the basic subjects and an intensive course on theoretical and practical educational psychology, there was a higher level of training considered from the angle of the teacher/pupil relationship and determined by the need to relate to African and Cameroonian realities, and at the same time to prepare people to take an effective part in the transformation of their environment and in national development.   Hence the emphasis on the study of works of Black African literature, particularly those which have a rural setting, and on the study of social phenomena, particularly those which illustrate the complementary nature of the relationship between town and country, and hence the even greater stress laid on the psychology of the African child.   Hence also the special importance of the study of the teaching language and particularly the relationship between the spoken and written word, the use of new methods of teaching mathematics, the practical applications for science in the spheres of agriculture and health, information on

1. Request to the United Nations Development Programme (Special Fund)— Project for the establishment of a rurally oriented primary teacher training institute, 1967.   43 p.

the uses of technology in a rural environment, and practical work connected with agriculture, hygiene and health.

These principles and general guidelines were just as applicable to in-service training courses for teachers as to the pre-service training courses. No one doubted the need for in-service training and it seemed natural that ENIR should be made responsible for this. Thus, the request to UNDP included in-service courses for primary inspectors and educational advisers lasting for three months. The teaching staff at teacher training institutes was also to undergo two sessions of in-service training, one year to be spent abroad and one year at the pilot institute where they would work as additional staff.

In fact, the life of ENIR was to be very short, and the transformation to the IPAR (Institut de pédagogie appliquée à vocation rurale—Institute of Rurally Oriented Applied Education) was inevitable and rapid. With seventy teachers being trained each year, the goals could not be attained by means of pre-service training alone. The need for in-service training was recognized as being central. However, it was also necessary to know beforehand by means of what methods, curricula and perhaps even what new institutions, primary education was going to be able to achieve its new purposes. It quickly became evident, therefore, that research was required with a view to working out what soon proved to be a veritable reform of elementary education. Finally, it was obvious that new training would not be possible without the production of new teaching materials. Production facilities for these materials were considered so important and of such a specific nature that they justified a separate establishment.

The argument that pre-service training should be combined with in-service training, research and production was essentially contained in the original request. For example, the recommendation that: 'In-service training courses for teachers are imperative as the government obviously wishes all primary school-teachers to possess the same qualifications as the young teachers who graduate from the pilot institute. Therefore the training institution will organize seminars and a system of correspondence courses for the in-service training of teachers.' Further on it is stated that: 'The ruralization of primary education as it has been defined calls for a radical change in the content of education and, first of all, in curricula. Thus the participation of the teacher training institute in curriculum reform cannot under any circumstances be minimized.' Finally the text adds: 'The production of prototypes, textbooks and teaching materials is imperative in view of the adoption of new curricula differing radically from the old ones in their content and of the use of new teaching methods.'

Because of the radical novelty for the teacher implicit in the reform and the low qualifications of almost 13,000 out of the 15,000 teachers in the country, IPAR had to prepare a great deal of lesson material in the various subjects and all the documents required by the teachers. It was also necessary for new recruits or serving teachers to understand the goals of the reformed education and learn to use new methods. Therefore, the reform of teacher training and all teacher training schools and the elaboration of a ten-year in-service training plan was announced in the half-yearly report in the middle of 1972.

One particularly novel feature was the fact that, in the period 1967-72, there was a decisive reform which changed the aims and purposes of the whole of basic education and, through it, of education as a whole in the United Republic of Cameroon. This responsibility was placed in the hands of a single institution, and thus the means employed to achieve the aims were just as much an innovation as the aims themselves. It was possible within the one institution to interrelate pre-service and in-service training, research and development. IPAR planned and acted, but between the planning and the action came the decision, and this was made directly at the highest political level. The decision itself was an expression of will. As in other countries, the supreme political will was to be the main driving force for innovation in the United Republic of Cameroon, and it was owing to the constancy with which the policy was followed that innovation was able to make genuine headway and penetration. The President of the Republic gave it his personal prestige and authority and, in a speech which he made at the first graduation ceremony, he defended the ruralization of education. He clarified this by saying, 'When I refer to the ruralization of education I do not mean a cut-price education of peasants' children. Ruralization means the adaptation of education to the actual conditions of this country, which is essentially agricultural.' In view of the scope and importance of the operation, the government opted for simplicity and effectiveness in order to be certain of rapid progress.

In order to appreciate the essential interface between the primary education reforms and teacher training, it is important to describe briefly the new type of primary school-teacher. He is now called a 'teacher-community leader' *(instituteur-animateur)*, a concept which embraces a new way of teaching, new attitudes and a new style of training. The teacher will no longer be the schoolmaster from whom the pupils receive orders and knowledge. His mission is to stimulate their minds and provide them with the instruments which they will put to use in order to think, learn, act and create. Thus, the teacher has a vocation to educate, through community leadership, sectors of the population other than schoolchildren—for example, adolescents who have already left school but who have not yet begun an active working life, or working adults with families. His role does not stop at the school gate. Outside school and after school, he is still a teacher; within school, during school hours he is already a community leader. The school has a double function: an in-school function, which is to educate pupils according to the new perspective, and an out-of-school function, which is to organize adult community activities. The trainee teacher must be prepared for a three-fold task: (a) a specialist in ruralized education; (b) a certified teacher who will be a permanent adviser to less-qualified colleagues; (c) a permanent intermediary in the organization of local community activities.

By making the village or the neighbourhood a real structure into which the young people can fit, the ruralized primary school becomes the starting point for community promotion, which is essential to the country's development. However well trained the pupil may be, his desire to work for progress may well be sapped if it encounters the inertia of an adult community which is hostile to change, and which does not allow the child to apply his knowledge and skills. If the teacher's activity is exercised only within the school, the pupil leaving school may be paralysed by tradition. The teachers will therefore be taught how to arouse interest among the adult section of the community in economic development and socio-cultural advancement, so that they welcome and encourage the activities of the pupils leaving school. The desire for adults to work towards transformation will be greatly facilitated if the village has a model provided by the school (poultry-house, garden, plantation, canteen, latrines, clean water source). The adults will gradually imitate the school if it provides them with examples of action to transform the environment and which satisfy their desire for profit, health and amusement. The school will become a centre of influence, and the teacher will be asked to guide and organize the adults' efforts to achieve a better life. However, as the government says, the teacher is not required to be a hero: he is asked to be the schoolmaster. A good educator is a leader. It is much easier for the teacher to be a leader in his *school* by encouraging a spirit of co-operation, initiative and creativity, and by encouraging practical work in the environment. He is not expected to become a *community* leader in a village where many habits are long-established. His leadership arises through his teaching activity, in leading the community to desire and achieve a change. Thus a teacher should obtain real participation from his students in all work undertaken at school, so as to transform the school gradually into a co-operative for thought and action. To give leadership in the community, the teacher must exercise the functions first of all in his school. He will only be able to do this if he is trained in a teacher training institute which is itself a living model of this concept. Thus we have the training institute as a 'living model' for the organization of activities in the rural school, and the rural school as a model for the organization of village activities.

It will be noted that, unlike some views of the concept of the role of the teacher, the second function—that of community leadership—is designed less to extend his field of action than to prevent the first field of action from proving sterile and vain. Leadership in the adult community is not an end in itself but a means to ensure that the training provided for the children will be easily and effectively employed in action by the environment. The attempt is to put adults in a frame of mind which inclines them to authorize the application of the adolescents' knowledge and skill. Motivation for community activity will be provided by the conventional community leaders. Leadership through organization and work will arise from the example shown by the school. This example will be provided by the teacher acting within the school environment. The innovation, therefore, contains elements of continuity and change. Thus the rural school puts foremost among its objectives the acquisition of three principal abilities: (a) the ability to think and to express oneself; (b) the ability to act; and (c) the ability to learn. 'Preparation for life is nowadays assessed in terms of ability rather than of knowledge. The adult in our modern societies must be capable of thinking logically and of expressing himself, of taking initiatives and of acting, of continuing to learn in order to adapt himself to change and to retrain for another occupation if necessary' [1].

The rural school is concerned with the acquisition of knowledge of two different types. The first may be called instrumental knowledge, where the school will, of course, continue to teach the standard subjects—language, arithmetic, non-verbal means of expression. But these, rooted in the setting of Cameroonian life and culture, will serve as instruments to study situations arising in the environment and to find an answer or a solution to them [2]. Acquisition of this type of knowledge is of decisive importance and is indeed the key to any ruralized primary education. The second type of knowledge will endeavour to get the pupil to know his environment well with a view to transforming it. Thus, a traditional compartmentalization of subjects will be replaced by interdisciplinarity. This is desirable because the greater the compartmentalization of subjects, the harder it is to prevent a similar compartmentalization occurring between pupils, between teacher and taught, between school and community. The best cornerstone for interdisciplinarity is the study of the environment. Knowledge will also be directed towards practical applications. Henceforth, there are two sides to each lesson: the pupil acquires a certain knowledge; and the practical work sessions add to this a certain know-how. The school thereby naturally finds its place again within the village. However, as pointed out most perceptively by Raymond Lallez, for the innovation to become established and to achieve its objectives, centres of innovation need to seek out and identify in the environment such elements as may be incorporated in their constructive work: for example, people who can exert in and on the environment a certain influence which will be all the stronger because they have never left that environment. The existence of such people, who could be the real intermediaries for community leadership, both for the adult community and for teams of children, can help to establish an educational network in the environment which it is the aim to transform, firmly based on that environment and anchored to its strong points. The integration into the education system of resource persons living and working in the community would help to build up around the ruralized school a consensus without which it has little chance of exerting influence and thriving.

The radical change in post-graduate training at Ahmadu Bello University in Nigeria illustrates one way in which the interface between 'conventional' teacher training and the schools can be made productive. In many developing countries the dominant theme of their current approach to education is to make it relevant and meaningful in terms of the urgent demands for change and development apparent to their own particular societies.

The extension of the teacher's role into the community, which is fully described in the United Republic of Cameroon, has also been a feature of rurally and community-oriented teacher training programmes in the Kakata Institute of Liberia, the Namatomba project in Uganda, the Burumbu Teachers' College in Sierra Leone, and others.

This role extension can be seen in the important but limited initiative in Nigeria and, much more comprehensively, in the wide-ranging innovation and reform in Cameroon. If has been the argument of this book that the three cycles of education and training to which teachers should be exposed provide a valid and helpful structure within which to rethink approaches to education and training. However, when giving a full description of the nature and implications of the second and third cycles in Cameroon, it was essential to describe the new role which the teacher was being expected to play. It is hoped that such an example, as well as those in the appendixes, will be of interest to those countries seeking to develop a more effective and relevant system of teacher education.

REFERENCES

1. Becquelin, J. *Interim report, 1967-1972.* Yaoundé, 1972. 37 p. (CMR. 11-IPAR.)
2. *La réforme de l'enseignement au Cameroun.* Yaoundé, IPAR, 1972.

Concluding note

As indicated in the introduction to this book, the authors consider that the more intimate contact and closer interdependence of the countries of the world make it more and more necessary to share ideas about the development of basic social institutions. The threads of common experience are more important than the distances they span. Many of the examples given in this book are of developing countries. It is not only that the problems are often more acute in such countries but also that they are more apparent and are being tackled with a directness and vigour that seem hard to emulate in more developed countries. However, all countries need to take similar steps in that an understanding of the complexity of the role of the teacher is essential before specific reforms in teacher education are put in hand. However carefully the various stages of education and training may be defined and refined in any country, it is essential to begin as we have begun in this particular text with a realistic definition of the role that a teacher is expected to play. The necessity for this initial step is as important in developed as in developing countries. It is vital, however, that it should not stop there: mere description is not enough.

The questions that must follow concern not only what is, but what ought to be; not only what teachers do, but what society needs; not only how the school is organized, but how its organization should relate to the community with which it should be demonstrably involved. Moving on from an analysis of the role of the teacher in the first part of the book, we have sought to demonstrate the way in which the teacher's personal education, initial professional training and his continuing training throughout his working life provide for an essential sequence which we believe should be adopted universally as a basis for teacher education and training.

We have seen that the cycle of education and training is only part of a much larger cycle. In the well-known Unesco publication education was seen as 'Learning to be'. Like life or the seasons, education is itself cyclical. The institutionalization of teaching and learning represents one of the few genuinely universal characteristics of modern society. The concerns of teacher education, however, are only a variation on a more universal theme seen in a particularly acute form in many developing countries. These are, for example, how to maintain continuity and at the same time respond to change, how to enable one generation to speak to another, and how to cultivate variety and uniqueness while ensuring that all men share the basic concepts that are essential for world co-operation and peace.

The educational world represented at the thirty-fifth session of the International Conference on Education showed little patience with the extreme views of the de-schoolers and those who wished to overturn totally the established system. On the other hand, there was even less support for continuation of what for many was the traditional isolation of the school from the urgent needs of contemporary society. This places a double burden on teacher education: it needs to prepare students to cope effectively with the school as it is but, even more significantly, to possess the skills, the understanding and the insight to be leaders for change in what, in many societies, are increasingly irrelevant educational institutions.

Thus, the first cycle—that of personal education—must give the teacher a sense of his own personal value and his capacity to help him with the resolution of many of the problems with which his own society is faced. The initial training stage should sharpen his perspectives and focus his training and experience upon achieving real competence and a desire to go on learning. The final stage may be seen by many people as the most critical of all: that is the continuing education and support of the teacher throughout his working life.

One of the most important tests which can be applied to any society is that presented by an examination of its schools and other educational establishments. It is most revealing to know whether society expects its teachers and schools to be authoritarian or democratic, student-centred or teacher-dominated, selective or comprehensive, open or closed, flexible or rigid. There is ample evidence that many people in all countries have an urgent desire to re-school their society, and there is an emerging consensus about what is now required of education. While some of the concerns are obviously connected with economic and vocational development, others are more reflective of an anxiety about the growing alienation of the young, and the need for the schools to enable children to achieve a better social and emotional balance and sense of personal value. More than any other activity, educational practices will ultimately have most effect upon the human condition. It is to be hoped that all concerned with the educational enterprise will find material of value in this book. None of the reforms, however, will be achieved unless political will and professional commitment join together to demonstrate that one of the priorities of the last quarter of this century should be the reform of the education and training of those who must bear the main responsibility for the education of children.

Some characteristics
of less-developed regions

Central to the understanding of what can be achieved in teacher education is an awareness of the problems of the developing countries. Some of the main difficulties facing the least-developed countries were recently discussed by their representatives. Below is an account of their main concerns. The least-developed countries are, in *Africa*: Botswana, Burundi, Benin, Chad, Ethiopia, Guinea, Lesotho, Mali, Malawi, Niger, Rwanda, Somalia, Sudan, Uganda, United Republic of Tanzania, Upper Volta; in *Asia and Oceania*: Afghanistan, Bhutan, Laos, Maldives, Nepal, Sikkim, Western Samoa, Yemen; and in *Latin America*: Haiti.

At the meeting in Paris[1] following the thirty-fifth International Conference on Education, senior officials of the Ministries of Education of the countries agreed that education could play an important role in fighting poverty and promoting development, but that the 'inherited' systems of education were not suitable to perform this role. There was, therefore, a need to introduce profound educational reforms in order that they may respond adequately to new national development needs and objectives. It was also necessary to reallocate the necessary resources to support decisions. It was pointed out that educational strategies in the past promoting quantitative development, emphasizing the requirement of the modern sector and often neglecting the needs of the rural sector, had in many cases hampered development and created problems. It resulted, on the one hand, in an increase in the number of educated unemployed, in a nation of rural youths migrating to urban centres and overseas in search of jobs and, on the other hand, in a lack of properly qualified people to fill jobs in some critical areas of development, all of which created a general sense of disappointment and frustration.

It was agreed that education should be geared, on the one hand, to tackle

---

1. Unesco. *Final report on meeting of senior officials of the ministries of education of the twenty-five least developed countries.* Paris, 1975. 30 p. (ED/MD/39.) [Mimeographed.]

the critical problems of poverty and underdevelopment, like food, health and nutrition, housing, clothing, etc., and, on the other, to train the skilled manpower at various levels and types necessary to improve the quality of life of the entire population. For this purpose it was necessary to look at education and training as an integral part of an over-all national development process. The planning of educational strategies should take into account and respond to the changes occurring in all the other sectors. The right to fundamental education for all was recognized, but great obstacles in the way were also noted, such as the lack of adequate financial resources, lack of trained manpower and community leadership to guide the implementation of reforms, traditional attitudes which do not favour change, and the non-availability of adequate expertise and scientific data on new forms of education.

Some noted that in many cases reforms led to the creation of two parallel systems: the formal academic system for the élite, and the non-formal training programme for the underprivileged, which increased inequalities rather than reduced them. On the other hand, total radical change of education systems was often costly and risky. Therefore there was a need to be careful in making the fundamental choices and in translating them into integrated educational training programmes. A course of planning of alternative strategies was required, based on a review of policy objectives and existing systems, and taking fully into account possible innovations and alternative resource possibilities in terms of both finance and trained personnel.

While the participants thought that education for productive work was one of the most vital instruments for fighting poverty, it was also recognized that education alone cannot be effective in the process of rural transformation and of mobilizing human resources for development purposes. It has a complementary role in the process of promoting socio-economic transformation of traditional societies, as well as in values and attitudes towards active life. It must, however, be supported by actual improvements in work opportunities in the rural sector. It was also recognized that there is an area of traditional value systems and attitudes towards practical programmes and work which parents, as well as teachers and teacher trainers, are sometimes reluctant to accept in non-academic orientations. The incentive systems in some of the less-developed countries are also hardly conducive to drastic changes in this respect. The meeting decided that, while national and international resources are certainly insufficiently sharing the risk of innovations in the education/work field, the lack of a methodological framework for translating an innovative idea in this area into practical experiments that can be evaluated may sometimes be more serious than the resource constraint.

The need for research and exchange of information in this area was stressed. Thus it was agreed that research based on experimentation should be action-oriented and focused on problems related to the renewal of education systems with a view to rendering them relevant and efficient. Such research should concentrate not only on collecting and analysing relevant quantitative data related to enrolments, school-age populations, active population, manpower requirements, etc., but also, more particularly, on qualitative aspects related to development and appropriate curricula and national languages, development of attitudes and aptitudes favourable to national development among the population, and new forms of education, formal and non-formal, geared to meet national development objectives. It should also focus on efficiency aspects of education like low-cost alternatives, the reduction of unit costs, etc., and on developing appropriate planning and management techniques—in particular, for organizing and implementing programmes of mass education concentrating on local development needs. The research efforts should be followed by large scale experimentation and innovations which would involve risk-sharing on the part of donors.

Approaches to teacher education and training

Examples from less-developed regions of the world:

INITIAL TRAINING

The Philippines

Innovations in initial training for teaching were developed from a number of basic factors about the country. In the 1971 census it was shown that 68 per cent of the population lived in rural areas. However, very few young men and women from village schools who went to college ever returned to their home *barrio* to help to transform their communities: most settled permanently in cities like Manila, Cebu, Iloilo. However, the Educational Development Decree of 1972 declared that the 'policy of the Government was to ensure within the context of a free and democratic system maximum contribution of the educational system to the attainment of the following national development goals: (a) to achieve and maintain an accelerating rate of economic development and social progress; (b) to assure the maximum participation of all the people in the attainment and enjoyment of the benefits of such growth; and (c) to strengthen national consciousness and promote desirable cultural values in a changing world.'

Thus, in the Philippines the Department of Education and Culture has viewed the initial training of teachers in the context of the national, political, economic and social realities, and the availability of human and material resources that will contribute to the attainment of national development goals. In effect, the schools are seen as making one of the major contributions to the achievement of the 'new society'—a major movement towards a participatory democracy and, therefore, calling for major reforms in the content and method of education. The role of the teacher has been considerably broadened so that he becomes an agent of local production in books and curriculum materials, a part-time civic leader, a social worker; he is expected to be more skilled in audio-visual education—in fact, he becomes a motivator, a guide, a consultant, a helper, a friend who knows a little better or a little more, so that the individual group to which his ability in a particular subject area places him will learn as much and as fast as his learning power and effort will allow. The movement is rapidly towards that of social integrator, attitude changer, community worker, with a particular emphasis upon the rural area. For this reason, the Philippine Association for Teacher Education has produced a revised teacher education curriculum which integrates all teacher preparation programmes for elementary and secondary school teaching, reducing the cost of teacher education through a reduction of the number of units or credit hours for the whole course.

Because teachers are expected to play key roles in rural transformation, as well as in the development of employable skills, a new concept of student teaching is the main thrust of recent revisions in the Bachelor of Science in Education at the University of Philippines College of Education (UPCE). In the Innovative Teacher Education Programme there has been a change from the previous arrangement where two semesters of teacher education were carried out at the university's High School and at one of the schools in Quezon City; in future, during the last semester of study at UPCE, students will not have any more academic courses, but during the first half of the semester they will practise teaching at the High School, and during the second half they will practise teaching in a rural school. The teaching practice in the rural school will be a total experience in which the student-teacher becomes part of the faculty of a school participating in all its operations as an integral part of the system, whether it be classroom instruction, attending meetings, dealing with parents and the community, or engaging in non-formal activities. Such an experience will help the prospective teacher to develop insights into the world of school, rural community and the larger society, and understand the positive, cognitive and affective processes, so that he can evoke and develop them instead of inhibiting their growth.

It is felt that this kind of teaching apprenticeship will prepare teachers to assume multiple roles, especially with regard to rural transformation, health and nutrition and the development of employable skills in the rural setting, where such extension services of teachers are urgently needed. It should also enable the student to understand the community as a social structure with its primary values, economy and patterns of behaviour. This is to help prepare them for non-formal educational activities which are increasingly important in the national plan for human resource development. It will also involve learning the culture of the school, where the reference cultures of community and bureaucracy converge. In this way, they experience the actualities of teaching, the limitations and constraints of the profession, and begin to understand the behaviour of children and youth in their context, so that they can help accelerate the acquisition of basic literary and communication skills and development of values. The innovation in initial training is also related to the theme of the Asian Programme of Educational Innovation for Development (APEID) sponsored workshop on teacher education and curricula for development. The National Research and Development Centre for Teacher Education has embarked, with the assistance of Unicef and Unesco on a special project to 'identify the new tasks and skills required of primary/elementary teachers to meet new roles in the national development and the production of sample curriculum materials for in-service and pre-service education of teachers'. The study will no doubt call upon other work that has been done, such as that of Professor Manalang on the Philippine rural school and that of L.B. Soriano. However, one of the most significant aspects of the development of initial training in the Philippines is the strong awareness that in-service training methods should relate directly to the changed political goals of the Philippines and also to the social and economic balance of the country's population, particularly its rural nature.

Indonesia

The decision in Indonesia to establish the Office of Educational Development and the presidential decree giving the Minister of Education and Culture the responsibility for over-all planning and control of educational institutions was vital in enabling an assessment to be made of current developments in education in that vast country. The assistance of Unesco and the Ford Foundation was crucial in shaping the new institution into a working unit. With a population of around 119 million—about 76 million of whom live on the islands of Java and Madura, and the other 43 million on three other major islands and countless smaller islands—the planning problems of Indonesia are peculiarly challenging and complex. Thus, the national assessment of education project had become a major strategy for guiding Indonesia in the difficult task of establishing priorities where resources are scarce. While it is inappropriate to discuss the range of innovations in planning, development, and evaluation in primary, secondary, non-formal and higher education explored by the national assessment project, the existence of such a broad-ranging and continuing national evaluation is important if the teacher-training element is to be properly orchestrated. Indeed, teacher training may be regarded as one of the most sensitive and interactive parts of the education system, coming often as a nodal point between school, community and higher education.

In Indonesia the Minister of Education has stated that the country can no longer solve its quantitative problems by quantitative means, by which he meant to underline a brutal fact: Indonesia (like most countries in South-East Asia) cannot expect to train enough teachers or build enough schools to meet the present and the future increase in the number of school-eligible children. A mere continuation of education systems based on European models of fifty or sixty years ago is no longer appropriate. The Abepura project in West

Irian aimed at improving the quality of education by concentrating on teacher training. For this reason, a new training centre was constructed in Abepura about sixteen kilometres from Jayapura. The centre, the efforts of the education authorities and of the team of Unesco experts were combined. In addition to reforms in teaching methods and approaches, the project challenges the old idea of a school being a place where children sit from eight in the morning until four in the afternoon for a predetermined number of years. It is accepted that the next thirty years will see great changes in the practice of education, but it will not be possible to build schools or provide teachers to enable all the children to attend a formal school: many will have to learn in special centres or even in their homes, where radio and television will be the teachers.

The centres will have a few instructors, rooms and workshops where the practical application of lessons can be carried out. The project is also looking at the provision of continuing education. Currently, however, the approach is on a threefold front: audio-visual aids, science and practical subjects. The project uses flannelgraphs, charts, diagrams and drawings, simple projectors and, more importantly, radio. A local education broadcasting service has been set up to broadcast first to teachers, later to children in the classroom, and to communities. Over the radio the children are told about the universe in which they live, beginning with their village, its environs, the climate, the soil, the plants and trees, the animals, the rivers and mountains, the atmosphere and the sky. Then they are encouraged to explore beyond the village to the district, to the province, to Indonesia, to Asia, to the world and to the universe.

Abepura has become a centre for educational change with a large number of courses being held to assist in the spread of modern ideas in all branches of education. The nearby University of Tjenderawasih has been working together with the new centre and has itself formed an association with an established university in the United States (University of Southern Illinois).

The emphasis upon quality in Indonesia does not mean that they are ignoring the problem of quantity but, rather, seeing it in perspective. For example, in 1973 there were about 425,000 primary teachers in Indonesia. At the end of the next five-year plan *(Repelita II)* it is estimated that there will be a need for 525,000 teachers, a figure which is based upon a teacher/student ratio of 1:40. Similar increases in other areas of education are obviously needed. Because, however, of the continuing high birth-rate, the provision of universal primary and secondary education is still a very long way away. Therefore, the status and salaries of existing teachers have been substantially improved in order to provide the base for the long-term goal of a well-trained profession of high standing coming from a consolidated teacher training programme. The integrated structure of the training institution is concerned with: (a) preparing teachers; (b) developing research on teaching and teacher education; (c) developing the capabilities to serve various kinds of training programmes for various educational personnel.   The aim of the integrated teacher-training system is to produce a new kind of teacher who is capable of flexibility and response to curriculum change and who will be a facilitator of self-reliant learning.   Rather than being only tellers of facts, teachers must also become organizers of learning, be able to pass this skill on to the learners and also to be stimulators of continuing learning.

THE INTERFACE BETWEEN INITIAL AND IN-SERVICE TRAINING

As will already be clear from the examples given above, a marked feature of teacher training in less-developed regions is the way in which the two stages of initial and in-service tend to interact with each other and, indeed, in some cases to overlap completely.   In the developed regions of the world the two 'sub-systems' tend to be quite separate, with initial training providing the basic teaching qualification, and in-service training normally following after the teacher has gained a certain amount of experience.   The proposed scheme of induction discussed in relation to the United Kingdom is a variant of this normal model coming rather closer to the approach of many less-developed regions.   However, the different styles of relationship between initial and in-service training mark one of the most substantial differences between the approach of less- and more-developed regions.   Nepal provides one example of the way in which the interface is deliberately operated.

In Nepal an action research project was proposed to develop a field-oriented sequence in the primary teacher training programme.   This was put forward by the Institute of Education at Tribhuvan University and accepted that the skills, concepts and attitudes that teachers presently have must provide a starting point for developing more effective teaching competencies. Therefore, the first phase of the project was devoted to research into teachers' behaviour in the classroom and their attitudes towards teaching and the nature of learning.   The expectations and attitudes of parents and education officers were also researched.   This background research provided a detailed picture of the teacher/learning environment of the schools which was used as a basis for developing a list of competencies that a primary teacher should have in order to teach effectively in a primary school.   These competencies were then accepted as their objectives for an experimental second semester sequence in the primary teacher training programme.   It was decided to implement these objectives at the Butal Campus Institute of Education with a class of twenty-eight randomly selected pre-service and in-service teachers. The objectives of the experimental semester were organized according to relevant topics called modules.   The modules were as follows: (a) teaching resource; (b) teaching technique; (c) evaluation technique; (d) grouping technique; (e) construction of instructional material; (f) community relations and school welfare; (g) extra-curricular activity; (h) lesson planning; and (i) teaching practice. Often concepts and methods were, of course, common to all subject areas, and there was a logical sequence in the way in which the topics were taught. The modules had an activity orientation in that the students were constantly using textbooks and curricula to develop and refine techniques which they practised with each other and used with a tutorial student or with a group of primary school children. Checklists have been developed as guidelines for developing different skills as one student-teacher observes another and completes a given checklist in order to provide feedback.

Data from the background research indicated that teachers viewed learning as primarily a process of memorization. This attitude is not likely to help achieve the present goal of the education system, which is to produce capable, development-oriented citizens. Therefore the project stresses learning as being the product of higher-level cognitive skills. Students are expected to write broader concepts and objectives, ask more open-ended, thought-provoking questions, and develop activities that give practice in a variety of cognitive skills. Students are evaluated according to their performance in class discussions and activities, micro-teaching situations, home assignments, primary class observations, unit and modular examinations and practice teaching. Special attention is paid to process evaluation in which the project itself is evaluated through staff meetings, informal talks with students and feedback forms completed by them, and visits by other institute staff. The Nepal experiment provides another example of the interface between initial and in-service training, with particular reference to the need to change the attitudes and behaviour patterns of the teachers who work in the schools.

Further notes on teacher education in developing countries

The first group are derived from the report of a technical working group, 21-30 October 1975, on alternative structures and methods in teacher education produced by the Asian Centre of Educational Innovation for Development, published by the Unesco Regional Office for Education in Asia, Bangkok, 1975.

1. Thailand

A project carried out by the staff of Udornthani Teachers' College, Thailand, since 1974 is the Udornthani project for educational reform by means of teacher training. The prime objective is to create a better educational environment in the rural villages in Thailand. Teachers in the rural villages of the north-eastern part of Thailand are expected to be change-agents in the process of educational development in rural villages and are expected to take leadership roles in promoting innovation for rural transformation. A college research and development centre has been created in order to support the operation of the college, and the emphasis upon fieldwork has been changed from urban schools to rural schools, and many aspects of the student teaching experience will be in non-formal as well as formal education.

2. Malaysia

In Malaysia there is a commitment to a kind of agricultural education that did not exist before. Intensive programmes are offered to teachers during the school holidays to help them implement the new agricultural science syllabus for secondary schools which includes both practical experience as well as basic theory. There is mobile in-service education in which teachers attend weekend courses at selected in-service centres in their respective areas. Mobile in-service training was started as a pilot project in Johor, and the aim was to determine whether effective training could be carried out by having small groups of about twenty-five teachers assemble for weekend sessions. Five locations were selected, and lecturers from the teacher training college met with those teachers at one of these locations every weekend for five weeks. A second round of instruction was held, and lecturers again met with these teachers in each of the five centres. The course content was directed at the immediate needs of the teachers. Areas of need were identified, and such topics as lesson planning, teaching methods, budgeting and technical subject-matter were discussed. The project was productive, indigenous and sensitive to national needs. It was expected that 155 agricultural science teachers in the secondary schools in Johor State would be reached by these in-service courses twice each year. The project is highly feasible, since on-the-spot training eliminates taking the teachers away from their job locations. The project is problem-oriented and adopts a systematic approach towards supplying trained teachers in agricultural science in secondary schools. The expansion of the project to other states in Malaysia is being envisaged as well as the involvement of the Agricultural University in the training of lecturers and teacher educators.

3. India

The Centre for Advanced Study in Education in the University of Baroda was recognized by the University Grants Commission of the Government of India in 1964. Two recent innovations have been the establishment of a semester system and the increased use of programmed material in teacher education. Under the semester system the approach used was one of study, group discussion, persuasion, orientation and that of developing conviction. Major organizational changes related to the transfer of responsibility for course content from the university authorities to the subject teachers, the transfer of responsibility for evaluation and grading from external examiners to the teacher educators, the setting up of an evaluation unit among the teachers of the department, and the linking of the student teaching programme with research on micro-teaching. Although of Western origin, the innovations have a local base because they were planned to meet local needs, and the programme material developed will be printed and put on the market by the institution.

4. Thailand

Thailand asserted that 'most teacher education programmes provide for formal coursework followed by student teaching with the implicit assumption that the prospective teacher is ready and well prepared to fulfil a range of professional responsibilities in the school. Experiences have shown that this is not so. Teacher education should therefore be the responsibility of the whole profession, not just the teachers' colleges or universities, and the community must plan both pre-service teacher education and in-service teacher education in close co-operation.' They also note that recruitment of teacher educators in Thailand tends to overstress academic background as opposed to experience. What are needed are perceptive, imaginative, knowledgeable and dedicated persons and effective procedures and instruments to discover and assess those qualities required. Research and development of such instruments and procedures call for immediate action.

5. Singapore

The Republic of Singapore indicated that there was provision of half-pay leave for teachers to pursue courses abroad for six months at any one time. This is normally available after the teacher has completed six years resident service.

6. Egypt

The Arab Republic of Egypt asserted that in their education system, because of rapid economic and social change, the concept of lifelong education is taken into consideration in preparing teachers. Teachers' preparation is only the first step in the process of self-development. Thus, developing the trainee's personality and his capacity for further growth is most important. The teacher is responsible for teaching the children how to learn, and to organize and guide their activities through collaborating with colleagues. Increasing emphasis is being given during training to the teaching practice period and in stressing knowledge about the child and his motivation, about his interests and abilities. Training for primary school-teachers consists of two years after the completion of the general secondary school. There is a central department for in-service training in the Ministry of Education and local departments in the Governorates, which plan to carry out systematic programmes for teachers at all levels. In-service training is not considered as a remedial measure to patch up deficiencies but as an instrument of permanent development and growth of teachers as both professionals and individuals. Thus the programmes are aimed at the creation of teachers who seek self-education, self-realization and self-development throughout their whole professional lives. In 1966 there was a Government Recommendation concerning the Status of Teachers which stated that 'authorities should promote the establishment of a wide system of in-service education free to all teachers'. The staff who are responsible for the in-service programmes within the two systems are regarded as equally important. In-service training for teachers is a co-operative process in which educational authorities, universities, teacher training institutions and schools themselves participate and have a share.

7. Sri Lanka

Many reforms were proposed in 1972. The institutionalized programmes in Sri Lanka are organized in twenty-eight teacher education institutes fairly evenly distributed in the island. Programmes aim to provide the teacher with basic knowledge and relevant skills supplemented with a period of active practice teaching. In view of the rapid changes, however, to which education is subjected, it is not in future intended to give the teachers 'a licence to teach'. It is intended as 'a licence for learning to teach' by adapting to new situations through continuous professional training and growth. The new education programme under implementation calls for certain management and organizational skills on the part of practising teachers. This aspect has been gradually instituted into the training programme through appropriately organized group-work and community development projects. The tests currently in use for the purpose of certification are basically achievement tests covering the subject matter of the respective courses. This approach is regarded as limited, and a form of continuous assessment throughout the duration of the course is being considered for implementation in the immediate future. Particular emphasis is also being put upon the need to have an induction programme for newly trained teachers, particularly those working in underprivileged, remote locations. In future the main purposes of teacher education are seen to be to provide the following:

1. A knowledge of child development, of the materials to be taught, of suitable methods of teaching it and the culture of the pupils;
2. Appropriate skills which enable the future teacher to teach, advise and guide his pupils, administer and manage his professional activities and respond sensitively to the pupils' community and culture with which he is involved;
3. Attitudes which should enable him to be positive without being aggressive, so that his example is likely to be emulated as he transmits explicitly and implicitly the national aims, ideals and social values.

8. Caribbean region

The University of the West Indies at St. Augustine, Trinidad, has been offering an in-service diploma in education programme since 1973. This was offered because it was estimated that only one in six of the country's secondary school-teachers had received postgraduate training. They now have an in-service diploma which is taken during the school vacations; the teachers attend a course at the university for a total of seven weeks—five weeks during the summer, one week at Christmas and one week at Easter. During the first two-and-a-half school terms the teachers return to the university on one afternoon a week, and are visited on average every two weeks by their curriculum tutor. The course has three major components: themes in education, curriculum studies and assignments. The advantages of the in-service over the pre-service training courses are that the in-service course is more economic. Furthermore, it deals with students already committed to careers in teaching and who can themselves bring experiences which enrich the course and enhance their appreciation of the relevance of problems dealt with.

The in-service diploma has stimulated teachers to become involved in a wide variety of educational activities, such as the foundation of the Association for Science Education of Trinidad and Tobago, working groups concerned with school counselling, and now substantial pressure for the establishment of a teachers' centre to provide the base for continuing education for teachers in the region. In future, training for secondary teachers may take place as shown on the accompanying diagram.

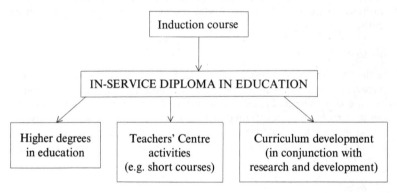

9. Kuwait

In the State of Kuwait the Ministry of Education has provided one-year supplementary evening courses for teachers, and those who successfully complete the course are awarded special increments in salary. There are also training programmes covering a wide range of educational personnel, including kindergarten teachers, English teachers at secondary school, technical inspectors, mathematics teachers, teachers of technical subjects. In 1970/71 there were only 569 in-service trainees. In 1973/74 the number had reached 3,140 out of a total number of teachers, headmasters and inspectors of 13,100.

10. Pakistan

In Pakistan the initial training for elementary teachers has been reduced over the last decade to a one-year course. It is intended to make this a more intensive training programme on a short-term basis, but soon to replace it by a two-year training course or the new three-year professional college course.

11. Republic of Korea

In the Republic of Korea there is considerable emphasis upon research, with a number of educational research institutes, including the National Institute of Education, which is a governmental research component within the Ministry of Education. Established in 1974, its major task is to carry out studies on educational policy as well as in-service teacher training. The Korean Educational Development Institute supports educational reform activities and operates a complete educational radio-television system. Broadcasting started in 1975 to air educational programmes to the demonstration schools throughout the nation. The Korean Institute for Research in Behavioural Sciences recruits and trains for respective researches in behavioural sciences. The work of the Institute ranges over fields of learning, social research, organizational behaviour and child development. There are also provincial and county institutes for educational research and research activities at various school levels.

12. Qatar

In the State of Qatar statistics prove that 85 per cent of the teachers in the preparatory and secondary schools are not educationally qualified although they are university graduates. Thus, an evening programme was provided to enable them to obtain a general diploma in education. The course lasts over a period of one-and-a-half academic years. Those who perform best get the chance to attend postgraduate courses. 150 teachers have currently enrolled in the programme.

13. India

In India the National Council of Educational Research and Training (NCERT) is continuing to organize summer institutes for science teachers at secondary schools. A scheme of in-service education has been prepared in order to enable all teachers to undergo in-service training once every five years and to become acquainted with modern developments in education.

14. Libya

In the Libyan Arab Republic in-service courses were provided in 1973/74 for 2,800 trainees.

15. Iraq

In Iraq within the Ministry of Education the Director-General of Educational Supervision and Teacher Training is responsible for the pre-service training of primary teachers and in-service training of primary and secondary teachers and educational leaders. A special unit for training the serving primary teachers by the multi-media approach was set up in 1973. The budgetary provision for teacher training has been trebled over the last three years. The multi-media approach as applied to the in-service training of primary teachers is based upon indirect forms of training, such as self-study assignments, supplementary reading, video-taped materials and radio-television programmes, with more direct methods of training, such as weekly seminars and workshops, on-the-job supervision and special courses. The target for 1975/76 is 1,500 primary teachers rising to 2,000 in 1976/77. In 1975/76 in-service training courses were also provided for primary school supervisors in order to improve the impact of supervisory activities on primary education and prepare the supervisors to act as field tutors for the teachers undergoing the one-year refresher course by the multi-media approach in their respective districts.

16. *Malawi*

In Malawi in-service training is undertaken by the Ministry of Education. All primary teachers are required to attend orientation courses organized in their districts by district education officers and inspectors during the first term of each academic year. Prior to the courses the district education and professional staff attend induction courses at the Ministry of Education in order to be briefed on new developments in the various primary curriculum subjects and the areas of weakness which need emphasizing. In order to improve the professional qualifications of the inadequately qualified primary school teachers, the Malawi Correspondence College runs a one-year upgrading course in two parts: part one is a correspondence course and part two is a five-week residential course. Both courses have been made possible because of the generous financial assistance of Unicef.

17. *Uganda*

In Uganda, also, a correspondence course was established in 1974 with the assistance of Unicef. Again, there is a correspondence element and a residential sequence of instruction. This has increased very substantially the number of teachers in higher categories. There are three purely in-service teachers' colleges in Uganda, and in 1974 they widened their scope to include experienced secondary graduates who were teaching in primary school. It is now possible for a primary teacher to advance through a series of in-service courses from a grade-two primary school position to becoming a degree holder teaching at a teachers' training college.

Recommendation No. 69 to the Ministries of Education concerning the changing role of the teacher and its influence on preparation for the profession and on in-service training

PREAMBLE

The International Conference on Education, convened by the United Nations Educational, Scientific and Cultural Organization, meeting in Geneva, at its thirty-fifth session, held from the twenty-seventh of August to the fourth of September, nineteen hundred and seventy-five,

Having regard to the relevant conventions, recommendations and declarations adopted at the international level, which are applicable to educational personnel, and more particularly to the Recommendation concerning the Status of Teachers, adopted by the special Intergovernmental Conference (1966) and the Revised Recommendation concerning Technical and Vocational Education, adopted by the General Conference of Unesco at its eighteenth session (1974),

Considering the rapid changes brought about by economic, scientific, technological, social and cultural progress in the modern societies as well as national aspirations,

Recognizing that changes in the teacher's role resulting from changes in society and in education have an effect on initial and on in-service education of various categories of teachers, and other personnel in education, as well as on their status and conditions of work,

The International Conference on Education,

Adopts on the third of September, nineteen hundred and seventy-five, and submits for consideration by the Ministers responsible for education and the competent authorities and agencies in the various States and appropriate international bodies, the following recommendation:

A. UNDERLYING PRINCIPLES

1. Coherent policy and action in the field of teacher education and in the field of their employment and conditions of work should be based on the following principles:

(a) Whatever are or will be the changes in the education system, the teacher-learner relationship will remain at the centre of the educational process and therefore better preparation of educational personnel constitutes one of the essential factors of educational development and an important condition for any renovation in education.

(b) To improve the contribution that education makes to international, national, social, economic and cultural development, fresh efforts in teacher education are required but these presuppose that education authorities in Member States take account of the directions of change in the role of the teacher and the factors involved.

(c) All appropriate forces of the society should be involved in the definition of the aims and objectives of education and consequently of teacher education. In this definition of purposes and objectives, teachers should take a responsible part, together with their professional associations or groups.

(d) All aspects of teacher education, including access thereto, should be free from any form of discrimination on grounds of race, colour, sex, religion, political origin, economic condition, etc.

(e) Specialists from other professions and other people from the community should be appropriately involved in the process of education.

B. THE ROLE OF THE TEACHER

2. Teachers and administrators of all categories and levels should be aware of the roles played by them in the present state and development of education. They should understand that their roles and functions are not fixed unchangeable categories, but are evolving under the influence of changes taking place in society and in the education system itself.

3. Despite the diversity of education systems and of arrangements for teacher education throughout the world, there is a general need for fresh national scrutiny, in a realistic manner, of the teachers' specific tasks and functions in terms of national policies and legislation. Such national analyses, with the participation of teachers themselves, should lead to the establishment of professional profiles for all categories of teachers and other educational personnel with clear definitions of the roles and functions assigned to them by the society.

4. Measures should be taken to ensure that conditions exist for serving teachers and future teachers to be aware of the changes in the teachers' roles and to be prepared for new roles and functions:

(a) The teacher is engaged more and more today in the implementation of new educational procedures, taking advantage of all the resources of modern educational devices and methods. He is an educator and a counsellor who tries to develop his pupils' abilities and interests and not merely to serve as a source of information and a transmitter of knowledge; the teacher plays a principal role in providing his pupils with a scientific world outlook.

(b) Since the role of the school is no longer limited to instruction, the teacher, apart from his instructional duties, has now to assume more responsibility, in collaboration with other educational agents in the community for the preparation of the young for community life, family life, productive activity, etc. The teacher should have more opportunity for involvement in extra-curricular and out-of-school activities, in guiding and counselling the pupils and their parents, and in organizing his pupils' leisure time activities.

(c) Teachers should be aware of the important role they are called upon to play in the local community as professionals and citizens, as agents of development and change and be given the possibility of practising that role.

(d) It should be recognized that the effectiveness of school education depends largely upon the development of new relationships between the teacher and his pupils, who become more active partners in the education process; between the teacher and his colleagues and other agents who may be called upon to co-operate with him; between the teacher and his pupils' parents and others in the community concerned with the process of education.

C. OTHER PROFESSIONALS AND SPECIALISTS IN EDUCATION

5. With the development and the continued diversification and enlargement of the function and programmes of educational establishments at various levels, the need may arise to use other professionals and specialists in the education system on a full-time or part-time basis to participate with the teachers in the realization of the education programme. This practice should be encouraged, taking into account the experience of Member States, and be recommended for wider implementation wherever it has produced positive results, provided that educational responsibility remains in the hands of qualified teachers.

6. In each case it is important to analyse the national situation in order to identify the categories of personnel desirable in the educational process apart from regular teachers and at the same time to identify and eliminate administrative or institutional obstacles which may retard or make it difficult for such personnel to participate widely in the education process.

7. The same analyses should be applied to other personnel appointed to assist teachers and school administrators in non-teaching duties, both in the administrative and in the technical sectors, in order to improve the efficiency of the school and of the teacher.

8. Other professionals and specialists engaged on a full-time or part-time basis should receive pedagogical training either prior to or during their work at the educational institution.

D. INFLUENCE OF THE CHANGING ROLE ON PREPARATION FOR THE PROFESSION AND ON IN-SERVICE EDUCATION

General considerations

9. If education is to meet the demands of our time and of the coming decades, the organization, content and methods of teacher education must be constantly improved. In particular situations, a search for new educational strategies and concepts should be undertaken, taking account of the special social and cultural conditions under which the school and the teachers must perform their basic functions.

10. In view of the continuous renovation and development of general and pedagogical knowledge, and of the constant change taking place in education systems and the increasingly creative character of pedagogical activities, it does not seem possible to equip the student teacher with knowledge and skills which would be sufficient for his whole professional life. Therefore, the initial preparation for the profession, pre-service education and training, should be considered as a first fundamental stage in the process of the continuous education of teachers.

11. Hence a comprehensive policy is needed to ensure that teacher education is reorganized as a continuous co-ordinated process which begins with pre-service preparation and continues throughout the teacher's professional career. In such a system, pre-service and in-service education should be integrated, fostering the concept of lifelong learning and the need for recurrent education.

12. In-service education should not only permit professional updating but should also ensure the necessary professional mobility by preparing educational personnel to assume new functions and responsibilities.

13. Such a comprehensive policy of teacher education should include provision for pre-service and in-service training of educational personnel of various categories and of various levels, including inspectors, supervisors and other administrators as well as other professionals and specialists engaged in education.

14. At the level of educational policy with regard to in-service education the four principles which it seems most important to apply are:
   (a) continuity designed to keep the teacher continually aware of new developments in the education system and in the field of educational research and to expand his knowledge and skills in his particular subjects;
   (b) comprehensiveness that will involve all those who participate in the education process—various categories of teachers, school administrators and inspectors, teacher educators and others;
   (c) establishment of an organizational framework with appropriate funding and staff provisions, making possible the participation of all educators in various forms of in-service education and the mobilization, in collaboration with all institutions concerned, of all the resources likely to contribute to such training;

(d) involvement of various categories of educational personnel in the definition of in-service teacher education policy, objectives and programmes and their implementation as well as in educational research.

Preparation for the profession

15. Taking into account the fact that there are, and always will be, changes in all aspects of social, cultural and educational life which will influence the roles and functions of teachers, it is essential to make future teachers aware of these changes and to prepare them for the profession with this in mind. This underlines particularly the importance of the development of the personality of the teacher in the course of his training and the development of his readiness and capacity for further training and self-education.

16. Within the context of existing educational legislation there should be flexibility for adapting rules, regulations, professional statutes, so as to facilitate progressive changes in the initial and continuing education of teachers, the formation of teacher teams which would include persons performing appropriate educational roles, the provision of incentives in career situations and prospects, etc. Accreditation and certification procedures should be geared to the new roles of teachers.

17. From the point of view of content, initial teacher education should enable the future teacher to acquire the necessary professional preparation for new roles and functions, and should provide a basis for continuing professional development in the framework of lifelong education for teachers. The development of the curriculum for teacher education courses should be linked closely with curriculum developments in the schools.

18. Considered from the point of view of general principles and aims, the programmes of initial teacher education should:

(a) Relate closely to roles and functions expected of the teacher today and prepare the future teacher not only for his instructional role but also for the variety of roles and functions demanded of him by the society and the development of education. Teachers are now more and more involved in various extra-curricular and out-of-school activities and should be prepared so that they will be able to combine teaching and up-bringing into the single process of developing personality.

(b) Prepare future teachers to use effectively and for the benefit of learners all the facilities and resources offered by the social and cultural environment.

(c) Give an opportunity for student teachers to experience these new roles and functions during the training period, by giving them responsibilities in the administration of teacher education institutions, by establishing closer links with various educational institutions and providing practical training so as to develop the students' initiative, responsiveness, resourcefulness and adaptability to change, and so enable them in the future to assume such new roles and functions as may appear.

(d) Provide for and ensure the student teachers' personal and professional self-development, so that they will be prepared to continue their education and development in the future either by self-education or by seeking to attend courses of in-service training and also prepare them to develop the same aptitudes in their pupils.

(e) Include adequate provision for general and professional, theoretical and practical preparation. The studies of specialization should be up to date and interdisciplinary in character and cover not only the facts but also the fundamental concepts, principles, structures of subjects so that students acquire an interdisciplinary framework within which they can continue to gain new knowledge independently during their professional life, taking account of the latest developments in the field of their specialization.

(f) Include ample provision for professional development, both theoretical and practical, including introduction to problems of educational research and its application, to elements of experimental technique in education in order to facilitate teacher participation in educational research and strengthen the links between training and research.

(g) Prepare the teacher for the effective use of educational technology, including the media of mass communication.

In-service education

19. Continuing education should be an integral part of the teacher education process and should therefore be arranged on a regular basis for all categories of educational personnel. Procedures should be as flexible as possible and adaptable to teacher's individual needs and to the special features of each region, taking into account developments in the different specialities and the extension of knowledge.

20. The functions of teacher education institutions should be extended not only to provide for the pre-service education of teachers but also to contribute substantially towards their further education; it is thus desirable that these institutions provide pre-service education and continuing education.

21. Special regional centres should also be developed for this purpose and also to provide initial in-service education for those teachers, particularly in developing countries, who did not receive adequate preparation before starting teaching.

22. Teachers' organizations should be encouraged to contribute to the continuing education of teachers by initiating opportunities for teachers to meet and work together on common problems. Conferences, seminars and courses organized by teachers' organizations may represent a significant measure in encouraging teacher development by the profession itself.

23. Self-education of teachers should be considered as an important element in their continuing education. The educational authorities and educational research and

documentation centres should help the teachers to organize their individual in-service education by providing guidance, the necessary documentation and literature, library facilities, etc., and by making the necessary time available.

24. In order to make continuing education more effective and to reach educators in remote regions, extensive use should be made of radio, TV and correspondence courses. The combination of short full-time courses with long periods of multimedia programmes, including radio, TV and correspondence courses may provide one immediate solution of in-service education of the broad mass of teachers.

25. The strengthening of the continuing education of teachers as required at all levels of the system, from early childhood education to the tertiary level and adult education, will require considerable efforts on the part of education authorities. Such efforts include the quantitative analysis of teacher supply and demand in the country and the working out of national or regional plans for the continuing education of teachers.

26. Present rules, regulations and statutes should be so modified as to recognize the importance, necessity and effect of in-service education, to take into account the developments in its organization which have already occurred and to provide a legal right for all educational personnel to take part in continuing education.

27. Measures should be taken to give all full-time or part-time specialists working in education the opportunity for in-service education and at the same time to ensure that their professional experience benefits other teachers.

E. STATUS OF EDUCATIONAL PERSONNEL

28. (a) It should be recognized that the social and economic status of teachers and the level of appreciation of their role are important for the quantitative and qualitative development of education;

    (b) Special attention should be paid to the status of women teachers and their educational opportunities, especially their reintegration into the educational service after absence due to family responsibilities.

29. It is desirable, however, that the improvement and adaptation of the existing administrative and socio-economic status of teachers to new requirements should also permit an enlargement of scope so as to make the education function accessible to a much greater number of competent people available in the community, at least for part-time participation in the educational activities.

30. For this purpose, it is desirable that an administrative, social and economic status should be granted to these specialists consistent with their roles and functions.

31. The Recommendation concerning the Status of Teachers (1966) should also be revised in this sense, and its proper application should be promoted.

F. PARTICIPANTS IN THE EDUCATION OF TEACHERS

32. Whatever may be the intentions to improve or to reform the education of teachers, the practical realization of such intentions will greatly depend on the quality and initiative of those called upon to participate in this activity. In order to prepare future teachers to assume new roles, such persons should in their own turn be competent psychologically, scientifically, academically and practically to educate teachers in this way.

33. Consequently, those responsible for educational policy should give more attention, in general, to the problem of the preparation of those called upon to contribute to the education of teachers. The continuing education of such persons is an essential aspect of educational strategy, which involves, notably, the contribution of universities and specialized institutions. Resources devoted to these purposes are likely to have a maximum multiplier effect.

34. Those responsible for the education of teachers should have at their disposal all the necessary means of keeping abreast of progress achieved in the field of education and of new methodologies and approaches concerning their specific functions.

35. Such persons should be competent to prepare teachers and other educational personnel for various specializations and functions in education and also for professional mobility, and should be in a position to promote among them the right attitudes towards innovation and towards lifelong education.

G. REGIONAL AND INTERNATIONAL CO-OPERATION

36. Co-operation in the field of initial and in-service teacher education should be carried out at bilateral, regional and international levels. The effect of such co-operation will be:
   (a) to promote the formulation and to support the application of policies and plans for the pre-service and recurrent education of teachers and other specialists at all levels and for all types of education in order that education systems may better contribute to economic, scientific, technological, social and cultural progress;
   (b) to facilitate programmes and activities for the education of teachers, teacher educators and various full-time and part-time specialists required for improving formal and non-formal education at all levels;
   (c) to encourage structures, programmes and methods facilitating the introduction of appropriate innovations in initial and continuing education for all those who may be called upon to assume educational responsibilities;
   (d) to encourage the Member States to collect and to disseminate all possible information about their policies and plans concerning teacher education and also to undertake case studies and comparative studies of such policies and plans;

(e) to recognize the diversity of situations in the development of education, to work out appropriate strategies in the field of teacher education and to intensify policies of assistance in this respect.

37. Regional organizations and international organizations, like Unesco, interested in the training of educational personnel, should help to establish a world network of documentation and information centres likely to stimulate and to support renovative action undertaken in various States, fostering the exchange of information on innovations between the institutions and services responsible for initial and continuing training of educational personnel.

38. Unesco is invited to give priority in its programme to such important aspects of training of educational personnel as are mentioned in this Recommendation: to search for new strategies, roles and functions of various educational personnel, continuing education, wider participation of people other than regular teachers in education, etc. In particular, Unesco should seek to increase concerted international action to support developing countries in their efforts to provide systems of continuous education for their teachers.

39. It is desirable that Unesco, in collaboration with the Member States' competent authorities, should study the possibility of extending the scope of the Recommendation concerning the Status of Teachers (1966) so as to cover various categories of full-time and part-time educational personnel.

Bibliography

1. Asian Centre of Educational Innovation for Development. *Alternative structures and methods in teacher education.* Report of a technical working group, Kathmandu, October 1975. Bangkok, Unesco Regional Office for Education in Asia, 1975. 91 p.

2. Asian Centre of Educational Innovation for Development. *Teacher education and curriculum for development.* Report of a regional planning workshop, Quezon City, Philippines, May 1975. Bangkok, Unesco Regional Office for Education in Asia, 1975. 50 p.

3. Australia. Department of Education. *Development of education in Australia, 1973/74 and 1974/75.* Report to the thirty-fifth session of the International Conference on Education, Geneva, September 1975. 43 p., figs. [Mimeo.]

4. Australia. *The changing role of the teacher.* Paper presented at the thirty-fifth session of the International Conference on Education, Geneva, September 1975. 20 p. [Mimeo.]

5. Austria. Federal Ministry of Education and Arts. *Organization of education in 1973/75.* Report presented at the thirty-fifth session of the International Conference on Education, Geneva, September 1975. 31 p.

6. Austria. *The changing role of the teacher.* Report presented at the thirty-fifth session of the International Conference on Education, Geneva, September 1975. 12 p., bibl. [Mimeo.]

7. Ayman, I. *Educational innovation in Iran.* Paris, Unesco, 1974. 35 p., bibl. (IBE Experiments and innovations in education, Asian series, no. 10.) [Also published in French and Spanish.]

8. Bahrain. Ministry of Education. *Impact of population and manpower problems on strategies for educational development in Bahrein.* Report presented at the thirty-fifth session of the International Conference on Education, Geneva, September 1975. 9 p. [Mimeo.]

9. Bär, S.; Slomma, R. *Initial and further training of teachers in the G.D.R.* Berlin, Ministry of Education; Paris, Unesco, 1973. 52 p., figs.

10. Belgium. Ministries of National Education. *Education in Belgium: the main trends 1973-1975.* Report presented at the thirty-fifth session of the International Conference on Education, Geneva, September 1975. Brussels, 1975. 112 p., figs.

11. Bizot, Judithe. *Educational reform in Peru.* Paris, Unesco, 1975. 63 p. (IBE Experiments and innovations in education, no. 16.) [Also published in French and Spanish.]

12. Bowles, F., et al. *Sudan: higher education.* Paris, Unesco, 1974. 149 p., bibl., figs. (FR/UNDP/SUD.73/009/CONSULTANTS.) [Distribution limited.]

13. Bulgaria. Ministerstvo Narodnogo Prosveščeniya Narodnaya Respublika Bolgariya. *Obraeovanje v Narodnoj Respublike Bolgarii/Report on the development of education in the People's Republic of Bulgaria.* Presented at the thirty-fifth session of the International Conference on Education, Geneva, September 1975. Sofia, 1975. 171 p., figs. [Mimeo.]

14. Canada. Council of Ministers of Education and Department of the Secretary of State for Canada. *Report ...* Presented at the thirty-fifth session of the International Conference on Education, Geneva, September 1975. 52 p. [Mimeo.]

15. Clarke, S.C.T.; Coutts, H.T. *Toward teacher education in the year 2000,* Edmonton, University of Alberta, 1975. 26 p. [Mimeo.]

16. Cuba. Ministerio de Educación. *Organización de la educación 1973-1975: informe de la República de Cuba a la XXXV Conferencia Internacional de Educación/Rapport de la République de Cuba à la XXXVᵉ Conférence Internationale de l'Education/Report of the Republic of Cuba to the XXXVth International Conference on Public Education.* Geneva, September 1975. 179 p.

17. Cyprus. Ministry of Education. *The changing role of the teacher.* Reply to the inquiry of Unesco: International Bureau of Education. 1974. 5 p. [Mimeo.]

18. Cyprus. *National report on the development of Cyprus education over the last two years 1973-1975/Rapport national sur le développement de l'enseignement à Chypre durant les deux dernières années 1973-1975.* 1975. 4 p. [Mimeo.]

19. Czechoslovakia. Ministry of Education of Czech Socialist Republic/Ministry of Education of Slovak Socialist Republic. *Development of educational system in the Czechoslovak Socialist Republic during the school years 1973/74 and 1974/75.* 1975. 107 p.

20. Egypt. National Center for Educational Research. *The changing role of the teacher and its influence on preparation for the profession, and on in-service training.* Documentation Centre for Education, 1975. 36 p. [Mimeo.]

21. Emerson, L.M.S. *Staff training and access to education.* Paper presented at the thirty-fifth session of the International Conference on Education, Geneva, September 1975. 14 p., figs. (ED/BIE/CONFINT-ED/35/Ref. 7.) [Mimeo. Distribution limited. Also published in French, Russian and Spanish.]

22. Finland. Ministry of Education. *Educational development in Finland 1973-1975.* Helsinki, 1975. 126 p. (Reference publications, 7.)

23. Finland. Ministry of Education. *The changing role of the teacher and its influence on the preparation for the profession and in-service training.* 1974. 48 p. [Mimeo.]

24. France. Ministère de l'Education. *Le mouvement éducatif en France/The educational movement in France/Prodviženie prepodovaniya vo Francii/El movimiento educativo en Francia/1973/1975.* Paris, Institut National de Recherche et de Documentation Pédagogiques, [1975]. 261 p., figs.

25. German Democratic Republic. Ministry of Education. *Development of public education in the German Democratic Republic/Développement de l'éducation nationale en République démocratique allemande.* Berlin, 1975. 84 p.

26. German Democratic Republic. Ministry of Education and Academy of Educational Sciences. *The changing role of the teacher and its effect on pre-service and in-service training for the profession.* Paper presented at the thirty-fifth session of the International Conference on Education, Geneva, September 1975. 22 p. [Mimeo.]

27. Germany, Federal Republic of. Standing Conference of Ministers of Culture and Education of the Länder in the Federal Republic of Germany. *Report on the development of education 1973-75.* Prepared for the thirty-fifth session of the International Conference on Education, Geneva, September 1975. Bonn, 1975. 25 p. [Mimeo.]

28. Germany, Federal Republic of. Secretariat of the Standing Conference of the Ministers of Education and Cultural Affairs. *The changing role of the teacher and its effects on teacher training.* Paper presented at the thirty-fifth session of the International Conference on Education, Geneva, September 1975. 16 p. [Mimeo.]

29. Ghana. Ministry of Education. *The new structure and content of education for Ghana.* Accra-Tema, 1974. 9 p.

30. Greece. Ministry of National Education and Religion. *Education in Greece.* Athens, Directorate of General Education, 1975. 26 p., figs.

31. Hawes, H.W.R.; Ozigi, A.O. *Post-graduate teacher training: a Nigerian alternative*. Paris, Unesco, 1975. 53 p. (IBE Experiments and innovations in education, no. 20.) [Also published in French and Spanish.]

32. Houston, W.R. *Performance education: strategies and resources for developing a competency-based teacher education program*. Albany, New York State Education Department, 1972. 137 p.

33. Huberman, A.M. *Understanding change in education: an introduction*. Paris, Unesco, 1973. 99 p. (IBE Experiments and innovations in education, no. 4.) [Also published in French and Spanish.]

34. Hungary. Vengerskaya Narodnaya Respublika Ministerstov Prosveščeniya. *Doklad o razvitii narodnogo obrazovaniya/Report on educational progress in 1973/75*. Presented at he thirty-fifth session of the International Conference on Education, Geneva, September 1975. 92 p. [Mimeo.]

35. India. Ministry of Education and Social Welfare. *Education in India*. Report presented at the thirty-fifth International Conference on Education, Geneva, September 1975. New Delhi, 1975. 35 p., illus.

36. Indonesia. Office of Educational Development (BPP), Ministry of Education and Culture. *Educational innovation in Indonesia*. Paris, Unesco, 1975. 50 p., bibl. (IBE Experiments and innovations in education, no. 13) [Also published in French and Spanish.]

37. Indonesia. *The changing role of the teacher and its influence on preparation for the profession and on in-service training*. Paper presented at the thirty-fifth session of the International Conference on Education. 36 p., figs. [Mimeo.]

38. International Conference on Education, thirty-fifth session, Geneva, 1975. *Final report*. Paris, Unesco; Geneva, International Bureau of Education, 1975. [Also published in Arabic, French, Russian and Spanish.]

39. International Teachers Organizations. *The teacher's role and training*. Paper prepared for the thirty-fifth session of the International Conference on Education, Geneva, September 1975. Paris, Unesco, 1975. 18 p. (ED/BIE/CONFINTED 35/Ref. 6.) [Distribution limited. Also published in French, Russian and Spanish.]

40. Iraq. Directorate General of Educational Planning. *Development of education in Iraq during 1973/74 and 1974/75*. A report presented to the thirty-fifth session of the International Conference on Education at Geneva, September 1975. Baghdad, 1975. 29 p., bibl., figs. [Mimeo.]

41. Ireland. Department of Education. *The organisation of education in Ireland during 1974/1975 and major trends in educational development in*

1973/74 and 1974/75. Report presented to the thirty-fifth session of the International Conference on Education, Geneva, September 1975. 18 p. [Mimeo.]

42. Italy. Ministry of Public Instruction. *Le mouvement éducatif au cours des années 1973-75/Movimento educativo negli anni 1973-75/The educational movement in the years 1973-75.* Report presented to the thirty-fifth International Conference on Education, Geneva, September 1975. 292 p., figs.

43. Ivory Coast. Ministry of National Education. *Education by television 1968-1980.* Vol. III: *Report of the missions for the evaluation of educational television in Niger, El Salvador and American Samoa.* n.d. 11 p., figs. [Mimeo.]

44. Japan. Japanese National Commission for Unesco. *The changing role of the teacher and its influence on preparation for the profession and on in-service training.* Report presented to the thirty-fifth session of the International Conference on Education, Geneva, September 1975. 7 p. [Mimeo.]

45. Japan. Ministry of Education, Science and Culture. *Development of education in Japan 1973/74-1974/75.* Report presented at the thirty-fifth session of the International Conference on Education, Geneva, September 1975. 15 p., bibl., figs. [Mimeo.]

46. Jordan. Ministry of Education. *A report to the XXXVth session of the International Conference on Education.* Geneva, September 1975. 41 p., bibl., figs. [Mimeo.]

47. Kohn, E.: Postler, F. *Polytechnical education in the German Democratic Republic.* Dresden, Ministry of Education of the G.D.R., 1973. 59 p., illus.

48. Republic of Korea. Korean National Commission for Unesco. *Social change and problems of teacher training in Korea.* Paper presented at the thirty-fifth session of the International Conference on Education, Geneva, September 1975. 34 p. [Mimeo.]

49. Republic of Korea. Ministry of Education. *Report on major trends in educational development in 1973/74 and 1974/75.* Presented at the thirty-fifth session of the International Conference on Education, Geneva, September 1975. 45 p., bibl. [Mimeo.]

50. Kuwait. Ministry of Education, Department of Cultural Relations. *The changing role of the teacher and its influence on preparation for the profession and on in-service training in Kuwait.* Presented at the thirty-fifth session of the International Conference on Education, Geneva, September 1975. 7 p. [Mimeo.]

51. Laderrière, P. Trends and innovations in teacher education. *Educational documentation and information* (Paris, Unesco), no. 195, 2nd quarter 1975, 80 p.

52. Lallez, R. *An experiment in the ruralization of education: IPAR and the Cameroonian reform.* Paris, Unesco, 1974. 113 p., bibl. (IBE Experiments and innovations in education, 8) [Also published in French and Spanish.]

53. Lesotho. Ministry of Education. *Report to the XXXVth session of the International Conference on Education, Geneva, September 1975.* 3 p. [Mimeo.]

54. Libyan Arab Republic. Ministry of Education. *A concise national report on educational developments in the Libyan Arab Republic during the two academic years 1973/1974-1974/1975.* Tripoli, National Commission for Education, Science and Culture, 1975. 23 p., fig. [Also published in Arabic.]

55. Malawi. *Report on developments in education in Malawi: 1973-75.* Paper presented at the thirty-fifth session of the International Conference on Education, Geneva, September 1975. 11 p. [Mimeo.]

56. Malaysia. Ministry of Education, Teacher Training Division. *The changing role of the teacher and its influence on preparation for the profession and on in-service training.* Paper presented to the thirty-fifth session of the International Conference on Education, Geneva, September 1975. 8 p. [Mimeo.]

57. Malta. *Developments in the system of pre-service and in-service training of teachers in Malta.* Paper prepared for the thirty-fifth session of the International Conference on Education, Geneva, September 1975. 6 p. [Mimeo.]

58. Manalang, Priscilla S. *Multiple roles of the Filipino teacher.* Paper presented at a regional planning workshop, Quezon City, Philippines, May 1975. Bangkok, Unesco Regional Office for Education in Asia, 1975. 10 p., bibl. (ROEA-75/APEID-RPW.TT.CD/RD 1.1.) [Distribution limited.]

59. Mauritius. Ministry of Education and Cultural Affairs. *Report on educational developments 1972-1974.* Presented at the thirty-fifth session of the International Conference on Education, Geneva, September 1975. 4 p., figs. [Mimeo.]

60. Morales, A.T.; Ramos, D.P.G. *Problems, issues and strategies relevant to national development: Philippine experience.* Paper presented at a regional planning workshop, Quezon City, Philippines, May 1975. Bangkok, Unesco Regional Office for Education in Asia, 1975. 7 p. (ROEA-75/APEID-RPW.TT.CD/6.11.) [Distribution limited.]

61. Mongolia. *The development of the Mongolian people's education from 1973 to 1975.* Report to the thirty-fifth session of the International Conference on Education. Geneva, IBE, 1975. 7 p. [Mimeo.]

62. Netherlands. Ministry of Education and Science. *Contours of a future education system in the Netherlands: summary of a discussion memorandum.* The Hague, 1975. 18 p.

63. Netherlands. Ministry of Education and Science. *Secondary school teacher training in the Netherlands.* The Hague, 1971. 19 p. (Docinform 300 E.).

64. Netherlands. Ministry of Education and Science. *Primary school teacher training.* The Hague, 1972. 11 p. (Docinform 288.)

65. New Zealand. *The changing role of the teacher and its influence on preparation for the profession and on in-service training.* Paper presented at the thirty-fifth session of the International Conference on Education, Geneva, September 1975. 19 p., figs. [Mimeo.]

66. New Zealand. *Education in New Zealand 1973-1975.* Report prepared for the thirty-fifth session of the International Conference on Education, Geneva, September 1975. 23 p., figs. [Mimeo.]

67. Nigeria. Federal Ministry of Education. *A report on education in Nigeria to the XXXVth session of the International Conference on Education.* Geneva, September 1975. 13 p. [Mimeo.]

68. Nigeria. *State and development of teacher education.* Report to the thirty-fifth session of the International Conference on Education, Geneva, September 1975. 2 p. [Mimeo.]

69. Norway. *Annual report on developments in education in Norway 1973/74 and 1974/75.* Oslo, 1975. 20 p., bibl., figs. [Mimeo.]

70. Norway. *The changing role of the teacher.* Paper prepared for the thirty-fifth session of the International Conference on Education, Geneva, September 1975. 17 p. [Mimeo.]

71. Norway. *The National Council for Innovation in Education: its structure and work.* Oslo, Forsøksrädet for skoleverket, n.d. 8 p.

72. Overseas Liaison Committee of the American Council on Education. *Report on the supply of secondary level teachers in English-speaking Africa.* Ann Arbor, MI, Michigan State University, 1974. 379 p., bibl., figs.

73. Pakistan. Ministry of Education. *Development of education in Pakistan 1973/75.* Report presented at the thirty-fifth session of the International Conference on Education, Geneva, September 1975. 97 p., figs.

74. Panna Lal Pradhan. *Nepal.* Paper presented at a regional planning workshop, Quezon City, Philippines, May 1975. Bangkok, Unesco

Regional Office for Education in Asia, 1975. 7 p. (ROEA-75/APEID-RPW.TT.CD/6.9) [Distribution limited.]

75. Philippines. *The changing role of the teacher and its influence on preparation for the profession and on in-service training.* Paper presented at the thirty-fifth session of the International Conference on Education, Geneva, September 1975. 11 p. [Mimeo.]

76. Poland. Ministry of Education. *The development of education in the Polish People's Republic, 1973-1975.* Report presented at the thirty-fifth session of the International Conference on Education, Geneva, September 1975. Warszawa, 1975. 33 p.

77. Postlethwaite, T.N. *The training of expertise.* Working draft prepared for seminar on the evaluation of the qualitative aspects of education held by the International Institute for Educational Planning. Paris, 1974. 25 p. [Mimeo.]

78. Qatar. Ministry of Education and Youth Welfare. *Development of education in Qatar (1973/74 and 1974/75).* Report to the thirty-fifth session of the International Conference on Education, Geneva, September 1975. 31 p. [Also in Arabic.]

79. Qatar. *The changing role of the teacher.* Paper presented at the thirty-fifth session of the International Conference on Education, Geneva, September 1975. 3 p. [Mimeo.]

80. Saudi Arabia. Ministry of Education. *A report on the progress of education in Saudi Arabia during the two years 1973 and 1974.* Presented to the thirty-fifth session of the International Conference on Education, Geneva, September 1975. 43 p. [Mimeo.]

81. Singapore. [Paper presented at the XXXVth session of he International Conference on Education. Geneva, September 1975.] 24 p. [Mimeo.]

82. Spain. Ministerio de Educación y Ciencia. *El desarrollo de la educación en 1973-74 y 1974-75/Développement de l'éducation en 1973-74 et 1974-75/Educational development in 1973-74 and 1974-75.* Report presented at the thirty-fifth session of the International Conference on Education, Geneva, September 1975. 218 p.

83. Sri Lanka. *Development of education in Sri Lanka (Ceylon) in 1973/1974 and 1974/1975.* Report presented at the thirty-fifth session of the International Conference on Education, Geneva, September 1975. 29 p. [Mimeo.]

84. Sri Lanka. Ministry of Education. *The changing role of the teacher and its influence on preparation for the profession and on in-service training.* Report presented at the thirty-fifth session of the International Conference on Education, Geneva, September 1975. 15 p. [Mimeo.]

85. Sudan. Ministry of Education. *Major trends in education.* Report presented to the thirty-fifth session of the International Conference on Education, Geneva, September 1975. 19 p., figs.

86. Sudan. *The implications of the changing role for pre-service and in-service training of teachers.* Paper presented to the thirty-fifth session of the International Conference on Education, Geneva, September 1975. 7 p. [Mimeo.]

87. Sweden. Ministry of Education. *Development of education in 1973/74 and 1974/75.* Report presented at the thirty-fifth session of the International Conference on Education, Geneva, September 1975. 11 p. [Mimeo.]

88. Sweden. *[Information for OECD with reference to the conference on teacher policies]* Contribution by the Swedish authorities to the OECD Conference on Teacher Policies, Paris, November 1974. 14 p.

89. Switzerland. Swiss Educational Documentation Centre. *Education in Switzerland.* Geneva, 1974. 47 p. [Also published in French.]

90. Thailand. *The changing role of the teacher and its influence on preparation for the profession and on in-service training in Thailand.* Paper presented to the thirty-fifth International Conference on Education, Geneva, September 1975. 32 p. [Mimeo.]

91. Thailand. Ministry of Education. *Educational development in Thailand (1973-1975).* Report to the thirty-fifth session of the International Conference on Education, Geneva, September 1975. 24 p., bibl., figs.

92. Togo. Ministry of National Education. *Report on the evolution of education during the years 1973-1975.* Presented to the thirty-fifth session of the International Conference on Education, Geneva, September 1975. 6 p., figs. [Mimeo.]

93. Uganda. National Commission for Unesco. *Educational development in Uganda 1973/75.* Prepared for the thirty-fifth session of the International Conference on Education, Geneva, September 1975. Kampala, 1975. 32 p., illus.

94. Unesco. *Final report on meeting of senior officials of the ministries of education of the twenty-five least developed countries, Paris, September 1975.* 30 p. (ED/MD/39.) [Mimeo.]

95. Unesco. *International standard classification of education.* Working document at thirty-fifth session of the International Conference on Education, Geneva, September 1975. (ED/BIE/CONFINTED/35/5.) [Distribution limited.]

96. Unesco. *Note on the Unesco-ILO recommendation (1966) concerning the status of teachers.* Presented at the thirty-fifth session of the International Conference on Education, Geneva, September 1975. 7 p. (ED/ BIE/CONFINTED/35/Ref. 3.) [Distribution limited.]

97. Unesco. *Recommendation of the Commission on the changing role of the teacher and its influence on preparation for the profession and on in-service training.* Paper presented at the thirty-fifth session of the International Conference on Education, Geneva, September 1975. 8 p. (ED/BIE/ CONFINTED 35/7.) [Distribution limited.]

98. Unesco. *Report of the commission on the changing role of the teacher and its influence on preparation for the profession and on in-service training.* Presented at the thirty-fifth session of the International Conference on Education, Geneva, September 1975. 11 p. (ED/BIE/CONFINTED 35/8.) [Distribution limited.]

99. Unesco. Role, function and status of the teacher. *Educational documentation and information* (Paris, Unesco), no. 194, 1st quarter 1975. 55 p.

100. Unesco. *Strategies for the training of educators: how modern techniques and methods can help.* Paper prepared by the Division of Methods, Materials and Techniques of Unesco for the thirty-fifth session of the International Conference on Education at Geneva, September 1975. Paris, 1975. 8 p. (ED/BIE/CONFINTED/35/Ref. 5.) [Distribution limited.]

101. Unesco. *Teachers and other professionals in education: new profiles and new status.* Paper prepared by the Division of Methods, Materials and Techniques and the Division of Training of Educational Personnel of Unesco for the thirty-fifth session of the International Conference on Education, Geneva, September 1975. Paris, 1975. 10 p. (ED/BIE/ CONFINTED 35/Ref. 4.) [Distribution limited.]

102. Unesco. *The changing role of the teacher and its influence on preparation for the profession and on in-service training.* An inquiry by Unesco: International Bureau of Education. Geneva, 1974. 19 p. (BIE/CON-FINTED 35/Prep. 1.) [Mimeo.]

103. Unesco Regional Office for Education in Asia. *The role of teachers in out-of-school education.* Report of an Asian regional meeting, Manila, November 1973. Bangkok, 1974. 62 p., bibl. [Mimeo.]

104. Ukrainian Soviet Socialist Republic. *Rozvitok narodnoi osviti v Ukrains'kij Radyans'kij Socialističnij Recpublici y 1973-74 i 1974-75 navčal'nih rokah/Development of public education in the Ukrainian Soviet Socialist Republic in the course of the school years 1973-74 and 1974-75/Progrès dans l'instruction publique en République Socialiste Soviétique*

d'Ukraine aux cours des années scolaires 1973-74 et 1974-75/Desarrollo de la instruccion publica en la Republica Socialista Sovietica de Ucrania durante los años escolares 1973-74 y 1974-75. Address to the thirty-fifth session of the International Conference on Education, Geneva, September 1975. Kiev, 1975. 174 p., illus.

105. Union of Soviet Socialist Republics. Ministry of Education. *Development of the educational system in the U.S.S.R.* Presented at the thirty-fifth session of the International Conference on Education, Geneva, September 1975. 27 p. [Mimeo.]

106. United Kingdom. Department of Education and Science. *Major trends.* Paper presented to the thirty-fifth session of the International Conference on Education, Geneva, September 1975. 11 p. [Mimeo.]

107. United Kingdom. Department of Education and Science. *Reply to I.L.O./Unesco questionnaire on recommendation concerning the status of teachers.* n.d. 22 p. [Mimeo.]

108. United Kingdom. Department of Education and Science. *Report on the development of education in the United Kingdom 1973-1975.* Presented at the thirty-fifth session of the International Conference on Education, Geneva, September 1975. 57 p. [Also published in French.]

109. United Kingdom. Department of Education and Science. *The changing role of the teacher and its influence on preparation for the profession and on in-service training.* Paper presented at the thirty-fifth session of the International Conference on Education. Geneva, 1975. 8 p. [Mimeo.]

110. United Kingdom. Northern Ireland Department of Education. *The changing role of the teacher, and its influence on preparation for the profession and on in-service training.* Report to the thirty-fifth session of the International Conference on Education, Geneva, September 1975. 17 p. [Mimeo.]

111. United Kingdom. Scottish Education Department. *The changing role of the teacher and its influence on preparation for the profession and on in-service training.* Paper presented at the thirty-fifth session of the International Conference on Education, Geneva, September 1975. 21 p. [Mimeo.]

112. Upper Volta. Ministry of National Education. *Brief data on the evolution of education in Upper Volta from 1973 to 1975.* Presented at the thirty-fifth session of the International Conference on Education, Geneva, September 1975. 3 p. [Mimeo.]

113. United States of America. *Implications of the changing role for pre-service and in-service training.* Paper presented at the thirty-fifth session of the International Conference on Education, Geneva, September 1975. 42 p., bibl. [Mimeo.]

114. United States of America. Department of Health, Education and Welfare. *Progress of education in the United States of America: 1972-73 and 1973-74*. Report for the thirty-fifth session of the International Conference on Education, Geneva, September 1975. Washington, United States Government Printing Office, 1975. 75 p., bibl.

115. University of the West Indies School of Education. *The in-service training of teachers*. 1975. 4 p. [Mimeo.]

116. Yugoslavia. Yugoslav Commission for Co-operation with Unesco and the Institute for Studies in Education. *Development and changes in education in Yugoslavia 1973-1975*. Paper prepared for the thirty-fifth session of the International Conference on Education, Geneva, September 1975. Belgrade, 1975. 44 p., figs. [Mimeo.]

Index